The Indigenous Welfare Economy and the CDEP Scheme

Edited by F. Morphy and W.G. Sanders

ANU

THE AUSTRALIAN NATIONAL UNIVERSITY

E PRESS

Centre for Aboriginal Economic Policy Research
The Australian National University, Canberra

Research Monograph No. 20
2001

ANU

E PRESS

Published by ANU E Press
The Australian National University
Canberra ACT 0200, Australia
Email: anuepress@anu.edu.au
Web: http://epress.anu.edu.au

Previously published by the Centre for Aboriginal Economic Policy Research,
The Australian National University

National Library of Australia
Cataloguing-in-publication entry.

The Indigenous Welfare Economy and the CDEP Scheme.

Includes index

ISBN 1 920942 04 1
ISBN 0 975122 93 2 (Online document)

1. Community Development Employment Projects (Australia). 2. Federal aid to
community development - Australia. 3. Aboriginal Australians - Employment -
Government policy. 4. Employment subsidies - Australia. I. Morphy, Frances,
1949- . II. Sanders, W.

331.699915

Designed by Green Words & Images (GWi)
Cover design by Brendon McKinley

Foreword

The Centre for Aboriginal Economic Policy Research (CAEPR) is an independent research centre within The Australian National University (ANU). Its funding comes from four sources: Aboriginal and Torres Strait Islander Commission (ATSIC), ANU, Department of Family and Community Services (DFACS) and its own consultancy activities. CAEPR's mission, as defined in its strategic plan, is to contribute to better outcomes for Indigenous people by independently monitoring changes in socio-economic status, influencing policy formation, and informing constructive debate. CAEPR does this through research that combines academic excellence of the highest standards with policy relevance, objectivity, and realism. Its two principal aims are to enhance CAEPR's role in research which leads to constructive policy debates and improved outcomes for Indigenous Australians, and to broaden Indigenous engagement with CAEPR's research and improve dissemination of CAEPR's research findings.

In November 2000 CAEPR, in conjunction with the Reshaping Australian Institutions (RAI) project of ANU's Research School of Social Sciences, organised a conference, 'The Indigenous Welfare Economy and the Community Development Employment Projects (CDEP) Scheme: Autonomy, Dependence, Self Determination and Mutual Obligation'. Convened in part to mark CAEPR's tenth anniversary, it was a wonderfully diverse gathering of delegates from Indigenous communities and organisations from all over Australia, from the bureaucracy, from key agencies and from academia. This CAEPR Research Monograph is one of the outcomes, and its contents reflect all that diversity of perspective and opinion. Professor Frank Castles, convener of the RAI project, welcomed delegates to the conference and I would personally like to thank him for his enthusiastic support for the conference. The cost of producing the monograph has been assisted in part by the financial support provided by Professor Castles and the RAI project.

In its early planning phase the conference was to focus on the CDEP scheme as a unique Indigenous institution, but in the light of the government's agenda to reform and reshape the institutions of Australian welfare, it seemed critical to broaden the focus of the conference to engage both the Indigenous welfare economy and the CDEP scheme, and their interrelationships. That broader focus will be evident to the reader of the monograph.

A blueprint for Australian welfare reform has recently been provided to the Howard government by the Reference Group on Welfare Reform, chaired by Patrick McClure. At the centre of the McClure vision is the principle of 'mutual obligation', which calls for a new relationship between welfare recipients and the state. Much of the language associated with this 'new' concept suggests that this will be a more caring and sensitive engagement, but at this early stage it seems that many of the proposals being considered by government, especially where they include compulsion, do not support this rhetoric.

This publication is timely because the debate is well under way, yet the marginal and diverse circumstances of Indigenous Australia, while very well documented, have not been adequately considered by the proponents of radical change. It is difficult to reconcile the rhetoric of mutual obligation as a vehicle for enhanced economic and social participation for those at risk of exclusion, with government's avowed policy embrace of the market and globalisation (although as this foreword is being penned that embrace, in an election year, seems to be loosening somewhat). It is of great concern that, to date, there has been so little active engagement between Indigenous Australians and proponents of welfare reform, and that what little engagement there has been has tended primarily to favour, rather than challenge, the reform agenda.

If poverty and social exclusion are complex and multidimensional problems in mainstream Australian society, how much more complex and multidimensional are these issues for Indigenous Australian individuals, families, and communities that are often *remotely* located, socio-economically disadvantaged, and in tense, ambivalent relations with the Australian state? Put another way, how reconciled are Indigenous and other Australians in our society and how similar are their visions for Australia's future?

In the early 1960s, universalist assumptions were embedded in a policy called 'assimilation'. Its definition, paraphrased a little so as not to cause offence, was as follows:

> The policy of assimilation means that all Indigenous Australians are expected eventually to attain the same manner of living as other Australians, to live as members of a single Australian community, enjoying the same rights and privileges, accepting the same responsibilities, observing the same customs and influenced by the same beliefs as other Australians.

It could be said that there are some worrying resonances here with McClure's communitarian vision.

In many situations, especially in the rural and *remote* areas where the CDEP scheme is widespread, Indigenous Australians have very different cultural values from the majority values that underpin key emerging notions like mutual obligation, social partnerships, and participation support. In other situations, Indigenous Australians can be partially or fully linked to the wider society, even if only by marriage or residential integration. While the McClure Report calls for sensitivity to cultural difference, it unfortunately says very little that is substantive about how it is to be accommodated in the new welfare paradigm of mutual obligation.

The subtitle of the conference, 'Autonomy, Dependence, Self Determination and Mutual Obligation', captures elements of this tension. In the final two decades of the twentieth century, many Indigenous communities enjoyed unprecedented levels of autonomy, underwritten by high levels of dependence. At times this was 'active' as in the CDEP, at other times 'passive' as with the dole. This is one manifestation of self determination. The crucial issue, addressed by many papers at the conference and now in this volume, is how Indigenous self determination and the rights agenda, which argues for the unique and inherent rights of Indigenous Australians, will sit with (or in opposition to) the proposed 'mutual obligation' of welfare reform. This is an issue of ongoing debate in Australian social policy arena.

As this monograph is being completed, the Howard government has made its first tentative steps to reform the CDEP scheme in the May 2001 Budget and with its 'new' policy framework *Australians Working Together*. The emphasis now, in regions where there are 'viable' labour markets, is on CDEP as a stepping stone to mainstream employment; in areas where there is no viable labour market, resources have been earmarked for Community Participation Agreements and community capacity building to ensure that CDEP participation generates outcomes of benefit to each participating community. These policy changes are to be tentatively piloted in the 2001–02 financial year, and the outcomes of these changes will require careful evaluation.

All the full written papers submitted for the volume were refereed by a specialist CAEPR editorial committee.

Professor Jon Altman
Director, CAEPR
August 2001

Contents

Foreword   iii

List of figures   xi

List of tables   xi

Abbreviations and acronyms   xiii

Introduction   1

Will Sanders and Frances Morphy

Part I: Overviews   3

1. Welfare and social justice for Indigenous Australians   5

   Brian Butler

2. CDEP, racial discrimination, and social justice   11

   William Jonas

3. The changing social security policy context: Implications for the CDEP program   19

   Peter Saunders

4. Community development in the context of welfare dependence   31

   David Martin

5. The political dimensions of community development   39

   Tim Rowse

6. Adjusting balances: Reshaping the CDEP scheme after 20 good years   47

   Will Sanders

Part II: Policy perspectives and issues   51

7. Welfare dependence, mutual obligation, and the CDEP scheme: Lessons from community research and an overseas initiative   53

   Diane Smith

8. The Indigenous Employment Policy: A preliminary evaluation   67

   Peter Shergold

9. Reforming the CDEP scheme   75

   Terry Whitby

10. Myth-making and the delivery of banking and financial services to   81
Indigenous Australians in regional and *remote* Australia

Neil Westbury

11. Demographic challenges to the future of CDEP   95

John Taylor and Boyd Hunter

12. Training by doing: Pathways through CDEP   109

Shirley Campbell and Jerry Schwab

Part III: Regional studies   123

13. 'Mutual obligation', the CDEP scheme, and development: 125
Prospects in *remote* Australia

Jon Altman

14. CDEP and careers: Some good news and some bad news from Torres Strait   135

Bill Arthur

15. CDEP as conduit to the 'real' economy? The Port Augusta case   143

Matthew Gray and Elaine Thacker

16. Yuendumu CDEP: The Warlpiri work ethic and Kardiya staff turnover   153

Yasmine Musharbash

17. Outstations and CDEP: The Western Arrernte in central Australia   167

Diane Austin-Broos

18. CDEP in Victoria: A case study of Worn Gundidj   177

Raymond Madden

Part IV: Community perspectives   185

19. The community game: Aboriginal self definition at the local level   187

Frances Peters-Little

20. CDEP and the sub-economy: Milking the CDEP cow dry   193

Phil Bartlett

21. Measuring expropriation: Enumeration of opportunity costs imposed   199
on the *remote* community of Burringurrah, Western Australia

Daniel Kean

22. A part of the local economy: Junjuwa Community/Bunuba Inc.,   203
Western Australia

Rowena Mouda

23. Self determination and CDEP: Tjurma Homelands Council, South Australia 205

   Katalin Mindszenty

24. Job creation and 'mutual obligation': Tapatjatjaka Community 207
   Government Council, Northern Territory

   Harry Scott

25. Regional development and CDEP: Tjuwanpa Outstation Resource 209
   Centre, Northern Territory

   John Nicholas

26. Catering for mobility and diversity: Bawinanga Aboriginal 211
   Corporation CDEP, Northern Territory

   Rupert Manners

27. Resourcing CDEP: The case of East Gippsland Aboriginal CDEP 213
   Co-operative, Victoria

   Lionel Dukakis

28. Adequate funding as a question of equity: Lake Tyers Aboriginal 215
   Trust CDEP, Victoria

   Siva Nalliah

29. Supporting employment inside and outside the community: 217
   Woorabinda CDEP, Queensland

   Elizabeth Young

30. Creating opportunities for training and employment: Tharawal 221
   Local Aboriginal Land Council CDEP, Western Sydney

   Wendy Ann Lewis

31. Using the system to our advantage: Redfern Aboriginal Corporation CDEP, 225
   Sydney

   Bruce Loomes

32. CDEP: A journey not a destination 227

   Stephen Humphries

Postscript 231
Tim Rowse

Index 235
Notes on the contributors 243

List of figures and tables

Figures

Fig. 11.1 Projected trends in Indigenous unemployment rates, 1996–2006   100

Fig. 11.2 Jobs required to achieve equity in unemployment rates, 1996–2006   100

Fig. 14.1 A generalised picture of CDEP, Torres Strait, 1999   136

Fig. 14.2 How young people look for and get jobs or training, Torres Strait, 1999   137

Fig. 14.3 Training sponsors, Torres Strait, 1999   137

Fig. 14.4 Devices thought useful for career, Torres Strait, 1999   138

Fig. 14.5 Preferred form of work, Torres Strait, 1999   139

Fig. 14.6 Reason for working or training, Torres Strait, 1999   139

Fig. 14.7 Qualities valued in work, Torres Strait, 1999   140

Fig. 15.1 Organisational structure of Bungala CDEP, 2000   145

Fig. 16.1 Participant numbers, Yuendumu CDEP, 1998–2000   154

Fig. 16.2 Turnover of CDEP managers in relation to participant numbers, Yuendumu CDEP, 1998–2001   154

Fig. 18.1 Organisational structure of Worn Gundidj corporate CDEP, 2001   178

Fig. 20.1 The fat CDEP 'cow', as she was   195

Fig. 20.2 The starved CDEP 'cow', as she is now   195

Tables

Table 10.1 Indigenous share of the outback population, 1981–1996   82

Table 11.1 Revised Indigenous employment estimates, 1996–2006   98

Table 11.2 Revised estimates of Indigenous employment growth required to maintain the status quo or to achieve employment equality, 1996–2006   99

Table 11.3 Estimates of Indigenous unemployment need, 1996–2006   101

Table 15.1 Sources of income, Bungala, 1995–96 to 1999–2000   147

Table 15.2 Movements to unsubsidised employment, Bungala, 1996–2000   149

Table 16.1 Highest educational qualification (15 years and older), Yuendumu, 1996   155

Table 16.2 Occupations of Indigenous and non-Indigenous population, Yuendumu, 1996   156

Table 16.3 CDEP projects at Yuendumu, 2001   157

Table 16.4 Non-Indigenous managerial turnover at Yuendumu, 1995–2000   160

Abbreviations and acronyms

ABS	Australian Bureau of Statistics
ABSTUDY	Aboriginal Study Assistance Scheme
AFDC	Aid to Families with Dependent Children (USA)
AGPS	Australian Government Publishing Service
AIAS	Australian Institute of Aboriginal Studies (now AIATSIS)
AIATSIS	Australian Institute of Aboriginal and Torres Strait Islander Studies
AIFS	Australian Institute of Family Studies
ANTA	Australian National Training Authority
ANTARAC	Australian National Training Authority Research Advisory Council
ANU	The Australian National University
ATM	Automatic Teller Machine
ATSIC	Aboriginal and Torres Strait Islander Commission
ATSICOEA	Aboriginal and Torres Strait Islander Commission Office of Evaluation and Audit
ATSIPTAC	Aboriginal and Torres Strait Islander Peoples Training Advisory Council
AWA	Australian Workplace Agreement
CA	Certified Agreement
CAEPR	Centre for Aboriginal Economic Policy Research (ANU)
CAR	Council for Aboriginal Reconciliation
CDEP	Community Development Employment Projects
CDFI	Community Development Financial Institutions Fund (USA)
CEO	Chief Executive Officer
ICERD	International Convention on the Elimination of All Forms of Racial Discrimination
CES	Commonwealth Employment Service
CESCR	Committee on Economic, Social and Cultural Rights

CGC	Commonwealth Grants Commission
CHIP	Community Housing and Infrastructure Program
CPS	CDEP Participant Supplement
CRA	*Community Reinvestment Act* (USA)
CRCAP	Canadian Royal Commission on Aboriginal Peoples
CRES	Centre for Resource and Environmental Studies (ANU)
CSIRO	Commonwealth Scientific and Industrial Research Organisation
DEET	Department of Employment, Education and Training
DEETYA	Department of Employment, Education, Training, and Youth Affairs
DETYA	Department of Education, Training, and Youth Affairs
DEWRSB	Department of Employment, Workplace Relations and Small Business
DFACS	Department of Family and Community Services
DSS	Department of Social Security
EITC	Earned Income Tax Credit (USA)
ESRA	Employment Services Regulatory Agency
GST	Goods and Services Tax
HREOC	Human Rights and Equal Opportunity Commission
IDA	Individual Development Account (USA)
IEC	Indigenous Employment Centre
ICESCR	International Covenant on Economic, Social and Cultural Rights
IEP	Indigenous Employment Policy
ILO	International Labour Organisation
ILOC	Indigenous Local Area
LFS	Labour Force Survey
NARU	North Australia Research Unit (ANU)
NATSIS	National Aboriginal and Torres Strait Islander Survey
NEIS	New Enterprise Incentive Scheme

NSA	New Start Allowance
OEA	Office of Evaluation and Audit (ATSIC)
OECD	Organisation for Economic Cooperation and Development
PRC	Papunya Regional Council
RAI	Reshaping Australian Institutions project (RSSS, ANU)
R&M	Repair and Maintenance
RDC	Racial Discrimination Commissioner
RTC	Rural Transaction Centre
RTO	Registered Training Organisation
SD	Statistical Division
SES	Specialised Enumeration Strategy
SIPF	Special Indigenous Personal Form
SPRC	Social Policy Research Centre (UNSW)
SSD	Statistical Sub-Division
STEP	Structured Training and Employment Projects
TAFE	Technical and Further Education
TANF	Temporary Aid for Needy Families (USA)
TCU	Traditional Credit Union
UB	Unemployment Benefit
UNSW	University of new South Wales
WFTC	Working Families Tax Credit (UK)
WFTD	Work for the Dole

Introduction

Will Sanders and Frances Morphy

The aim of the conference on which this volume is based was to encourage debate and discussion about the Indigenous welfare economy and, in particular, one major manifestation of that economy, the long-running and now widespread Community Development Employment Projects (CDEP) scheme. Many conferences on Indigenous issues institute (and institutionalise) debate between academic researchers, or between the bureaucrats charged with implementing and delivering policy, and sometimes between the two, but few deliberately engage in an extended way with the views of the people who are the subject of discussion. This conference was different, and so too is the volume which results from it. Representatives from many CDEP organisations were present at the conference; they not only debated from the floor in response to the issues raised by the academics and policy makers and implementers, but also presented their own view of CDEP—and their CDEPs—in the sessions of the conference designated as the 'Community perspectives forum'.

The term 'welfare' has both positive and negative connotations, and so too does the phrase 'the Indigenous welfare economy'. In using this phrase for the conference title, it was not our intention to suggest either a positive or a negative judgment about the substantial reliance of Indigenous Australians on government welfare payments for income. There was a time, before the 1960s, when Indigenous Australians were legislatively excluded from the social security system and such reliance was impossible. In the 1960s, Indigenous people and their supporters fought long and hard for social security rights as citizenship entitlements. Once these entitlements were gained, however, new issues arose. There was concern about the degree of reliance on these payments that was developing among Indigenous people and about whether this was good for Indigenous communities.

The CDEP scheme arose in the mid 1970s in response to the increasing payment of unemployment benefits in *remote* Aboriginal communities with few formal labour market employment opportunities. This payment was seen by some as unhelpful and inappropriate in these circumstances. So an alternative was developed whereby the Commonwealth's Aboriginal affairs administration, rather than the social security administration, made payments to Aboriginal communities roughly equivalent to community members' unemployment payment entitlements, in order for communities to employ their members on a part time basis. The CDEP scheme, as it was called, began in just 12 *remote* Aboriginal communities in 1977. It immediately proved popular and faced demands for expansion from other Indigenous communities. From the mid 1980s CDEP was allowed to expand not only into other Indigenous communities in *remote* areas but also into Indigenous communities in more southern, densely settled areas of Australia. Today CDEP operates through approximately 300 Indigenous community-based organisations, and over 30 000 Indigenous people, or about one-third of all Indigenous people in employment, participate in the scheme.

The CDEP scheme is a major adaptation of the Australian government social welfare system to the social and economic circumstances of Indigenous people. It is both long-running and widespread and deserves, therefore, to be thoroughly examined in any debate and discussion about the Indigenous welfare economy more generally. The perspectives presented at the November 2000 conference and in this publication are those of elected Indigenous representatives, government policy makers, academics, and CDEP administrators. These are extremely varied perspectives, yet almost all are supportive of CDEP without being uncritical of it. CDEP is seen as a flexible and proven program which can be further improved, but which has already achieved much. It has encouraged the building of Indigenous political authority, as well as employment and community development. It has even in some instances encouraged the development of Indigenous business enterprises.

This volume is divided into four parts, roughly corresponding to the named sessions of the conference. Part I contains overview papers which place the CDEP program in its wider cultural, socio-political, and economic context. The papers in Part II address policy and policy-related issues which impact directly, or indirectly, on the structure and function of the CDEP program and of individual projects. In Part III are found research-based case-studies of particular CDEP projects in their regional context, drawn from the Northern Territory, South Australia, and Victoria. The majority of the spoken contributions (but not, alas, the video presentations) from the 'Community perspectives forum' are found in written form in Part IV. Most are case studies, from the perspective of the actors themselves, of particular CDEP projects. They provide a telling counterpoint to the other sections of the book, taking up and providing a grass-roots view of many of the themes and concerns that are expressed there. The two opening papers of Part IV address more general topics: Frances Peters-Little examines critically the concept of 'community' as it is applied in Indigenous affairs and used by Indigenous people, and Phil Bartlett, deploying a striking image of CDEP as a cow being milked dry, discourses on the multiple functions of today's CDEP projects.

In recent debates about the Indigenous welfare economy, CDEP has probably not been given the attention it deserves. CDEP shows us the sorts of adaptations of the welfare system to the circumstances of Indigenous Australians which have been possible in the past. As a pointer to the future it has the virtue of being grounded not just in vague ideas, but in existing experience and policy practice. The Australian welfare system can better serve the interests of Indigenous people than at present, but there are no miracle cures out there waiting to be discovered. What is needed is to pay attention to, and to learn from, past practical adaptation and experience. Hopefully this volume will contribute to that important endeavour.

PART I

OVERVIEWS

1. Welfare and social justice for Indigenous Australians[1]

Brian Butler

Introduction

Aboriginal and Torres Strait Islander peoples are just as keen as the government is to address welfare and social justice issues. These have to be understood in the context of the early European settlement of this country, which destroyed the structure of our way of life and cultural values, and led to the dispossession of our land. Our peoples still face what is described by the Commonwealth Grants Commission (CGC) in a recent draft report (CGC 2000) as 'the historical legacy of exclusion from the mainstream provisions of Australian society'. It is imperative that we understand the importance of these underlying issues. From the early settlement period until the referendum of 1967, the majority of our peoples never really had a fair go in education or employment, and they were certainly not in a position to exercise autonomy, or self determination about their future. This power was exercised by governments and still is to this day.

Our peoples were exposed to the welfare support system as a necessity, not by desire. They were forced to live in an alien environment, and dependence on the welfare support system of course meant access to the cash economy. As a result our peoples encountered many social problems such as alcohol and substance abuse, ill health, poor housing, brushes with the law, and racism and discrimination. These factors in turn impacted on their ability to attain relevant and appropriate levels of education and labour market skills to enhance their employment and social skills. We are faced with the reality of the legacy of dispossession and dislocation that have weakened or destroyed the economic bases of many Aboriginal and Torres Strait Islander societies. These experiences have left many without social context, relevant skills, or opportunities to move beyond a reliance on welfare.

One factor that has not received enough attention is racism. No government has yet fully considered this as a major issue which warrants changes in its policies so that it can be addressed in the delivery of essential services to Aboriginal and Torres Strait Islander clients. Despite legal sanctions against racism and discrimination, our people still experience overt and tacit racism in this country (see Bartlett, Ch. 20, this volume). It is rare, for example, to be served by an Aboriginal or Torres Strait Islander shop assistant. Racism can be addressed through structural changes in the delivery of services. Governments and policy makers should be aware of the fact that, as Noel Pearson (2000) said, 'welfare dependency makes people even more vulnerable to the degradations of racism'.

Attempts have been made, and programs introduced specifically to address Aboriginal and Torres Strait Islander peoples' welfare and social justice issues. Yet since the recognition of our peoples as Australian citizens in 1967, none of these programs have effectively addressed these issues. They may have slowed down the process of dislocation, or improved conditions a little, but governments certainly have not found the right solution. The dislocation of Aboriginal and Torres Strait Islander societies has not been arrested. Wrong decisions on welfare reform have the potential to exacerbate the circumstances of our peoples. This is surely an outcome to which no government would aspire.

Principles of welfare reform

As ATSIC commissioner with portfolio responsibility for social justice I have taken a close interest in the government's current welfare reform agenda. I have visited many of our communities around the country, and have seen the reliance of many of our peoples on the social welfare system. The structure of Australian welfare is an issue of critical significance for our peoples. The demographics of our population, compared to that of the general Australian population—including the higher proportion of people living in *remote* locations, the greater proportion of single parent families, and the greater prevalence of illness—force reliance on Australia's social security safety net.

In recognition of the potentially negative impact of welfare reforms on our peoples, ATSIC, in consultation with welfare experts from academic and public sector institutions, ATSIC Commissioners, and Regional Councillors, drafted a response to the Reference Group on Welfare Reform's recent report (McClure 2000). ATSIC proposed seven policy principles as a starting point for further action on welfare reform. In summary these principles emphasised the necessity for consultation and negotiation, and stressed that any welfare reform should be focused on addressing the underlying causes of Indigenous disadvantage, and that Indigenous welfare recipients should not suffer financial loss due to welfare reform.

The safety net

The two key aspects of the welfare report that are of concern to our peoples are the safety net, and participation issues. The safety net provides access to payment for people whose life circumstances do not enable them to participate in employment. Access to such payments is non-negotiable and should not be subject to mutual obligation requirements. Participation support, on the other hand, represents a range of largely positive measures to assist people to obtain employment.

It is important to understand that for a large number of our peoples, the safety net is not yet in place. For example, people may be eligible for, but not accessing, any form of payment (see Smith, Ch. 7, this volume). There may be no access to Centrelink staff or offices in the places where they live. These inequalities must be addressed before discussion of reforms to the system can even begin. Once the safety net is available fairly for all Australians, steps must be put in place to empower people to participate fully in Australian society. Welfare in the form of the safety net is never going to lead to economic independence for our peoples. Empowerment does not come from merely reforming the welfare structures.

Reliance on welfare payments means subsisting on or below poverty levels of income. The term 'welfare reliance' assumes that people choose or want to remain poor. No Aboriginal or Torres Strait Islander person would choose or want to continue to live in the circumstances that many currently do—living in cars, not being able to afford basics like shoes and clothing, going without in order that their children may eat. It is very difficult to conceive of how a person in such circumstances might realistically front up for a job interview.

Employment

The availability of employment is a crucial factor in regard to the introduction of the concept of mutual obligation. The Aboriginal and Torres Strait Islander unemployment rate is estimated at 26 per cent. This contrasts with a national average of less than 7 per cent. If the 33 000 people employed on CDEP are classified as unemployed, the Indigenous unemployment rate is closer to 40 per cent.

The need to address employment in reforming welfare is emphasised in the ATSIC report, *The Job Still Ahead* (Taylor & Hunter 1998). If Aboriginal and Torres Strait Islander employment continues only at the rate current at the time of the 1996 Census, the direct welfare cost to the government increases from about $800 million in 1996 to $1.1 billion by 2006 (see also Taylor & Hunter, Ch. 11, this volume). However, if Aboriginal and Torres Strait Islander unemployment can be reduced to the same level as that of the overall population (remembering that this was at 9 per cent in 1996, not the current 6.3 per cent), the government would save $274 million by 2006 *and* receive additional tax income of $177 million. This is a turnaround in the order of $450 million in government revenues. Surely, some of this potential saving can be used now to assist our people into employment and to break the cycle of welfare.

The role of CDEP

Currently CDEP keeps 33 000 of our people out of the welfare system. However, the ATSIC Board acknowledges that the CDEP scheme is no substitute for mainstream employment outcomes for our people where these opportunities exist.

Welfare reform can be transformative. Structures that empower communities and individuals will emerge as our peoples are accorded their right to take control of their lives and destinies. Our people have already demonstrated their capacity for innovation, by the way in which 33 000 of them have embraced CDEP. It is not the solution, but it is useful tool in building community. Empowerment emerges through the process that involves our peoples in making decisions about their own futures (see Rowse, Ch. 5, this volume).

Mutual obligation

Many of our people actively support the concept of social obligation; it is consistent with the traditional strong cultural value placed upon fulfilling obligations to the extended family and community. And ATSIC supports the adoption of a broad interpretation of the concept of mutual obligation. It advocates a flexible approach that ensures the protection of 'the right of everyone to social security', which Australia has recognised through becoming a signatory to the International Covenant on Economic, Social and Cultural Rights (ICESCR). Any mutual obligation regime must recognise this right.

Our people have led the way in mutual obligation since 1976, by foregoing their individual social security entitlements, volunteering to work for their communities, and building social structures that support our people through CDEP. The CDEP scheme is a good model for how mutual obligation and social partnerships can be effectively achieved while providing work for participants and benefiting the community.

It is essential that Commonwealth, State, and local governments recognise the welfare and social support that our organisations, including CDEPs, are providing to our communities, and that they develop better linkages between these community organisations in the effective delivery of their programs and social welfare services.

Service delivery

Indigenous community organisations, including CDEP schemes, are already delivering a substantial proportion of this country's welfare and social support workload, covering for inadequate welfare support and servicing in many communities throughout the country (see the contributions to Part IV, this volume). Inadequate resourcing leads to the commonly heard criticism that these community organisations display an inability to deliver. All levels of government, as well as the private sector, should acknowledge their social obligation to deliver social support mechanisms, particularly by way of increased employment for our peoples.

Reforms to income support and service delivery will not work unless the underlying causes of difficulty are addressed. The cultural and locational diversity of our peoples coupled with the effects of racism call for different sets of service delivery structures. The diversity of the Indigenous Australian community must be adequately reflected at all levels of the participation support structures, with our people employed in all types of positions at Centrelink, the Job Network and other support agencies and private providers.

Government agencies must model an understanding of diversity and commitment to tackling racism, not only in their recruitment strategies but also in all their policy and program delivery. All agencies at all levels of government have Indigenous clients. It is time these service delivery agencies considered ATSIC as the last resort for Aboriginal and Torres Strait Islander peoples, and not as the first provider. Current practice results in the ATSIC budget being used for safety net issues, rather than as a base for true empowerment and economic development.

Governments are making an effort to move away from the concept of 'one size fits all' solutions in relation to mainstream policy. They need also to move away from it in Aboriginal and Torres Strait Islander policy.

Empowerment and control

In an announcement on 15 October 2000 concerning the 'Peak forum to support Indigenous families and communities', the then Minister, John Herron, stated that: 'Indigenous people know what their problems are and have good ideas on how to address them. Governments need to recognise this and support [I]ndigenous communities to work together to tackle their own issues' (Herron & Newman 2000). ATSIC supports this statement but stresses that it needs to translate into genuine engagement with our people at the community level, not merely through the conduct of national forums but in ensuring that measures taken on the ground are developed in collaboration with local communities.

Once we begin moving control of programs and policy to the community level to control links between programs, we also begin moving away from the model that Aboriginal and Torres Strait Islander communities are simply 'recipients' of services. Communities can then use different programs for common purposes supporting overall community development.

Conclusion

The economic and social welfare issues faced by our people in the new millennium are varied and complex. It is critical that no one be financially worse off under the proposed reforms, nor overburdened by an inflexible participation regime. Welfare reform cannot be isolated from other issues. There is little point in reforming welfare assistance to our peoples unless efforts are also made to address the underlying issues that force them onto welfare, and to address the basic questions of health, housing and employment.

These issues cannot be addressed by people, whether they be black or white, who are *remote* from what is actually taking place in our communities. The communities need to exercise control over programs and policies at the local level to ensure their needs and aspirations are met.

Notes

1. This paper is dedicated to the late Dr Kumantjayi Perkins.

References

Commonwealth Grants Commission (CGC) 2000. Draft Report of the Indigenous Funding Inquiry, *Discussion Paper IFI 2000/2*, October 2000, CGC, Canberra.

Herron, J. and Newman, J. 2000. 'Peak forum to support Indigenous families and communities', Joint media release, 15 October 2000.

McClure, P. (Chair) 2000. Participation Support for a More Equitable Society: Final Report of the Reference Group on Welfare Reform, July 2000 [the McClure Report], DFACS, Canberra.

Pearson, N. 2000. *Our Right to Take Responsibility*, Noel Pearson and Associates, Cairns, Qld.

Taylor, J. and Hunter, B. 1998. *The Job Still Ahead: Economic Costs of Continuing Indigenous Employment Disparity*, Office of Public Affairs, ATSIC, Canberra.

2. CDEP, racial discrimination and social justice

William Jonas

Introduction

In this paper I will address the human rights dimensions of CDEP in relation to the principles of racial non-discrimination and 'special measures', and also in relation to the concepts of formal and substantive equality. In 1997 a report by the Human Rights and Equal Opportunity Commission's (HREOC's) Race Discrimination Commissioner (RDC), *The CDEP Scheme and Racial Discrimination* (HREOC 1997, henceforth the HREOC Review), found that the CDEP scheme did not appear to raise any significant issue of racial discrimination, although it had some specific concerns with the administration of the scheme. Since then changes have been made in light of most of the recommendations from this review and an independent ATSIC review. There are, however, ongoing issues concerning the place of the CDEP scheme in the broader context of government obligations to address Indigenous disadvantage and ensure equitable social, economic and cultural participation. I shall focus later in the paper on the question of the extent to which a scheme such as the CDEP can operate as a special measure for meeting Indigenous employment need in what is our current climate of supposedly practical reconciliation.

The CDEP scheme has had a significant place in the history of struggle for Indigenous rights, specifically in the context of gaining access to the national social security system in the mid 1970s. Although the DSS removed specific and discriminatory references to Aboriginal people from its Act in 1966, full access to social security benefits did not occur for Indigenous people until the late 1970s, and, in some *remote* communities, not until the early 1980s.

The first CDEP scheme, which was started at Bamyili as an alternative to 'sit-down' money, developed in response to some of the problems associated with the social impact on communities of introducing cash incomes through the social security system. It should be emphasised that CDEP was an Indigenous alternative proposed by the community itself and not a 'solution' imposed by government (HREOC 1997: 1–5). The set of issues surrounding CDEP has resonances in current debates about Indigenous people and welfare passivity. Noel Pearson's observations on the detrimental effects of the post 1967 era of 'rights without responsibilities' and 'support without reciprocation' on Indigenous communities have become well-known in this context. In his recent Ben Chifley Memorial Lecture, 'The light on the hill', he stated:

> The irony of our newly won citizenship in 1967 was that after we became citizens with equal rights and the theoretical right to equal pay, we lost the meagre foothold that we had in the real economy and we became almost comprehensively dependent upon passive welfare for our livelihood. Because we find thirty years later that life in the safety net for three decades and two generations has produced a social disaster (Pearson 2000: 6–7).

The CDEP scheme emerges both as a product of, and as an alternative to, the advancement of Indigenous citizenship rights through accessing the social security system. As such, it is a form of support *with* reciprocation, which has led to its inevitable comparison with the 'work-for-the-dole' program. Its evolution as an adaptation to the employment circumstances and labour market realities of Indigenous Australians in the post 1967 'rights' era has made it difficult to define. It has been variously described as an employment program; a form of income and a form of welfare benefits; a source of training or skilling; community development; a transition to employment in the mainstream labour market; a substitute provider of essential services; a source of community cohesion and cultural maintenance; an Indigenous initiative; and even a form of self determination. The definition which is most interesting for the purposes of this paper is that of CDEP as a 'special measure', and the extent to which the scheme qualifies for that category.

CDEP and human rights

The HREOC Review (HREOC 1997) was conducted by the RDC at the request of Aboriginal and Torres Strait Islander communities and organisations who expressed concern about the treatment of CDEP participants. The main brief of this report was to assess whether any aspect of the treatment of CDEP participants is racially discriminatory under Federal human rights law. The human rights principles most relevant to the CDEP scheme are those of equality, non-discrimination and special measures. The principles of equality before the law and non-discrimination are expressed in the International Convention on the Elimination of All Forms of Racial Discrimination (ICERD), to which Australia is a party, as follows:

> States Parties undertake to prohibit and eliminate racial discrimination in all its forms and to guarantee the right of everyone, without distinction as to race, colour, or national or ethnic origin, to equality before the law (ICERD 1965: Art. 5).

The essential feature of the principle of equality is the understanding that the 'promotion of equality does not necessitate the rejection of difference' (Acting Aboriginal and Torres Strait Islander Social Justice Commissioner 1998: 31). In his now classic statement, Judge Tanaka of the International Court of Justice explained this concept as follows:

> The principle of equality before the law does not mean the absolute equality, namely the equal treatment of men without regard to individual, concrete circumstances, but it means the relative equality, namely the principle to treat equally what are equal and unequally what are unequal . . . To treat unequal matters differently according to their inequality is not only permitted but required (Tanaka 1966: 303–4, 305).

There are two approaches to equality contrasted in this passage. The first is often referred to as the substantive equality model, or the provision of equality *in fact*. This approach takes into account 'individual, concrete circumstances', including racially-specific aspects of discrimination such as socio-economic disadvantage, historical subordination, and a failure to recognise cultural difference (Acting Aboriginal and Torres Strait Islander Social Justice Commissioner 1998: 31–2). Such an approach acknowledges, for example, that

Indigenous people are disadvantaged in Australian society and permits the differential treatment of Indigenous people in order to redress this disadvantage and to achieve their equality in society.

The alternative approach—often referred to as formal equality—relies on the notion that all people should be treated identically regardless of their differing circumstances. It presumes that a 'level playing field' exists for all social participants, and that everyone is on an equal footing to start with. As Dr Michael Wooldridge, the Minister for Health and Aged Care, has stated in relation to the delivery of health services to Indigenous Australians: 'This is, of course, a false view of justice that offers those who are disadvantaged nothing. Justice does not mean treating everyone the same' (1998: 2–3). This understanding of equality in terms of 'treating everyone the same' stands in contrast to the principle of equality as it has developed under international law. In adopting a substantive equality approach, international law indicates that there are two types of differential treatment that are 'legitimate' and therefore not discriminatory. These are firstly, actions that constitute 'special measures' and secondly, those which recognise and protect the distinct cultural characteristics of minority groups.

The rationale for allowing 'special measures' is that historical patterns of racism entrench disadvantage, and that more than the prohibition of racial discrimination is required to overcome the resulting racial inequality. Special measures are deliberately designed to offer targeted assistance to those who have been historically disadvantaged by discrimination. Where there has been ongoing and systematic discrimination against a particular group, whether it be on the basis of race, sex, or religion, for example, there needs to be a period whereby such a group is given a chance to catch up. Otherwise mere formal equality of treatment will result in further entrenchment of the discrimination that such a group has inherited.

The HREOC Review (1997) found that the CDEP scheme did not appear to raise any significant issue of racial discrimination. While the CDEP scheme is race-based and applies only to Aboriginal and Torres Strait Islander peoples, it is designed to deal with the disadvantage experienced by Indigenous communities in their access to social security and mainstream labour market programs and opportunities. Moreover, it seeks to do so in ways that enhance the economic, social and cultural rights of Indigenous peoples. The CDEP scheme is also not racially discriminatory in so far as it does not disadvantage non-Indigenous people. A further finding of the report was that the CDEP scheme is adapted to the concrete circumstances of Indigenous communities, particularly, for example, in overcoming difficulties faced by those in *remote* locations. Whether the scheme constitutes a 'special measure' is a more complex issue that is discussed below.

The report had some specific concerns, however, with the administration of the scheme. Many of these related to the lack of consistency shown by Commonwealth agencies in the treatment of income derived from the CDEP scheme. Serious inequities were caused by the definition of CDEP as a Commonwealth-funded program under the 1991 provisions of the *Social Security Act* which barred CDEP participants from becoming DSS customers and receiving the same services and allowances as others. The CDEP scheme was also inconsistent in its treatment of pensioners.

Following the findings of the HREOC Review and also those of ATSIC's independent review of the CDEP scheme, changes were introduced to address these inequities in the *Further 1998 Budget Legislation Amendment (Social Security) Bill 1999*. This came into effect in March 2000.

CDEP in the broader policy context

The discussion so far has been concerned with whether the CDEP scheme itself operates in ways that are racially discriminatory. I now turn to a consideration of how the CDEP scheme relates to the broader landscape of initiatives to address Indigenous inequality and disadvantage, and whether it can be considered a special measure in regard to unemployment.

Article 2 of the International Covenant on Economic, Social and Cultural Rights (ICESCR), to which Australia is a party, places obligations on states to ensure that economic, social, and cultural rights are exercisable in a non-discriminatory manner, as well as 'to take steps', that is, to apply special measures, to achieve the full realisation of these rights, which includes the right to work. In interpreting the scope of the obligation 'to take steps', the Committee on Economic, Social and Cultural Rights (CESCR) has indicated that there is a threshold level of enjoyment of economic, social and cultural rights that states must provide. State parties to ICESCR have a 'minimum core obligation to ensure the satisfaction of, at the very least, minimum essential levels of each of the rights', and must be able to demonstrate that 'every effort has been made to use all resources...to satisfy...those minimum obligations' (CESCR 1999: Para. 10). The Committee has also acknowledged that full recognition of these rights will be realised *progressively*, over a period of time, since 'the full realization of all economic, social and cultural rights will generally not be able to be achieved in a short period of time' (CESCR 1999: Para. 10).

Despite all the rhetoric championing 'practical reconciliation' in recent years, a concerted approach to the progressive realisation of Indigenous people's economic, social and cultural rights in Australia is still clearly lacking. In 1999 the Australia Institute published a study on 'Public expenditure on services for Indigenous people' (Neutze, Sanders & Jones 1999) across the 'four pillars' of the government's stated commitment Indigenous disadvantage—education, emplyment, health and housing. One of the findings of this study was that: 'While Indigenous people benefit substantially more than other Australians from specific programs, they benefit substantially less from many, much bigger, general programs' (Neutze, Sanders & Jones 1999: xii). In the area of unemployment, the CDEP scheme is a major element contributing to this pattern. While the Indigenous unemployed receive 35 per cent less expenditure from general programs, they receive 48 per cent more when Indigenous-specific programs are added. This is a reflection of the significant role of the CDEP scheme in supporting the Indigenous unemployed. While the total number of CDEP participants is difficult to identify in census data, the Australia Institute study found that even with conservative estimates, '[t]he figures suggest that about as many Indigenous people participate in CDEP as access general unemployment payments' (Neutze, Sanders & Jones 1999: 25–6.)

Even so, government expenditure on Indigenous employment is still relatively low in comparison to need. Using CDEP-adjusted figures for the Indigenous unemployed, the Australia Institute study found that the Indigenous unemployment rate was approximately four and one-half times the non-Indigenous rate. Indigenous people also experienced higher levels of long-term unemployment than any other group. The study concluded that given the greater level of need, '[i]t would seem reasonable then to suggest that specific measures to encourage Indigenous people into employment are well justified, alongside general measures' (Neutze, Sanders & Jones 1999: 28).

It should also be noted that CDEP accounts for approximately one-third of ATSIC's program budget. This is reflective of a general trend to see ATSIC as the main provider for Indigenous affairs rather than as a supplementary provider created to take up the slack of provision that should be coming from all levels of government to address Indigenous disadvantage. The CDEP scheme itself takes up the slack by providing specific employment, training, and community development initiatives for Indigenous people. At times, it even substitutes for a lack of service delivery and programs, becoming the 'entry point' for government in some instances.

A further issue that needs consideration is the potentially greater level of Indigenous employment need in the near future because of the age structure of the Indigenous population (see also Ch. 11, this volume). The Indigenous population aged 15 years and over is expected to grow at 2 per cent per annum over the decade from 1996, compared to 1 per cent for the rest of the population. About 65 000 Indigenous people will be added to the working-age population within this decade. It is estimated that, as a result, 'at best the unemployment rate of Indigenous people will remain unchanged, at worst it will increase' (Altman 2000: 16, citing Taylor & Hunter 1998). Altman has predicted that as a consequence of greater Indigenous employment need in the first decade of twenty-first century, '[t]he costs to government of low income disparity are estimated to grow and maintenance of unemployment levels at current unacceptably low levels will remain dependent on continued expansion of the CDEP Scheme' (2000: 16).

These comments draw attention to the inadequacy of CDEP as a special measure in the face of the continuing escalation in levels of Indigenous employment need and inequality. One of the advantages of the CDEP program is that it has evolved and adapted in response to the uniqueness of Indigenous labour force circumstances, and has significant social, economic, and cultural benefits such as supporting traditional cultural aspects of community life, and contributing to social cohesion and the viability of communities in *remote* areas. It is arguable, however, whether the CDEP scheme constitutes a 'special measure' or a merely 'form of reasonable differentiation'. A 'form of reasonable differentiation' is the term used by the ICERD Committee for differential practices or treatment adapted to the circumstances of a particular racial group that are not able to be characterised as 'special measures' but do not constitute racial discrimination.[1] The HREOC Review noted that the CDEP Scheme 'is beneficial in nature and *contains elements* that could be described as "special measure" under the RDA [or *Racial Discrimination Act 1975*]' (1997: vii, emphasis added). The Australia Institute study described the CDEP scheme in qualified terms as:

not as clearly and unequivocally an 'Indigenous specific' program as some others. Indeed it can in some ways be thought of as 'appropriate' adaptation of general unemployment payments to the different economic and labour market circumstances of Indigenous Australians (Neutze, Sanders & Jones 1999: 29).

One of the features of 'special measures' is that they should provide targeted assistance to particular disadvantaged groups within a prescribed time-frame—that is, they must have assessable objectives to be met within a certain period—until equality is achieved. Special measures are to be withdrawn when they have completed the job that they were established to do. This is when the cycle of discrimination is broken and the target group is no longer in need of special treatment.

While the CESCR acknowledges that the full realisation of all rights will occur progressively over a period of time, there is an obligation for states 'to move as expeditiously and effectively as possible towards that goal'. This requires the implementation of special measures in ways that are 'deliberate, concrete and targeted as clearly as possible towards meeting the obligations recognized in the Covenant' CESCR 1990: Para 2).

As recent analyses of Indigenous levels of health, housing, education, and employment indicate, there is certainly no evidence that Indigenous Australians no longer suffer the effects of past discrimination. In the case of the CDEP scheme, when it is considered as a measure for meeting employment need, its lack of a prescribed time-frame and employment goals implies that it exists to support a problem perceived as intractable or maybe just not worthy of significant commitment to redress. As ATSIC's 1997 Spicer Review observed, CDEP runs the risk of becoming a 'life-time destination' for the Indigenous unemployed rather than a 'conduit to other employment options' (Spicer 1997: 4).

In assessing the question of what kind of special measures or what form of progressive realisation of Indigenous employment rights is necessary, it is worth considering the notion of social cost rather than looking to programs such as CDEP to maintain the status quo. In its Final Report (1996), the Canadian Royal Commission on Aboriginal Peoples (CRCAP) argued that the current approach to Indigenous disadvantage results in two forms of 'social cost' to the nation: costs associated with the economic marginalisation of Indigenous people, and costs incurred as governments attempt to address social problems through remedial programs (CRCAP 1996: 23). The Commission proposed that an extensive effort to overcome indigenous disadvantage was necessary, and that it would require the application of substantial resources by government, over a 20-year cycle, to restructure the relationship between indigenous and non-indigenous people. The Commission argued that this type of commitment would not only change the circumstances of aboriginal people but lead to the progressive reduction and eventual elimination of the social costs accrued due to indigenous disadvantage.

In the Australian context, CAEPR has made similar observations about the social cost of the lack of parity between Indigenous and other Australians in the labour force. Taylor and Hunter estimate that:

If Indigenous unemployment was reduced to the same level as that commensurate with the rest of the population, and assuming that this latter rate remained constant, then the savings to government in payments to the unemployed, in 1996 dollars, would be around $193 million by the year 2001 and $274 million by 2006 with much lower unemployment bills of $112 and $126 million respectively.

On the credit side, the tax return of achieving parity in labour force status would approximate $177 million by 2006. However, by shifting all Indigenous people who want to work from welfare dependence to unsubsidised employment would increase tax revenue by $250 million (in 1996 dollars). Furthermore, this would enhance national production and provide large social policy returns in areas such as health (1998: iv).

Conclusion

Some of the outstanding issues surrounding the CDEP scheme and Indigenous employment do not sit well in relation to the Commonwealth government's avowed commitment to practical reconciliation. In July 1999, the government introduced its Indigenous Employment Policy (IEP) to be implemented by DEWRSB (see Shergold, Ch. 8, this volume). This policy offers incentives to increase Indigenous people's participation within the private sector and seeks to support the development of Indigenous small business. While this kind of policy is a step in the right direction, it is clear that a more thorough and comprehensive range of special measures are needed in addition to CDEP and the IEP to address Indigenous disadvantage in regard to unemployment.

This is why a 'rights'-based approach has such a valuable role to play in prompting government to take responsibility for the effects on its Indigenous constituents of past and continuing inequities. The notion of a rights-based approach to Indigenous disadvantage has been associated of late with a loss of responsibility on the part of Indigenous people (see Pearson 2000). But the reason why such an approach to reviewing the social justice implications of the CDEP scheme and Indigenous employment need is so important, is that it requests a significant commitment from government to address Indigenous disadvantage with adequate special measures. The development of appropriate and effective special measures does not necessarily mean a commitment to greater welfare passivity. It can lead, instead, to building on the inroads already made by the CDEP scheme on Indigenous unemployment. This should entail serious application to the question of how an adequate investment can be made in building both the financial and the human capacity to address Indigenous employment need, particularly for the future of our young people.

Notes

1. The ICERD Committee observes 'that a differentiation of treatment will not constitute discrimination if the criteria for such differentiation, judged against the objectives and purposes of the Convention are legitimate.' Cited in the HREOC Review (1997: 41).

References

Acting Aboriginal and Torres Strait Islander Social Justice Commissioner 1998. *Native Title Report*, HREOC, Sydney.

Altman, J.C. 2000. 'The economic status of Indigenous Australians', *CAEPR Discussion Paper No. 193*, CAEPR, ANU, Canberra.

Canadian Royal Commission on Aboriginal Peoples (CRCAP) 1996. *Report of the Royal Commission on Aboriginal Peoples*, Volume 5, *Renewal: A Twenty Year Commitment*, Canada Communication Group, Ottawa.

Committee on Economic, Social and Cultural Rights (CESCR) 1999. The Nature of States Parties Obligations (Art. 2, par. 1), 14/12/90 , CESCR General Comment 3 (General Comments), Office of the United Nations High Commissioner for Human Rights, Geneva.

Neutze, M., Sanders, W. and Jones, G. 1999. 'Public expenditure on services for Indigenous people: Education, employment, health and housing', *Discussion Paper No. 24*, The Australia Institute, Canberra.

Pearson, N. 2000. 'The light on the hill', Ben Chifley Memorial Lecture, presented at Bathurst Panthers Leagues Club, Bathurst, Saturday 12 August 2000.

Human Rights and Equal Opportunity Commission (HREOC) 1997. *The CDEP Scheme and Racial Discrimination: A Report by the Race Discrimination Commissioner,* Commonwealth of Australia, Canberra.

Spicer, I. 1997. *Independent Review of the Community Development Employment Projects (CDEP) Scheme* [The Spicer Review], Office of Public Affairs, ATSIC, Canberra.

Tanaka, J. 1966. *South West Africa Case (Second Phase)*, ICJ Rep. 6.

Taylor, J. and Hunter, B. 1998. *The Job Still Ahead: Economic Costs of Continuing Indigenous Employment Disparity*, Office of Public Affairs, ATSIC, Canberra.

Wooldridge, M. 1998. 'Aboriginal health: The ethical challenges', Speech delivered at the Caroline Chisholm Centre for Health Ethics, 6 August 1998.

3. The changing social security policy context: Implications for the CDEP program

Peter Saunders

Introduction: Inequality and unemployment

There is a certain irony in the fact that at a time when Western industrial economies are entering their eighth year of solid economic growth, attention has focused on the limitations of the social security system. Governments, for long prepared to tolerate rising income inequality as the price to be paid for increased reliance on market flexibility and market forces, see joblessness and the unequal distribution of (paid) work as requiring a policy response.

Although unemployment has fallen markedly in some Organisation for Economic Cooperation and Development (OECD) countries, including Canada, Denmark, Ireland, New Zealand, the UK and the USA, elsewhere it has either fallen only modestly or actually increased. For the OECD as a whole, the unemployment rate is projected to fall by less than one percentage point between 1997 and 2001 despite average growth over the period of around 3 per cent per annum (OECD 2000). The decline of unemployment in countries such as the UK, USA and New Zealand has been accompanied by substantial rises in income inequality (Easton 2000; Smeeding 2000).

Considerable attention has focused on increasing inequality (particularly in the USA), yet as Nobel Prize winner Amartya Sen has pointed out, inequality in the US income distribution must be seen in the context of its low unemployment rate relative to Europe (Sen 2000). In Australia, this debate has been promoted by the recent report of the Reference Group on Welfare Reform (McClure 2000), which cites inequity in the distribution of work as an issue to be addressed, but makes no explicit reference to the need to reduce inequality in the distribution of income.

Has the combination of globalisation and technological change given rise to a new trade-off between inequality and unemployment? Or is it simply that an *ex ante* rise in inequality is the trigger for falling unemployment and declining *ex post* inequality? What has happened to the traditional argument that low unemployment is not only inherently desirable, but is also an effective way to reduce poverty and inequality? Is the only realistic path to lower unemployment for a country like Australia to follow the USA and accept a dose of rising inequality during the transition—and possibly also beyond it?

I think not. A recent study of the rise in US income inequality in the 1990s reveals the extent of the problem and highlights the factors that are driving it (Mishel, Bernstein & Schmitt 1999). Across the middle and lower sections of the US income distribution, the main culprit has been declining wages. Real hourly wage rates fell for the bottom 60 per cent of American workers between 1989 and 1997, resulting in a decline in real median earnings and a rise in median family income of less than US$300. In contrast, executive salaries have soared, increasing on average from 20 times those of the average production worker in 1989 to 116 times as high by 1997. In other words, it now takes the average US executive around two days to earn what the average production worker earns in a year.

Taxation has also played a major role, with the wealthiest 1 per cent of US families experiencing a decline in their annual tax bill of almost US$37 000 between 1977 and 1998. Even the inequities of Australia's Goods and Services Tax (GST) reforms pale in comparison against these figures. Much of the increase in American inequality has occurred (as it has in Australia) at the top of the distribution. Changes in tax policy are needed to bring the rich back within the sight of the rest of society, though there is little sign of this occurring in the foreseeable future in either country.

However, it is what has been happening at the *bottom* of the income distribution that has far greater implications for social security. As Australia follows US trends (though to a lesser degree), wages and working conditions are declining at the bottom of the distribution. This is leading inevitably to a situation where the attractiveness of work relative to social security is declining, making it more difficult to induce those on social security into the workforce.

The persistence of high unemployment is thus in part a direct consequence of the rise in earnings inequality and job insecurity generally. Strategies that attempt to coerce the unemployed and other jobless social security recipients back into work will fail (or, at best, achieve only limited success) unless they also address the issues of low wages, job security and unemployment.

At the same time, the changing nature of risk has undermined the support role of social security. One of the initial goals of the welfare state—as Giddens (2000) has emphasised—was to institutionalise the management of risk so as to offer protection against hazards such as disability or job loss that were seen as outside the control of individuals. Over time, however, moral hazard emerged as an issue, particularly as mass unemployment made it increasingly difficult to police eligibility by supplying job offers to welfare clients. We are now in a situation where, far from protecting the individual against uncontrollable external risks, social security allows individuals to avoid the internal risks associated with participating in an increasingly flexible (and thus precarious) labour market.

Thus, while it is entirely rational from the short-term perspective of individual welfare clients to avoid risk by minimising the effort put into job search activity, the longer-term consequence is to entrench them in a cycle of dependency and social exclusion. Over time, their human capital erodes and they become less attractive to employers, apparently confirming their own assessment of poor labour market prospects. Meanwhile, the welfare budget remains high, preventing government from cutting middle-class taxes. These kinds of arguments have caused the focus of social security policy for people of working age to shift away from meeting the needs of people when they are without work, to developing strategies for integrating them (back) into the world of paid work.

In reviewing some of the policy developments that are taking place in Australia and elsewhere, it is important to emphasise that changes are required both in the social security system and in the labour market. An important factor behind the difficulties facing the social security system relates to what is happening in the labour market. Without addressing these labour market issues, reform of the social security system will achieve only limited success.

Mutual obligation and the new welfare agenda

The McClure Report (McClure 2000) provides a blueprint for medium-term reform of the Australian social security system. Designed to encourage participation, it is built around the principle of mutual obligation—the idea that those who receive social support should be required to 'give something back to the community'. Some commentators are opposed to the idea of mutual obligation on the grounds that its compulsory nature involves a reduction in the rights of citizens, as articulated in social security legislation. However, the receipt of social security benefits has always involved an element of compulsion. Ever since unemployment benefit was first introduced in Australia in the 1940s, applicants have had to satisfy eligibility criteria that have included the requirement that they engage in active job search or other forms of approved activity.

I see nothing wrong in principle with the idea of compulsion—as long as it works in the interests of the client and his or her family and protects the legitimate interests of taxpayers. The key issues revolve around how things operate in practice. How much compulsion will be applied, with what degree of severity, how much assistance will be provided in the form of services, and what will be the consequences for those unable to achieve the participation outcomes expected of them? These practical questions are not addressed in any detail in the McClure Report, yet they are crucial to the functioning, impact and public acceptability of increased mutual obligation. Until we see the government's response to the report's recommendations and observe how the changes function in practice, it is difficult to reach any conclusion about the likely impact of mutual obligation on the prospects of the jobless (as opposed to the numbers receiving social security benefit).

A key concern with mutual obligation as developed in the McClure Report is not the idea itself, but its unbalanced application. Although mutual obligation involves imposing additional requirements on social security recipients, there are no parallel requirements (only expectations) on the other social partners—government, business and local communities. In relation to business, for example, there are many ways in which its obligations could be enforced through appropriate legislation, even if it involved increased taxation. If the social security system is to be tailored to ensure that the mutual obligation requirements on recipients are being met, should not the tax system serve the same purpose for the other social partners, particularly business?

Unless mutual obligation requirements are developed and imposed on all of the social partners, the McClure Report proposals will become the latest in a series of measures designed to make life increasingly difficult for those in receipt of social security. Even the impact of compulsion on job-seeking activity will be small unless action is also taken to address the labour market impediments facing those with few skills or little experience of the labour market. That is, unless compulsion is seen as a vehicle for further eroding the protections currently offered to those at the bottom of the labour market.

This is the US model, where minimum wages are very low, but where low-paid work is an option (in fact, the option) for those denied social security. Poverty on welfare is replaced by poverty in work, the work ethic is enforced, and the declining welfare bill provides the next round of tax cuts for the rich. Despite what some in the current government might wish, I do not see this as an approach acceptable to the vast majority of Australians.

What would most Australians be prepared to tolerate in terms of treatment of the unemployed and other groups? Some insight into this issue can be gained from the Social Policy Research Centre (SPRC) research on community attitudes to social and economic change based on a nationally representative sample of Australians undertaken in the middle of 1999 (Saunders, Thompson & Evans 2000). The results indicate that a high proportion of Australians see no end to the unemployment problem. Over three-quarters of respondents agreed that there will always be some unemployed people and that full employment is no longer a realisable goal. There was also a tendency to overestimate the level of unemployment and the incidence of long-term unemployment. At the same time, while less than 14 per cent agreed with the proposition that the unemployed 'only have themselves to blame', almost 44 per cent agreed that business should be required to create more jobs, while over 47 per cent agreed that solving unemployment is the government's responsibility (Eardley, Saunders & Evans 2000).

There is thus little evidence here of a one-sided approach to mutual obligation when it comes to addressing the unemployment problem. Indeed, there is strong community support for requiring more of business and government as well as of the unemployed themselves, and broad agreement that mutual obligation should be extended to all three groups, through specific proposals. This suggests that mutual obligation must be linked to the notion of social partnerships, which is given considerable emphasis in the McClure Report, with government having a major role in fostering community capacity.

When it comes to views on the generosity of support for the unemployed, clear differences begin to emerge. Around one-quarter of people think that too much support is provided to the young (under 25) unemployed, the long-term unemployed, people constantly in and out of work, and unemployed migrants. In contrast, less than 14 per cent thought that too much was provided to the unemployed with young children, and less than 2 per cent thought that this was so for the older (over 50) unemployed. This differentiation of views is consistent with recent attitudinal research for the Netherlands reported by van Oorschot (2000). That research indicates that public support for welfare benefits is greatest for those seen as having less control over their circumstances, those who most closely resemble the respondents, and those who are seen as having 'earned' their right to support. Support is greatest, in other words, for those who are powerless and deserving, but also most readily identifiable as part of the mainstream.

When the SPRC researchers asked about attitudes to activity test requirements such as requiring people to look for work, participate in work for the dole, or undergo training, they found a similar differentiation in what is considered reasonable, according to the circumstances of the unemployed person. In fact, the variation was greater according to the characteristics of the unemployed than according to the kinds of requirements imposed on them. While a large majority favoured requiring the young unemployed and, to a lesser degree, the long-term unemployed, to do just about anything as a condition of getting benefit, support for similar treatment of other groups of the unemployed was much lower. There was much greater reluctance to impose activity test requirements on the older unemployed and those with young children, and strong opposition when it came to people affected by a disability (Eardley, Saunders & Evans 2000: Table 7).

Australians thus do not seem inclined to offer unconditional support to the notion of mutual obligation as applied to all of the unemployed. There is strong agreement that government should play a greater role in solving the unemployment problem, even if this involves additional budget outlays. But there is almost no support for further deregulation of the labour market as a strategy for reducing unemployment, with less than one per cent citing this as one of the changes government should be making.

Although the participation support system proposed in the McClure Report represents a uniquely Australian response to the problems of unemployment and joblessness, strong parallels have been drawn with 'welfare to work' programs introduced in the USA and UK and elsewhere (e.g. the Netherlands). There are certainly many similarities. These include the imposition of work-focused requirements and sanctions for those who refuse to comply, the according of a supportive role to enabling services such as training and child care, an emphasis on encouraging self reliance and independence, and the need to involve other key stakeholders such as business and the community. But there are also important differences in the emphasis given to obligation as compared with other objectives, as well as in the design of specific policies introduced to achieve change.

Making work pay: Implications of US and UK experience for Australia

Australia has always had strong links and shared experiences with the UK and the USA, the two leading members of the liberal welfare state regime to which Australia belongs. There have been many exchanges of policy experience (and policy makers) between Australia and the UK, operating both through organisations like the OECD and on a direct bilateral basis. Although this is less true of Australia–USA relations in social policy, the USA is a natural place to look for empirical evidence on the impact (particularly the behavioural impact) of social policies. It is also the home of many of the most prominent liberal (and libertarian) welfare theorists and the country that has travelled for longest on the 'welfare to work' path.

Although it is natural for Australia to look to developments in those countries with which its welfare system has most in common, this should not prevent us from also studying the experience of other countries. There is a tendency in Australia to equate European welfare states with those of Scandinavia—where levels of social expenditure and taxation would terrify most Australian politicians. But there is in fact a considerable diversity of welfare size and experience within Europe and many lessons to be learnt from a careful study of the relevant experience of countries such as France, the Netherlands and Ireland.

Australia can also benefit from the experiences of our nearer neighbours, including not only our OECD partners Japan and Korea, but also others in a region where, even though state welfare plays a subsidiary role to family and civil society, welfare policies still provide many interesting lessons.

These comments notwithstanding, my focus here is on what we can learn from the recent social security experience of the USA and the UK. There is a good deal that is common in the recent welfare reform experience of Australia and these two countries. At the same time, as Julia Perry of the SPRC has observed, although these three countries speak the same welfare reform language, they do so with rather different accents (Perry 2000). One common thread running through what all three countries are trying to achieve is to increase the attractiveness of work compared to welfare through a combination of welfare conditionality and in-work benefits. The former is designed to modify the behaviour of social security recipients (possibly through coercive measures) in order to make them more prepared to seek (paid) work, while the latter is intended to make the transition to work more financially attractive to them. The differences arise in the scope and severity of conditionality and in the nature of the tax, benefit, and labour market changes designed to increase the attractiveness of work.

There is no doubt that the Earned Income Tax Credit (EITC), originally introduced in the USA in 1975 but greatly expanded in the early 1990s (Ellwood 2000), has increased the financial attractiveness of work for those on welfare—although not by as much as is often claimed, according to Wolfe (2000). The Temporary Aid for Needy Families (TANF) program introduced in 1996 as part of the *Personal Responsibility and Work Opportunity Reconciliation Act* placed a time limit on benefits for single parents. This introduced an element of compulsion into the welfare system that commentators like Lawrence Mead (2000) see as essential in achieving the welfare to work transition.

However, although Mead argues that the evidence on participation rates and poverty is consistent with the view that these programs have been successful, others agree with Giddens' (2000) assessment that 'the jury is still out' on this key question. There is less evidence, for example, that the fall in welfare receipt among US single mothers, although accompanied by increased employment participation, has resulted in increased incomes and lower poverty. There are, however, formidable problems in attributing what has happened to the EITC and TANF welfare reforms, as distinct from the booming US economy. The real test for the USA will come when the next recession arrives.

The other important aspect of the US situation is the labour market, specifically the low wages and working conditions of the low-paid. As Mishel, Bernstein and Schmitt (1999: Fig. 6I) have demonstrated, throughout the 1990s both male and female wages at the twentieth percentile are well below what is required to raise a family of four above the poverty line. In light of this, it is difficult to see how low-wage workers in the USA can be expected to work their way out of poverty. Despite the rhetoric about work being the most effective anti-poverty strategy, the US experience shows that this is not a practical reality if market forces are allowed to dictate what happens at the bottom of the labour market.

Indeed, Wolfe (2000) argues that the USA has not been successful in combining strong work incentives with an adequate welfare safety net that has eliminated poverty. The welfare system (and the welfare budget) may have shrunk, but poverty remains high and inequality continues to rise. The statistics are certainly impressive. As Danziger (1999) indicates, the number of Aid to Families with Dependent Children (AFDC)/TANF recipients fell from a peak of over 14 million in 1994 to 7.5 million by 1998, at a time when employment participation among single mothers increased to the same rate as that of married mothers. Yet the poverty rate for single mothers in 1997 was 35.1 per cent, virtually identical to the figure for 1979 (34.9 per cent) and 1989 (35.1 per cent).

In contrast to the US approach, the New Deal in the UK combines active labour market support for the unemployed with greater emphasis on the obligations of (and, increasingly, compulsion on) the unemployed to achieve financial independence through paid work. But the difference is that the strategy operates within a social security safety net designed to provide security and an adequate standard of living for the unemployed, sole parents, and people with disabilities who are not able to find work. Work itself has been made more financially attractive through the introduction of Working Families Tax Credit (WFTC) and an additional tax credit for those with child care costs (Grover & Stewart 2000).

But arguably the most significant element of the British approach—certainly the aspect that distinguishes it from the American model—is the introduction of a minimum wage. Although there have been criticisms that it has been set too low, two arguments in favour of the minimum wage are of particular interest in the Australian context. The first is that, in direct contrast to what has happened in the USA, a minimum wage has the potential to prevent the erosion of the welfare system in the face of downward wage pressures emanating in the labour market. It reflects the fundamental principle that a coherent welfare to work strategy requires a consistent set of welfare *and* wage policies. The other rationale for the UK minimum wage was that, since wages are spent locally, a minimum wage can assist in the regeneration of economically depressed regions by injecting additional spending power into the local economy (Grover & Stewart 2000).

It is clear from this discussion that there are both similarities and differences in the recent welfare to work policies of the USA and the UK. The similarities include the use of tax credits to raise the in-work income of low-wage earners, an increased reliance on the obligations of welfare recipients to find paid work, and (although not discussed explicitly above) the elimination of child poverty as a goal of social policy.

The differences are, however, both more important and of greater relevance to Australia. Whereas the USA has continued its *laissez faire* approach to the labour market, the UK has increased the role of labour market interventions as part of its overall strategy to forge a new ('third way') alignment between state and market in achieving economic and social objectives. The logic underpinning the US approach is that an increasingly competitive labour market will continue to drive down wages, making the welfare system unsustainable. In these circumstances, the state has a duty to warn welfare recipients that 'their days are numbered' and to take action (including coercion) to force them to compete in the labour market, assisted by tax credits and other programs consistent with a minimalist state, market economy.

In contrast, the UK's strategy recognises the need for a new approach to state welfare in a world increasingly dominated by market competition, in which paid work is the source of economic prosperity and an expression of personal identity. In this context, the means and ends of welfare may need to be revisited, but neither the welfare state nor those who rely on it should be abandoned. That, at least, is the essence of the UK experience under the Blair government.

Which country offers the better model for Australia? There are aspects of both in the vision and framework developed by the Reference Group on Welfare Reform (McClure 2000), although the strength of its commitment to social security (albeit it repackaged as social participation support) suggests a closer affinity with what is happening in the UK. Against this, the Howard government's labour market reform agenda has been strongly influenced by the US experience.

We cannot have it both ways. The logic developed above indicates that the social security system is not sustainable in an environment where the labour market is deregulated and where the wages of the low-paid are constantly falling. The need to lower benefits in order to maintain incentives will constantly erode the ability to provide an adequate level of support relative to need. Australia's traditional emphasis on poverty relief and a targeted, needs-based approach to adequacy suggests that it has more to learn from the UK experience than from what is happening in the USA—particularly when it comes to the labour market.

Implications for CDEP

What, if anything does this imply for the future of CDEP? I restrict myself to a few observations, prompted by the work of the Reference Group on Welfare Reform and by Noel Pearson's recent scathing attack on 'passive welfare' (Pearson 2000a, 2000b). Some time ago, Will Sanders described the CDEP scheme as 'sitting astride the welfare/work divide', by which he meant that it was primarily a welfare program, but with many of the attributes of an employment program (Sanders 1997; see also Sanders, Ch. 6, this volume). Now CDEP is located at the centre of the welfare–work stage, not because of any change in the program itself, but because welfare is now viewed as part of a spectrum leading to work in an era of mutual obligation.

Since its establishment on a pilot basis in 1977, CDEP has shown remarkable resilience in a period of constant welfare reform. It has also proved to be popular among the Indigenous community and its leaders (Altman 1997) and has recently been shown to generate additional income in the communities reliant on CDEP compared with other Indigenous communities (Altman & Gray 2000). Yet the fact remains that CDEP has not provided the basis for economic renewal in remote Indigenous communities.

Research undertaken by Gregory and Daly (1997) has relevance to this issue. They showed that although Indigenous Australian men had higher incomes than Native American men in the USA, Indigenous employment rates were much lower in Australia. Over the 1980s, while Native Americans maintained their employment level in the face of a 17 per cent fall in income, the incomes of Indigenous Australians rose by 10 per cent while their (non-CDEP) employment fell by one-quarter. This situation in Australia can only be overcome, the authors argued, by giving 'Aborigines currently residing in remote communities… access to the range of employment opportunities that are normally available to the White community in cities' (Gregory & Daly 1997: 118). The implication is that CDEP cannot provide a long-term solution to this problem, whatever its short-term popularity and effectiveness.

There are echoes of this line of argument in Noel Pearson's recent criticism of 'passive welfare', by which he means welfare provided as 'unconditional cash pay-outs to needy citizens of whom nothing further will be required' (Pearson 2000a: 137). Although CDEP does require something of its recipients and provides a modicum of control over local communities, Pearson emphasises that this should not divert attention from the fact that Indigenous Australians have been provided with social transfer income but have been dispossessed from the real economy (Pearson 2000b).

There is a certain similarity between Pearson's use of the term passive welfare and the moralistic tones which were expressed by Minister Newman in her 'welfare dependency' speech to the National Press Club prior to the establishment of the welfare review (Newman 1999). The difference is that whereas Senator Newman was arguing that requiring too little of non-Indigenous welfare recipients may have induced a 'culture of dependency' that has left individuals excluded from economic wealth and prosperity, for Indigenous Australians the problem is one of community exclusion based on systematic discrimination and dispossession.

Welfare reform alone will do little to resolve the problems identified by Noel Pearson. What is needed is the establishment and development of real productive economic activity in the Indigenous community. Welfare reform may be necessary to achieve this, but unless accompanied by economic reform its role will be, at best, only marginal. This paper has argued that the same is true of the role and impact of welfare reform generally. In light of this, the failure of CDEP to bring about economic revival is hardly surprising.

This is the main conclusion that flows from the arguments presented here. The major contemporary problems we face—structural unemployment, poverty, and inequality—are all basically economic in origin and their resolution requires policies that address these economic causes. That is why welfare reform must be accompanied by labour market reform in mainstream Australia, and why significant progress for Indigenous Australians will not be achieved without sweeping economic reform.

References

Altman, J.C. 1997. 'The CDEP scheme in a new policy environment: Options for change?' *CAEPR Discussion Paper No. 148*, CAEPR, ANU, Canberra.

—— and Gray, M.C. 2000. 'The effects of the CDEP scheme on the economic status of Indigenous Australians: Some analyses using the 1996 Census', *CAEPR Discussion Paper No. 195*, CAEPR, ANU, Canberra.

Danziger, S. 1999. 'Introduction: What are the early lessons?' in S. Danziger (ed.), *Economic Conditions and Welfare Reform*, W.E. Upjohn Institute for Employment Research, Michigan, MI.

Eardley, T., Saunders, P. and Evans, K. 2000. 'Community attitudes towards unemployment, activity testing and mutual obligation', *Australian Bulletin of Labour*, 26 (3): 211–35.

Easton, B. (2000), 'What has happened in New Zealand to income distribution and poverty levels?' in S. Shaver and P. Saunders (eds), *Social Policy for the 21st Century: Justice and Responsibiliy*, Vol. 2, *Reports and Proceedings No. 142*, SPRC, UNSW, Sydney.

Ellwood, D. 2000. 'The impact of the Earned Income Tax Credit and other social policy changes on work and marriage in the United States', *Australian Social Policy*, 1999 (1): 75–113.

Giddens, A. 2000. *The Third Way and Its Critics*, Polity Press, Cambridge.

Gregory, R.G. and Daly, A.E. 1997. 'Welfare and economic progress of Indigenous men of Australia and the US 1980–1990', *Economic Record*, 73 (221): 101–19.

Grover, C. and Stewart, J. 2000. 'Modernizing social security? Labour and its welfare-to-work strategy', *Social Policy and Administration*, 34 (3): 235–52.

McClure, P. (Chair) 2000. Participation Support for a More Equitable Society: Final Report of the Reference Group on Welfare Reform, July 2000 [the McClure Report], DFACS, Canberra.

Mead, L. 2000. 'Welfare reform and the family: Lessons for America', in P. Saunders (ed.), *Reforming the Australian Welfare State*, AIFS, Melbourne.

Mishel, L., Bernstein, J. and Schmitt, J. 1999. *The State of Working America, 1998–99*, Cornell University Press, Ithaca, NY.

Newman, J. 1999. 'The future of welfare in the 21st century', Telstra Address to the National Press Club, Canberra, 29 September 1999.

Organisation for Economic Cooperation and Development (OECD) 2000. *OECD Economic Outlook No. 67, June 2000*, OECD, Paris.

Pearson, N. 2000a. 'Passive welfare and the destruction of Indigenous society in Australia', in P. Saunders (ed.), *Reforming the Australian Welfare State*, AIFS, Melbourne.

—— 2000b. 'The light on the hill', Ben Chifley Memorial Lecture, presented at Bathurst Panthers League Club, Bathurst, Saturday 12 August 2000.

Perry, J. 2000. 'One language, three accents: Welfare reform in the US, UK and Australia', Paper presented to the AIFS Research Conference, Sydney, July 2000.

Sanders, W. 1997. 'Opportunities and problems astride the welfare/work divide: The CDEP scheme in Australian social policy', *CAEPR Discussion Paper No. 141*, CAEPR, ANU, Canberra.

Saunders, P., Thomson, C. and Evans, C. 2000. 'Social change and social policy: Results from a national survey of public opinion', *Discussion Paper No. 106*, SPRC, UNSW, Sydney.

Sen, A.K. 2000. *Development as Freedom* (pbk edn.), Anchor Books, New York.

Smeeding, T.M. 2000. 'Changing income inequality in OECD countries: Updated results from the Luxembourg Income Study (LIS)', in R. Hauser and I. Becker (eds), *The Personal Distribution of Income in an International Perspective*, Springer-Verlag, Berlin.

van Oorschot, W. 2000. 'Who should get what and why? On deservingness criteria and conditionality of solidarity among the public', *Policy and Politics*, 28 (1): 33–48.

Wolfe, B.L. 2000. 'Incentives, challenges and dilemmas of TANF', Paper presented to the Seventh International Research Seminar on 'Issues in Social Security', Sigtuna, Sweden, 17–20 June 2000.

4. Community development in the context of welfare dependence

David Martin

The beginning of the twenty-first century sees a number of quite fundamental challenges confronting the CDEP scheme, both at the policy level and at the level of local implementation. The first challenge arises from implications for the CDEP scheme of new international and Australian thinking about welfare policy in general. A second challenge concerns the establishment of meaningful and appropriate parameters for 'development' through the CDEP scheme which go beyond purely economic development. Another concerns the definition and operationalisation of an appropriate scope for the 'community' in which the particular CDEP scheme is operating.

CDEP and 'mutual obligation'

I first want to turn briefly to some of the issues emerging from new welfare policy thinking in Australia, which itself reflects international trends in countries such as the USA and the UK (see also in this volume Saunders, Ch. 3; Smith, Ch. 7; Westbury, Ch. 10). In essence, these new approaches to welfare replace the philosophy of the inherent entitlements of citizens to basic social and economic support by the state, with one in which the recipient of welfare benefits is expected to actively seek employment, to improve his or her employability, and to contribute to society in return for its support.

The cynic might take the view that much of this thinking derives from the increasing reluctance of government to fund the ever-expanding demand for welfare support, and its sensitivity to popular, if misinformed, hostility towards welfare recipients. At the same time, it has to be said that there is an increasing awareness of the corrosive effects on individuals and communities of long-term welfare dependence. This can be seen both in the report to government of the Reference Group on Welfare Reform, *Participation Support for a More Equitable Society* (McClure 2000) and in publications by the prominent Aboriginal intellectual and social activist, Noel Pearson, in particular *Our Right to Take Responsibility* (Pearson 2000).

The Reference Group argues that the welfare system must be judged by its capacity to assist people to participate both economically and socially, as well as by the adequacy of income support arrangements. The McClure Report identifies five features of its proposed Participation Support reforms, including 'mutual obligations' underpinned by a broader concept of social obligations, and 'social partnerships' as a key strategy for building community capacity. Similarly, Pearson argues for new partnerships to be forged between Indigenous people and their organisations, government, and other parties, and for 'reciprocity' to be reinstituted as a fundamental means by which the 'gammon' (false) welfare economy, which encourages passive dependence in Indigenous people, must be transformed to a 'real' economy.

While (as Jon Altman notes in Ch. 13 of this volume) neither Pearson's monograph nor the McClure Report pay much attention to the CDEP scheme, it could be argued that for almost a quarter of a century Indigenous people and their organisations have pioneered innovative means of instituting principles now espoused through the 'mutual obligation' framework. However, I would caution against assuming that the principles of CDEP schemes should be seen as unproblematically consistent with that policy framework.

Firstly, mutual obligation is held to lie essentially between the welfare recipient as an autonomous individual on the one hand, and government, representing the wider society, on the other. However, the obligations accorded significance by Indigenous people are typically not to the wider, largely non-Indigenous society, from which after all they have historically been excluded or at best marginalised; on the contrary, their obligations lie within Indigenous society itself, for example to specific kin or within 'family' networks.

From this perspective then, the form of mutual obligation which underlies CDEP schemes may be closer to the 'reciprocity' which Noel Pearson has argued is necessary to transform the passive welfare economy to a 'real' economy. Pearson argues in part that government is too *remote* from its citizens, and in particular does not have the moral authority with Indigenous people to appropriately enforce mutual obligations. Rather, these obligations must be demanded and implemented between the individual and his or her particular community, family and local group; it is at these levels that the terms must be established of the reciprocity to which able bodied community members should be bound (Pearson 2000: 85–7; see Martin 2001).

The core point being made here is that while in CDEP schemes mutual obligation lies essentially between the Indigenous individual and their own particular Indigenous group or community, in the wider policy framework the obligations lie between the individual and the wider society. I return to this point later in the paper.

A second point of difference is that the stated objective of the mutual obligation policy is to encourage greater self reliance and motivation in job seekers by encouraging them to take responsibility for, and to be more focused on, preparing for and searching for work. That is, mutual obligation is clearly concerned with moving individuals from welfare dependency to engagement with the formal market economy. As such, it is consistent with the increasing reliance upon market and quasi-market forces in areas of social as well as of economic policy. Its adoption as a policy principle is thus consistent with a view of people which sees them essentially in economic terms, as taking their place within a progressively more mobile workforce in an increasingly globalised economic order.

Such views of the relationship between society, the individual, and the economy are not necessarily widely held by Indigenous people themselves; in fact, they may well be rejected. Within Indigenous groups, value is typically placed on particular sets of relationships to other people within particular social networks (especially those of kinship), and on connections to specific regions and locales. Thus, while there is high mobility amongst Indigenous people, it tends to be mobility within a relatively bounded social geography. Indigenous people's world views and identities are thus often intensely locally based; the very idea of moving away from one's own family and place may be confronting or even frightening. The values accorded to such 'economic' matters as work, cash, consumer goods, entrepreneurship, investment, and productivity, may differ significantly from those which enable individuals and groups to compete effectively in the wider economy.

A third, and very important, point of difference lies in the focus of mutual obligation on individuals. It implicitly assumes that social and economic change should be driven through changes in the circumstances, skills, and opportunities of individuals. Equally, it assumes that the wider social problems which are associated with welfare dependency can be addressed through changing the circumstances of individual lives. However, this focus on the individual does not reflect common principles of Indigenous social, economic, and political organisation. Nor does it reflect the fact that the problems associated with the cumulative effects of historical exclusion, marginalisation, and now welfare dependency in many Indigenous societies, most particularly in the remote and rural Indigenous communities, are *systemic* in nature and of a scale absolutely unparalleled in contemporary non-Indigenous society. CDEP, if it is to truly be effective, must take account of the particular ways in which individual participants, in each scheme, are embedded within their social networks and groups, for example those of family and kin.

I have suggested a number of reasons why the current policy definition of mutual obligation does not necessarily sit easily with the CDEP scheme. I now turn briefly to consider what might be meant by the 'development' aspect of community development.

Community 'development' and CDEP

CDEP schemes have been operating in Indigenous communities since 1977. However, under the 1987 Aboriginal Economic Development Policy and more particularly since the Spicer Review of CDEP (Spicer 1997), the original emphasis on 'community development' has gradually been replaced, at the policy level at least, by a focus on the scheme's capacity to facilitate enterprise development and to prepare individuals for employment in the mainstream labour market (see Shergold, Ch. 8, this volume).

In practice, the goals of CDEP schemes continue to be rather more diverse. There are many schemes which do have a primarily economic focus, which provide training and work opportunities which enable participants, if they so choose, to move into the mainstream job market, and which in some cases have developed creative strategies for leveraging their competitive advantage for enterprise development. Such outcomes should be applauded, and strongly supported at both policy and resourcing levels. However, as an exclusive policy focus for the CDEP scheme, moving individuals into formal employment and enterprise development is, in my view, misguided for at least three reasons.

First, many Indigenous communities, particularly those in remote and rural regions, are located within regional economies in which such policy objectives are simply not achievable for more than a relatively insignificant minority of individuals. Structural factors such as the current poor health and educational levels of Indigenous people in many regions, together with 'locational disadvantage', that is, the lack of business development and employment opportunities in the areas in which many Indigenous people live, mean that it is simply not realistic for policy to be predicated upon moving significant numbers of Indigenous people from dependency on welfare payments to participation in the formal economy. In such circumstances, the challenge both for policy makers and for Indigenous people themselves is to develop creative responses to the objective reality that in many regions there will be continuing medium and long-term Indigenous dependence upon Government transfer payments, rather than simply reproducing the myth of economic development or even independence.

Second, an exclusive policy focus on a narrowly 'economic' form of development also denies the objective reality of distinctive Indigenous world-views—cultures—in which, typically, material goods play a different role than they do in non-Indigenous society. This is not to say that Indigenous people are necessarily caught in some time warp where the contemporary world of cash, consumer goods and so forth has no place. The evidence indicates the contrary. However, there is a strong commonality between the so-called 'traditionally oriented' Indigenous societies in the more remote regions and those in urban and rural areas, in that the formal economy based on the production, exchange and consumption of things, including cash, is embedded within a 'social economy' in which primacy is given to the connections between people rather than to the connections between people and things.

Third, a formally 'economic' focus for CDEP ignores the severely disadvantaged and sometimes quite dysfunctional state of many contemporary Indigenous communities, particularly those in rural and remote areas. It assumes that, somehow, meaningful employment, training, and enterprise development activities can take place within situations all too often characterised by chaos, conflict, and family and personal distress. It assumes that the intensity and scale of these personal and social problems, often wrongly attributed solely to welfare dependency, can be addressed through mechanisms which both enable, and ultimately compel, individuals to engage with the formal economy.

The challenge for CDEP is to return to the core concept of 'community development', in which economic development is but one factor, although one of central importance. This broader goal is consistent with the thrust of the recommendations of the McClure Report mentioned earlier. While affirming the policy framework of mutual obligation and the centrality of enabling people to find meaningful work, the McClure Report embeds mutual obligation within a wider framework of social obligations, stresses that there are a range of means by which individuals can participate in and demonstrate their obligations to society, and places the enhancement of 'community capacity' as a core policy goal. A more broadly based policy goal such as this suggests at the very least a sympathetic re-examination of the potential importance of community development as a core goal of the CDEP scheme, and challenges a narrowly economic or employment-based focus for the welfare system more generally, and particularly for CDEP.

CDEP should not be seen as the Indigenous equivalent of 'work for the dole'. It should be one of the means by which Indigenous communities are resourced to enhance and develop their social and capital infrastructure. Its goal of community development should not be confined to formal 'economic' development, but should include building on existing Indigenous values and capacities, developing the capacity of Indigenous groups and individuals to make strategic choices in their engagement with the wider society and economy, and helping Indigenous individuals and groups enhance their capacity to deal with the often difficult circumstances of their everyday lives.

What constitutes the 'community' in CDEP?

The concept of 'community' also needs careful examination in the context of CDEP. The term is widely used both by government and by Indigenous people and their organisations. Indigenous individuals and organisations will legitimate their position by reference to being community based. Equally, governments seek what they term 'community support' for their policies, and will legitimate policy changes in terms of this supposed support. However, Indigenous communities are highly complex and internally differentiated (see Frances Peters-Little, Ch. 19, this volume). Their existence as communities of interest is constituted largely in relation to the outside world. Their populations are differentiated in terms of the factors which continue to inform Indigenous political, social and economic relations—connections with ancestral lands and language, personal and group histories, ethnicity, and bearing on all of these, family and other local group affiliations.

Above all else, a fundamental component of Indigenous societies across Australia is the 'family'. Indigenous families however are not to be understood as merely 'extended' versions of non-Indigenous families. They are based on principles, in particular that of descent, which demonstrate direct continuity with the land-holding structures of pre-colonial Indigenous societies. They form the basic political, social and economic units of contemporary Indigenous society. Indigenous people typically do not operate in terms of their 'community'; rather, their place in the Indigenous world, and their responses to the non-Indigenous society, are established through their place as a member of their particular family (Sutton 1998: 55ff).

This has important implications for the implementation of the CDEP scheme. It has been argued throughout this paper that the CDEP scheme should take account of, rather than deny, the reality and validity of Indigenous values and practices. If Indigenous families form basic units of economic and social action, then it is important that this be taken into account, as far as possible, in the implementation of CDEP schemes.

What could this mean in practice? From the perspective of government, and of ATSIC, it is simply not feasible to fund a whole host of family-based CDEP schemes. Nor is it desirable from the Indigenous point of view; for one thing, small schemes would just not be administratively or logistically viable, as can be seen from the failure of many of the small Indigenous housing associations. Funding agencies need administratively competent, viable, CDEP organisations with the economies of scale and the ability to attract the necessary skilled staff.

Yet, within these organisations there is the capacity to plan and implement the allocation of resources, work programs, and other activities in such a way that autonomy and control at the local group level is facilitated. There are many ways in which this is already being done within CDEP schemes across Australia. Work gangs can be based on families or kin groups. Centrally administered regional CDEP schemes can allow for local residential communities to have effective control of their own work programs (see Gray & Thacker, Ch. 15 and Madden, Ch. 18 in this volume for cases in point). Even mechanisms for budgeting, program delivery and financial accounting can be developed so as to maximise control by relevant local groups, within an overall strategic direction set by the organisation as a whole. New technologies, including the Internet and accounting software, can be important tools in assisting the CDEP scheme to be accountable to, and maximise the control of, such local groups, as can more effective and accountable organisational structures.

An analogy—although it speaks to saltwater, rather than inland people—is that a CDEP scheme which gives maximum autonomy to its constituent families or other relevant sub-groups can be likened to a large jellyfish. From above, the jellyfish appears solid and bounded. Underneath, however, are myriad tentacles, each feeding and existing almost independently of the others.

Thus the community to which a CDEP scheme relates is not just an aggregation of individuals, as the non-Indigenous welfare policies would have it. Nor is it an undifferentiated entity. Rather, it is comprised of 'family' or other relevant sub-groupings which reflect basic Indigenously defined structures. It is these Indigenous groupings which should be the primary focus of CDEP, and of Indigenous welfare policy more generally.

Conclusion

During the 1988 bicentennial events, Indigenous people countered the dominant view of Australian history with their own, alternative view. Transcending the history of the denial of the reality and validity of Indigenous society and culture by the dominant society, the strong message from Indigenous people was: 'We have survived'. The policy of assimilation has been replaced by self determination and, more recently, self management, and the Indigenous view should be accorded the respect that is due. The CDEP scheme should not be utilised to provide a mechanism for a more subtle form of assimilation— not by overt prescription but by default.

Of course, all cultures change, and the situation in many Indigenous communities is truly desperate and must be addressed. But economic change is only one aspect of social change, and the full potential of the CDEP scheme will only be realised through its capacity to foster community development which includes, but is not limited to, economic development.

References

McClure, P. (Chair) 2000. Participation Support for a More Equitable Society: Final Report of the Reference Group on Welfare Reform, July 2000 [the McClure Report], DFACS, Canberra.

Martin, D.F. 2001. 'Is welfare dependency "welfare poison"? An assessment of Noel Pearson's proposals for Aboriginal welfare reform', *CAEPR Discussion Paper No. 213*, CAEPR, ANU, Canberra.

Pearson, N. 2000. *Our Right to Take Responsibility*, Noel Pearson and Associates, Cairns, Qld.

Spicer, I. 1997. *Independent Review of the Community Development Employment Projects (CDEP) Scheme* [The Spicer Review], Office of Public Affairs, ATSIC, Canberra.

Sutton, P. 1998. *Native Title and the Descent of Rights*, National Native Title Tribunal, Perth.

5. The political dimensions of community development

Tim Rowse

The self determination policy era has given rise to Indigenous political institutions with a mix of representative, service delivery, policy making and land owning functions. This 'Indigenous sector' is essential to the representation and satisfaction of Indigenous wishes. Without the Indigenous sector, Indigenous Australians would lack public policy recognition of their needs and aspirations; they would be invisible, as Indigenous people, within Australian society and they would be unable to make any demands, as Indigenous Australians, on Australian institutions. In short, the Indigenous sector is one of the defining material products of the Australian public policy change from 'assimilation' to 'self determination'. The Indigenous sector is what puts into practical effect the 'self' in self determination.

CDEP as political development

CDEP schemes make up an important component of the Indigenous sector. In this paper I want to highlight CDEP as a program of political development. Any CDEP scheme can be considered as an instance of Indigenous political authority. It is easy to 'forget' that CDEPs are political institutions whose aims include perpetuating and increasing their own empowerment. The 'labour market' focus of so much of the government effort to improve Indigenous welfare invites us to consider the outcomes of CDEP as either 'employment outcomes' or 'non-labour market outcomes' (ATSIC Office of Evaluation and Audit (ATSICOEA) 1997: i). Another policy publication lists the outcomes of CDEP under the headings 'Indigenous employment situation' and 'community development, social and cultural outcomes' (Spicer 1997: contents page). I suggest that the so-called 'non-labour market outcomes' and 'community development, social and cultural outcomes' of CDEP include the 'political' empowerment of Indigenous participants in CDEPs, and that this should be explicitly stated.

A CDEP scheme embodies a form of Indigenous authority, in three ways. First, CDEP schemes derive authority from the fact that the Commonwealth government endows them with money, and delegates to each scheme a great deal of discretion about how that money is to be spent. That discretion is not unlimited. The Commonwealth's grant of money is conditional on each CDEP scheme addressing certain policy objectives. However, these objectives are multiple, and it would be rather difficult to demonstrate that a CDEP scheme is not addressing any of the stated objectives of Commonwealth government policy. Thus although CDEP schemes derive their authority from the government giving them money, they have a high degree of autonomy. One of the most important expressions of that autonomy is that CDEPs can define 'work'. When ATSIC's Office of Evaluation and Audit (OEA) examined the range of definitions of 'work' used in urban CDEPs, it found that about three out of every five CDEPs in their survey paid people for 'home duties'. Across 53 CDEP schemes, 7 per cent of participants had their home duties recognised, and paid, as 'work' (ATSICOEA 1997: 17).

Second, the CDEP scheme exercises authority over the work-time of its participants. However, a CDEP scheme is unusual when compared with other 'bosses' who have authority over 'workers'; CDEP workers are, in some respects, like shareholders in the CDEP. Because CDEPs are community-based organisations, their managers are not only bosses over the participants, they are also, to some degree, the employees or servants of the scheme's participants.

Let me illustrate my first two points with some research findings. In 1997 ATSIC's OEA surveyed 53 coordinators of urban CDEPs. The OEA asked coordinators what aspects of CDEP were most in need of improvement. Interestingly, they ranked 'participant motivation' well behind 'project funding', 'training', 'paper work/redtape', and 'planning' (ATSICOEA 1997: 20). In other words, the coordinators were finding more difficulties in managing their relationship with ATSIC and other agencies than their relationship with participants. When the OEA asked about the problem of 'participant motivation', the coordinators offered a range of suggestions:

- the most frequently cited (43 per cent) was the provision of more meaningful and varied work in the CDEP;

- the next most frequently given suggestion (28 per cent) was the strict usage of the 'no work, no pay' policy; followed by

- the provision of better communication and participant involvement in the running of the CDEP (26 per cent);

- giving participants a warning followed by dismissal if absenteeism persists (17 per cent);

- provision of incentives such as pay bonuses and recognising the contribution of participants (17 per cent); and

- development of a good system for monitoring and enforcing attendance (13 per cent) (ATSICOEA 1997: 17).

This list of motivational strategies draws attention to two features of the political authority of CDEPs: the importance of sufficient autonomy, so that CDEPs can define work in a way that takes seriously participants' interests and needs, and the 'industrial democracy' factor—the wisdom, as managers see it, of involving participants in decision making.

The third and final way in which I see CDEP schemes as a form of Indigenous political authority, is that by being able to direct the collective working capacity of participants towards certain ends, the CDEP scheme becomes an effective player in the local political scene. That is, a CDEP scheme forms relationships with other organisations, whether they be other Indigenous organisations in the region, or the local shire or municipal council, or State or Territory and Commonwealth agencies that have responsibilities in the area. Sometimes these relationships take the form of contracts for the CDEP scheme to deliver a service. However, not all the significant relationships between CDEP schemes and other regional players are contracts of service. Sometimes CDEPs are effectively powerful simply because they deliver a service that no government agency has provided. (Although this is often seen as an unfair imposition on over-stretched CDEPs—see Bartlett, Ch. 20 and Kean, Ch. 21 of this volume— it is also a source of their bargaining power—see Nicholas, Ch.25, this volume.) Another reason a CDEP scheme may be a political player is because its leaders—its governing Board or Council and its senior managers—include some of the most experienced and hard-working Indigenous leaders in that region (see Lewis, Ch. 30, this volume). A CDEP scheme may be part of a power base for the emergence of a regional Indigenous leadership.

In making these three points about CDEPs as structures of Indigenous political authority, I am not saying anything new. However, it is important to make these political dimensions of CDEP explicit, because in the CDEP policy literature this political dimension tends to be taken for granted. For example, the Spicer Review (1997) remarked that CDEP 'can be described as an employment program, a community development program, and enterprise development program, a diversionary program, a skills development and work preparation program and/or a cultural maintenance program' (Spicer 1997: 24). I would like to add 'political development program' to that list of possibilities. Spicer might concur, because his very next sentence implies 'political development' without actually using that phrase: 'As CDEPs *have the ability to determine their own objectives, and the manner in which they are achieved*, features of all these programs can exist in any one community' (Spicer 1997: 24, emphasis added).

Spicer's phrase 'community development' might be interpreted to include 'political development'. However, the phrase 'community development' can mean so many different things to different people; any positive change in people's lives, such as a fall in alcohol consumption, can be counted as 'community development'. I want to promote 'political development' as an essential part of the vocabulary with which we discuss CDEP so that we can appreciate CDEP as one of the most significant steps ever taken in this country towards Indigenous self determination. I will later suggest a way to understand 'community development' in the context of CDEP.

Forgetting the political dimension

By insisting on the political dimensions of CDEP, I hope to bring back into our understanding something that we are in danger of forgetting. The then Aboriginal Affairs Minister, Ian Viner, first tabled guidelines for CDEP in the House of Representatives on 26 May 1977. The fourth of his four objectives was 'to maximise *the capacity* of Aboriginal communities *to determine* the use of their workforce' (Human Rights and Equal Opportunity Commission (HREOC) 1997: Appendix 2, p.59, emphasis added). One of CDEP's architects, 'Nugget' Coombs, suggested later that same year that those evaluating the new scheme should bear in mind that 'CDEP is not simply a means of providing employment as a source of a minimum cash income but *a training exercise in self-management* and increasing independence for the Aboriginal communities involved' (Coombs 1977: 1, emphasis added).

In the 23 years since Viner and Coombs wrote political objectives into the founding documents of CDEP, it has been too easy to evaluate CDEP as if it were only or mainly another strategy to counter 'welfare dependency'. For example, the Department of Social Security (DSS) asserted in 1997 that 'the philosophical basis of the scheme is to assist unemployed Indigenous Australians in their move away from welfare dependency towards self-reliance' (cited in HREOC 1997: 48). This is far too narrow a view of CDEP. By contrasting 'welfare dependency' with 'self-reliance', the DSS was ignoring the possibility that CDEP communities might develop their self reliance in the context of their continuing dependence on a certain form of welfare payments—CDEP. Self reliance is a term with more than one meaning. It may refer to an individual 'not relying on any kind of payment from the state', but it can mean other things too. These other forms of 'self reliance' are those envisaged by Viner—'the capacity ... to determine' how consolidated Unemployment Benefits are to be used—and by Coombs—'training ... in self-management'. We should avoid assuming that 'self determination' or ('self management') is possible only once people have moved outside the welfare system. If people get organised so as to use their welfare payments as they wish, and if governments do not impose narrow conditions on such uses, then we can have a form of self determination that is based on, and secured by, 'welfare dependency'. Unlike the author of that 1997 DSS letter, I believe that welfare payments can be the financial foundation for Indigenous self reliance. It all depends on *the political conditions* that are placed by the government on the transfer of funds to the CDEP scheme.

If we are to evaluate CDEP with a sensitivity which pays attention to its complexities, we must understand each CDEP scheme as an interlocking set of three political relationships: between the government and the eligible Indigenous participants, between those participants and the managers of each scheme, and between each scheme and the other organisations within its region.

Just as the emergence of the 'Indigenous sector' since the early 1970s is a new chapter in Australian political history, so CDEP is a unique program within the history of Australian social policy. Because it is unique it is very tempting to try to understand it by comparing it to some welfare program with which we are already familiar. It has been very common, in discussions of CDEP, to liken it to other programs—such as income support programs and job-training programs—and to evaluate it in such terms. No doubt there are elements of CDEP which cause it to resemble, in some ways, other social and industrial programs. One example has just been mentioned: DSS in 1997 chose to think of CDEP as if it were essentially aimed at getting its participants into jobs and so making them ineligible for welfare payments. Another way of understanding CDEP, which also falls into the trap of likening it to something with which we are familiar, has recently risen to prominence: is CDEP the Indigenous version of 'work for the dole' (WFTD)? And are both CDEP and WFTD the prototypes of the newly-acclaimed principle of 'mutual obligation'?

Work for the dole and mutual obligation

It is certainly tempting to understand CDEP as Australia's earliest experiment in 'mutual obligation'. I have tried to understand CDEP in such terms, but now I have my doubts. If there is a precedent for mutual obligation in Australian social policy it is not CDEP, but the (more recent) WFTD program introduced by the Howard government in October 1997. CDEP is not the Indigenous equivalent of WFTD.

Why is it misleading to liken CDEP to WFTD? The Spicer Review gave one answer to that question in 1997—an answer from the point of the view of the individual participants:

> WFTD participants retain their NSA (New Start Allowance) entitlement and are also paid a $20 per fortnight 'Community Work Supplement' to cover work related costs such as transport. They also retain all the 'extras' attached to NSA that are at present denied to CDEP participants (e.g. Rent Assistance, taxation rebates, access to advance payments). They are also able to access free child-care whereas this is not an automatic entitlement for CDEP participants (Spicer 1997: 46).

Governments have generally tried to calibrate the entitlements of CDEP and WFTD participants, to give them more equal 'baskets' of benefits, in order to oblige the principle of equity of entitlement among citizens. Indeed Spicer advocated such equalisations. However, we do not have to restrict our comparison of WFTD and CDEP to the viewpoint of the individual participants. While the baskets of entitlements may become more equal, there remain some important structural distinctions between WFTD and CDEP.

The essential difference between them, as I understand it, is that WFTD does not require the formation of an ongoing community-based political authority. In a WFTD scheme, the participants' primary relationship is with DFACS. They continue to receive NSA from the Department (including Centrelink). The host of the WFTD scheme is a relatively unimportant go-between in the relationship between NSA beneficiary and state authority. Although the WFTD host supervises and certifies each individual's performance of some work, that host's powers are less than those delegated to the managers of a CDEP scheme. CDEP schemes have more ongoing discretion about what is to be defined as 'work', for example.

Those in the WFTD schemes continue to be counted as unemployed. In CDEP, the relationship between participants and management is an employer–employee relationship. That is why the author of the Spicer Review thought it necessary to devote its longest chapter to discussing how best to apply the *Workplace Relations Act* to CDEPs. There is no employer–employee relationship in the WFTD scheme, and so there is no possibility for industrial relations law and culture to shape the social context in which people 'work for the dole'.

Both WFTD and CDEP schemes get administrative and capital grants, but the CDEP scheme also gets all the money equivalent to the Jobsearch Allowance and NSA that their participants would receive, and they have some discretion to draw on this money in funding their various expenditures on administration and capital items. This greater financial latitude that is afforded to CDEP structures would be magnified were a government to take up Spicer's recommendation that CDEP schemes be funded triennially. (It is clear from the contributions to the 'Community perspectives' section of this volume that CDEP managers aspire to more authority over the use of their diverse incomes than they have been allowed recently.)

In many places where there is a CDEP scheme—particularly in remote Australia, and more particularly on outstations—CDEP is one of the few administrative structures for that place, and in some cases the only administrative structure. As Spicer put it, 'in some localities, CDEP often represents the community itself. Without it, some remote communities would simply not exist' (1997: 1).

To sum up, in WFTD schemes DFACS–Centrelink has delegated far less authority to the host of the scheme than ATSIC has delegated to CDEP organisations. This difference is consistent with a marked cultural difference between the two presiding agencies. Compared with ATSIC, the administrative culture of DFACS is highly centralised; its senior officers are nervous about the possibility of the downward delegation of authority, lest that detract from the Department's well-deserved reputation for policing the fiscal delinquency of the poor. ATSIC, by contrast, seems to have weathered the storms of fiscal accountability and has secured a government mandate to delegate a great deal of authority to Regional Councils and to such clients of the Regional Councils as CDEP schemes.

'Mutual obligation' as industrial relations

All major political parties have endorsed, in general terms, the principle of mutual obligation. However, we are still in the early days of the development of that principle into operational social policy programs. Much of our comment about the forms to be taken by 'mutual obligation' must remain speculative. My speculation is that it is unlikely that CDEP will be a general precedent for 'mutual obligation' which, in Australia, is likely to become a punitive administration of social security entitlements, a raising of the bar of eligibility testing. According to the DFACS 1998–99 *Annual Report*, out of 72–96 000 people estimated to fall under the Department's mutual obligation requirement, 53 000 signed up to mutual obligation (not necessarily in WFTD schemes) and 23 000 were breached (in 1998–99) for not satisfying their mutual obligation requirements (DFACS 1999: 121). Certainly 'mutual obligation' provides new grounds for breaching.

If the state were to make CDEP its model for 'mutual obligation', it would have to foster the formation of CDEP-like community authorities all over Australia, and then it would have to delegate considerable powers to those entities. There is nothing in the statements made by either side of politics that promises such a transformation of Australian social policy. From the point of view of political elites who favour market solutions to problems of human survival, CDEP is not a model, but an exception—possibly an embarrassing or even dangerous exception. CDEP is an infringement on the privilege of private investors to define the conditions of material wellbeing through the market place. CDEP does more than compensate for the market's failure to provide jobs where Indigenous people live, it also throws into question the power of the market to define the nature and intensity of work. To illustrate this point, let us look at some recent reviews of CDEP.

I suggest that the term 'community' in CDEP can best be understood as a particular industrial relations culture. Participants in CDEPs are not like employees of a normal Australian employer. Earlier I likened CDEP participants to shareholders. Looking at it another way, the relationships within a CDEP are also a bit like the relationships among members of a mutual association. Ultimately, we must try to see each CDEP in its own terms, for a CDEP industrial framework seems nevertheless to be evolving. Spicer's Monash University industrial relations consultant posed the question: would it be better for CDEP management and participants to formalise their relationship as an Australian Workplace Agreement (AWA) or as a Certified Agreement (CA)?

After surveying a sample of CDEP managers, the consultant concluded that AWAs were inappropriate. For several reasons, it would be neither practical nor consistent with the communal aspirations of CDEPs to govern industrial relations through a series of individual contracts between management and participant. The 'values and principles' of AWAs are 'contrary to CDEP social or community development objectives' (Spicer 1997: 129). Even if all the individual contracts within a CDEP were written in the same terms, the consultant concluded, there was reason to doubt that CDEP managers had the skills or the inclination to use AWAs. Though CDEP managers did deal with their participants as individuals, they told the consultant that they preferred to keep such individual case-management on a purely informal basis. The managers' reported reasons for preferring certified agreements—whether negotiated with a union or not—are very interesting, and pertinent to the theme of this paper. The managers told the consultant that they thought it important that all CDEP personnel—managers and participants alike—were bound by an agreed set of rules, in order to discourage favouritism and to establish, in the eyes of all, the fairness and impartiality of the CDEP, and in order to bind managers and participants to the expressed wishes of the host community (Spicer 1997: 134–5).

> Thus, the main value in certified agreements for CDEPs appear to lie in potential benefits derived from having a self-determined level of formalisation of rules and regulations governing participation in CDEP. In comparison with AWAs, certified agreements were also seen as far more consistent with self determination and various consultative approaches to CDEP decision-making in operation at CDEP programs (Spicer 1997: 136).

Let me underline two points that emerge from the work of Spicer's Monash University industrial relations consultant.

- The managers conceived of themselves as working according to a community mandate. (This was not the only constraint that they were aware of, of course. They remarked also on the way that conditions of funding set a framework for their supervision.) The notion of a community mandate is clearly important in distinguishing CDEPs from other enterprises with which it might be compared. It serves as another reminder that CDEPs are structures of political authority.

- The managers, at least as reported by the Monash consultant, expressed their need for a set of rules that made their authority legitimate in the light of what they see as the participants' expectations.

These insights into the industrial relations culture of CDEPs are important because they help us to come to an understanding of that otherwise impossibly vague term 'community development'. The 'community' that CDEP constructs can be understood in quite specific terms as a set of *negotiated understandings* about what counts as work, what counts as effort, and what obligations bind 'management' and participants.

Conclusion: Market versus democracy

There are competing models of mutual obligation. One of them is CDEP; another is WFTD. With such different possible models, 'mutual obligation' has the potential to become a key political term whose practical meanings are continually contested. The main issue that would emerge from such a politics of 'mutual obligation' would be this: what is the nature of the authority that defines and enforces the obligations of individual welfare recipients? Is that authority a national bureaucracy, seeking to apply the same definitions of recipient compliance all over Australia, with no concessions to cultural or regional difference? Or is that authority a series of local community authorities, each delegated the discretion to define work in locally-relevant terms and each empowered to make its own assessment of the developmental needs of the individuals and communities it serves?

The rise of the Indigenous sector is the most important change in the Australian system of government since World War II. CDEP is one of the most interesting and challenging types of institution within that Indigenous sector. CDEP could be a model for the application of mutual obligation to the entire Australian welfare system, or it might merely continue to be understood as an expedient device for dealing with a temporary 'Indigenous problem'—helping 'them' to catch up with 'us'. There is a culture of mutual obligation in CDEP, but it is one which Australian governments are unlikely to find attractive. Governments are unlikely to use CDEP as a widely relevant model of mutual obligation because CDEP is also a model of how the demands of the market may be answered by the demands of democracy. For this reason, governments are more likely to try to reduce the autonomy of CDEPs and to regulate their internal culture so that they become more like the 'work for the dole' scheme.

References

Aboriginal and Torres Strait Islander Commission Office of Evaluation and Audit (ATSICOEA) 1997. *Evaluation of the Community Development Employment Projects Program: Final Report, September 1997*, ATSIC, Canberra.

Coombs, H.C. 1977. 'The application of CDEP in Aboriginal communities in the Eastern Zone of Western Australia', *Centre for Resource and Environmental Studies Working Paper HCC/3*, CRES, ANU, Canberra.

Department of Family and Community Services (DFACS) 1999. *Annual Report 1998–99*, DFACS, Canberra.

Human Rights and Equal Opportunity Commission (HREOC) 1997. *The CDEP Scheme and Racial Discrimination: A Report by the Race Discrimination Commissioner*, Commonwealth of Australia, Canberra.

Spicer, I. 1997. *Independent Review of the Community Development Employment Projects (CDEP) Scheme* [the Spicer Review], Office of Public Affairs, ATSIC, Canberra.

6. Adjusting balances: Reshaping the CDEP scheme after 20 good years

Will Sanders

Introduction

There are two simple ideas flagged in the title to this paper. The first is that the first 20 years of the CDEP scheme, from 1977 to 1997, were very clearly *good* years. From its tentative beginnings in just a few communities, the CDEP scheme proved enormously popular both with Indigenous communities and with governments. Over the years the scheme grew accordingly; indeed, it became the largest single program in the Commonwealth Indigenous affairs budget.

The second idea is that the CDEP scheme has always been a fairly delicate balancing act. It arose out of the extension of social security rights to Indigenous Australians and it has, ever since, tried to balance those rights with other policy imperatives—such as the desire to encourage employment, enterprise and community development.

In current debates about the Indigenous welfare economy, and how it might be improved or even surpassed, I do not think the CDEP scheme has been given enough attention. The scheme shows us what is possible in improving the Indigenous welfare economy and it also shows us some of the complex and delicate balances that have to be struck in order to realise these possibilities.

In this paper, I focus on some of those complex and delicate balances and how they continue to require adjustment, even after 20 good years for the CDEP scheme. Ultimately I want to argue that the reforms of the last two or three years have been moving the CDEP scheme in two quite different directions at once—towards the social security system on the one hand and towards greater employment outcomes on the other. I do not have a strong sense yet of whether this is, overall, a good or bad thing. My main objective, at this stage, is simply to try to understand why and how it is occurring. I will set the scene with a little bit of policy history, from the 1970s to the early 1990s.

Policy history

Although the CDEP scheme grew out of the extension of social security entitlements to Indigenous Australians, it was not, in the late 1970s and the 1980s, in any way formally linked to the social security system. The scheme was not recognised by or referred to in the social security legislation and it was administered, at Commonwealth level, almost entirely by the Indigenous affairs portfolio with little or no input from the social security portfolio. The link between the CDEP scheme and social security entitlement was simply an informal, notional financial offset. The CDEP scheme was outside the social security system, and participants in the scheme were essentially treated simply as low-income wage earners.

This changed somewhat in 1991 when a clause was introduced to the social security legislation which forbade participants in 'Commonwealth funded employment programs' from qualifying for unemployment payments—or New Start Allowance as it then became. CDEP was not mentioned specifically by name, but the intent of the reference to 'Commonwealth funded employment programs' was clear: CDEP participants would not under any circumstance be entitled to Newstart allowance because they were seen as already receiving another form of Commonwealth government income support.

This quite specific legislative provision opened up a new line of criticism of the CDEP scheme, which manifested itself in complaints to the Human Rights and Equal Opportunity Commission (HREOC) from CDEP scheme participants. These complaints, paraphrasing the voice of CDEP participants, were of roughly the following form:

> Seeing the social security legislation recognises us, CDEP participants, as Commonwealth income support recipients for the purposes of disqualifying us from New Start Allowance entitlement, why doesn't it also recognise us as income support recipients for the purposes of qualifying for such social security entitlements as rent assistance, health care cards and tax rebates available to beneficiaries, and for the further fringe benefits that can flow from income support recipient status such as concessional charges for various state and local government and privately provided services?

The HREOC Review

In 1995, HREOC directed its Race Discrimination Commissioner to investigate and report on these complaints. In her report in 1997, the Commissioner generally accepted the validity of the complaints and, although stopping short of making a finding of racial discrimination, was quite critical of the way the DSS and other government agencies treated CDEP participants. She argued that there was a lack of 'consistency' or 'uniformity' in the treatment of CDEP participants by government agencies which, in some situations, meant that they got the 'worst of all' treatments (HREOC 1997: ix).

The Race Discrimination Commissioner suggested that the solution to this 'worst of all worlds' treatment was to consider CDEP participants consistently and uniformly as 'ordinary wage earners'. To this end, she even contemplated the repeal of the 1991 provisions of the *Social Security Act* which had partially recognised the CDEP scheme as part of the Commonwealth income support system, and had hence forbidden CDEP participants from also qualifying for New Start Allowance (HREOC 1997: ix). However this repeal did not occur.

By late 1997, the DSS had also come to accept the validity of the complaints of CDEP scheme participants and was moving, in consultation with ATSIC, to resolve the issues in another way altogether. Its solution was to *extend* the recognition of CDEP participants within the social security system. CDEP scheme participants would become social security customers, while also being wage earners in relation to their local Indigenous community organisation. They would have a social security customer reference number and receive 'add on' entitlements as income support recipients from within the social security and tax systems, even though their basic entitlement would still be routed through ATSIC and the Indigenous community organisations administering CDEP as wages.

This is the arrangement which was foreshadowed in the 1998 Budget and which was slowly introduced during 1999 and 2000. The new social security service delivery agency, Centrelink, is now part of the CDEP scheme's administration and DFACS, which oversees social security system, also has a background policy presence. This reshaping of the CDEP scheme after 20 good years has brought it, and its participants, considerably closer to the social security system than ever before.

The Spicer Review

I now turn to another source of review and reshaping of the CDEP scheme altogether, the so-called Spicer Review (Spicer 1997). This review grew out of a freeze placed on the expansion of the CDEP scheme by the incoming Howard government in 1996. Previously, under Labor, CDEP had been able to expand by between 1200 and 1800 places per year. After a year of the Howard government's freeze, ATSIC sought to raise anew the issue of expansion and was told that, before expansion would be even contemplated, there would have to be an 'independent' review of the CDEP scheme. Hence the creation of the Spicer Review in the second half of 1997.

The Spicer Review began with the observation that up to one-third of CDEP participants did not then work, and that for them the scheme was no more than an alternative form of income support (Spicer 1997: 2). This 'sit-down money' element of CDEP was seen as both a wasted work resource and as a poor substitute for social security income support. These people would often be better off, financially, if they were clients of the social security system and, it was suggested, the CDEP scheme would also be better off, and more work-focused, without them. This push towards a more work-focused CDEP scheme was also seen as putting off the need for expansion since, for a couple of years at least, CDEP could supposedly expand internally, by offloading those on sit-down money onto the social security system and by increasing the proportion of participants who were working.

This set of reforms was essentially pursued by ATSIC once it became clear that the Howard government was not going to accept much expansion of CDEP. ATSIC was, in many ways, pushing CDEP away from the social security system. Those on CDEP who looked like social security recipients were being encouraged off, while those who stayed on CDEP were being encouraged to be more work-focused, possibly undertaking training and even being encouraged to move beyond the scheme into general, or mainstream employment.

Conclusion

At the policy level at least, the recent reshaping of CDEP has been a matter of adjusting balances within the scheme by moving in two directions at once. This movement has been both towards the social security system, as a result of (though not recommended by) the HREOC Review, and towards a greater employment focus as a result of the Spicer Review.

In an earlier paper I described CDEP as being 'astride the welfare/work divide in Australian social policy' (Sanders 1997). With this recent movement in two directions at once, CDEP is as firmly and awkwardly astride that divide as ever, though as I noted in that earlier paper, there are both opportunities and problems in that position, and the opportunities for CDEP have in general outweighed the problems.

I have not attempted here to make any overall judgment as to whether this recent pull in two directions has been a good or a bad thing for the CDEP scheme. I simply observe that this is what has occurred, and try to understand why. At the level of practice—rather than policy—it is debatable whether the CDEP scheme is in fact moving in two directions at once. It would seem to be very difficult to encourage people off the scheme onto social security payments because they are not working, while at the same time telling them they are indeed Centrelink customers, even while on CDEP. In practice, on the ground, the scheme may not have been moving in two directions at once; it may simply have been moving closer to the social security system, with some old and thorny issues about working and not working within the scheme remaining unresolved.

References

Human Rights and Equal Opportunity Commission (HREOC) 1997. *The CDEP Scheme and Racial Discrimination: A Report by the Race Discrimination Commissioner,* Commonwealth of Australia, Canberra.

Sanders, W. 1997. 'Opportunities and problems astride the welfare/work divide: The CDEP scheme in Australian social policy', *CAEPR Discussion Paper No. 141*, CAEPR, ANU, Canberra.

Spicer, I. 1997. *Independent Review of the Community Development Employment Projects (CDEP) Scheme* [the Spicer Review], Office of Public Affairs, ATSIC, Canberra.

PART II

POLICY PERSPECTIVES AND ISSUES

7. Welfare dependence, mutual obligation and the CDEP scheme: Lessons from community research and an overseas initiative

Diane Smith

Introduction: The policy threads

It is commonly asserted that Indigenous dependence on welfare is increasing; that it is a passive and debilitating experience rather than a valued citizenship entitlement. But to what extent is this actually the case? And if it is true, what policy tools and service delivery models might assist in addressing the situation?

The Federal government's current welfare reform agenda suggests the problem of welfare dependency can be met by moving 'beyond reliance on income support to self-sufficiency'. The concept of mutual obligation is proposed as a 'new participation framework' for facilitating this objective (Commonwealth of Australia 2001: 8; Newman 1999: 6–7). Mutual obligation is characterised by government as being 'both a right and the obligation to share in the benefits of economic and employment growth' (Newman 1999: 6). It will require unemployed people, and possibly persons in receipt of other types of welfare payments, to 'strive to improve their chances of getting jobs and actively look for work and give something back to the community that supports them' (Newman 1999: 4; see also Commonwealth of Australia 2001). It is not yet clear how the new social security reforms, and especially mutual obligation, will be applied to Indigenous people dependent upon welfare transfers.

This issue is especially pertinent because, since 1977, Indigenous communities have been able to participate voluntarily in the CDEP scheme. Individuals in the scheme transfer from the direct receipt of social security income to the receipt of equivalent levels of income for undertaking work coordinated by local CDEP organisations. In June 2000, some 30 600 people across 262 communities were participating in the CDEP scheme, and over half of these resided in remote locations (ATSIC 2000: 48). Thus participants in CDEP schemes are, in effect, already fulfilling mutual obligation by 'working for the dole'. It might also be possible for CDEP organisations to play a wider role at the community level, in translating proposed social security policies into practical and feasible options. But the prospect of such an enhanced role raises other questions concerning the effectiveness and funding of CDEP organisations, and the availability of community-based training and employment opportunities for Indigenous Australians. These policy threads—on welfare dependence, mutual obligation and possible future roles for the CDEP scheme—will be woven together here, so as to address the broader issue which links them all; namely, how social security income and services might be more effectively and appropriately delivered to Indigenous Australians in order to alleviate high levels of welfare dependence.

The historical transition of Indigenous Australians to welfare dependence is first described. There then follows a presentation of the detailed results of survey research on the current nature of welfare dependence being experienced by Indigenous families in two communities—Kuranda and Yuendumu.[1] In both communities, the CDEP scheme is a major component of the labour market. The important contribution of CDEP incomes to the welfare economies of households is highlighted. Recommendations for fine-tuning social security policy and service delivery are then outlined, with a focus on the potential capacity of CDEP organisations to provide assistance to a wider range of social security recipients. The type of policy framework best suited to implementing mutual obligation in Indigenous communities is explored.

The paper concludes with a review of a major initiative in the delivery of social security income and services to American Indian people, known as the Temporary Assistance to Needy Families (TANF). The US Federal government's Tribal TANF program has some similarities to the CDEP scheme, but it also shows some important differences in its policy and service delivery. While still in its early days of implementation, TANF has potential relevance for Indigenous welfare reform in Australia (see also Saunders, Ch. 3 and Westbury, Ch. 10, this volume).

The historical transition to welfare dependence

The changing relationship of Indigenous Australians to the social security system can be characterised as a transition from enforced exclusion up to the 1960s, to progressive inclusion over the last 30 years (Altman & Sanders 1995). That process of inclusion has been paralleled by growing levels of dependence on income support payments. Fisk (1985) estimated that social security payments constituted 47 per cent of all Aboriginal personal income in 1976 and 54 per cent in 1981, compared to a national rate estimated at 14 per cent for the whole of Australia. In 1974, the Australian Commission of Inquiry into Poverty reported an Indigenous poverty rate of 48 per cent (Brown, Hirschfeld & Smith 1974; Henderson 1975). There have been good economic reasons why Indigenous Australians actively asserted their right to take up income support payments from the 1970s onwards.

Some 30 years later, data about the progressive uptake of social security income by Indigenous Australians suggest that, in relative terms at least, welfare dependence has not greatly increased. In the National Aboriginal and Torres Strait Islander Survey (NATSIS) conducted in 1994, 55 per cent of respondents stated they received some form of social security payment as their main source of income. Amongst the wider Australian population, 13 per cent of households received their primary income from social security payments (Altman & Hunter 1998). This comparative rate is almost identical to Fisk's earlier estimates for the late 1970s and early 1980s (Fisk 1985).

However, a combination of factors indicate that while the relative state of Indigenous welfare dependence has not changed significantly over thirty years, there has been an absolute increase in the number of people reliant on income support payments. These factors include a 33 per cent increase in the Indigenous population between 1991 and 1996; the resulting dramatic increase in the Indigenous working-age population and the number of households; the youthful Indigenous demographic profile; and the continued failure of mainstream employment opportunities to keep pace with Indigenous population growth (see Daly & Smith 1999; Ross 1999; Taylor & Hunter 1998; Tesfaghiorghis & Gray 1991). In light of these factors, it seems likely that Indigenous dependence on social security income support will continue, if not increase, in both absolute and relative terms, unless drastic action is taken (see Taylor & Hunter, Ch. 11, this volume).

The community research project

There seems to be an almost neo-missionary zeal surrounding the current debate about Indigenous welfare dependence. While the debate is necessary, much of it is not new, and there seems to be a dearth of hard facts and practical solutions. This paper begins to address the lack of data by presenting preliminary survey research about the qualitative experience of welfare dependence within households, and its social, economic and structural consequences.[2]

In late 1998, CAEPR was commissioned by the Indigenous Policy Unit of DFACS to investigate the effectiveness and suitability of social security service delivery to Indigenous families with children, and to consider the related policy implications.[3] The research is being carried out over a four-year period during which approximately 60 households in the two communities of Kuranda and Yuendumu will be surveyed each year (see Smith 2000).

The research project aims to obtain qualitative and quantitative data through a mix of methodologies. These include the conduct of informal group discussions; interviews with key individuals working in regional education, health, housing and finance institutions; the elicitation of household genealogies; and the repeated administration of household questionnaires via a key reference person. The success of the field-based research has been highly dependent on the support of the local communities and the use of Indigenous field assistants to facilitate the interviewing process (Smith 2000; see also Hunter & Smith 2000). The validity and relevance of the household data have been enhanced by an analysis of relevant national census and aggregate Centrelink administrative data.

The terms of reference for the project include identifying, in each community:

- the household and family organisational structures and composition;
- the nature of household welfare economies, based on the sources of individual members' incomes;
- the key cultural parameters of child care;
- patterns of mobility of children and adults household members; and
- family members' own perceptions of welfare service delivery.

The household questionnaires covered a total of 418 individuals who were the members of the households at the time of the interviews in 1999.[4]

Welfare dependence and work: The community survey data

When household income by source is considered, it is clear that social security payments constitute the core component of income for the surveyed households. In the 28 Kuranda households, the 180 people (adults and children) in residence are overwhelmingly welfare dependent, with the households receiving a total of 96 social security-related payments. In Kuranda, 77 per cent received their primary source of income from a social security payment, 20 per cent from CDEP, and 3 per cent from wages. In Yuendumu, 71 per cent of all adults received their primary source of income from a social security payment, 19 per cent received it from a CDEP income, and 10 per cent received a wages income. In both communities, 100 per cent of the surveyed households had at least one adult receiving a welfare payment, and the majority had several adults receiving a range of social security payments. For many households, total income per person per fortnight was under $300, with 40 per cent getting less than $200 per fortnight.

The research indicates that individuals in both communities are locked into a fortnightly pattern of immediate consumption, lending, and borrowing linked to the payment of social security income support. Many are living in a 'feast and famine' cycle where certain family members—in particular, children and the aged—are vulnerable to any fluctuations in income and care. Such a pattern leaves individuals with little capacity to save (see Westbury, Ch. 10, this volume). This situation is tempered, however, by facilities made available through CDEP organisations and Centre Pay, whereby individuals can have regular deductions made from their incomes for the payment of recurrent bills. These facilities provide a valued form of budgeting and de facto savings for many people.

Family members rely heavily on other relatives sharing available cash and resources with them. They also regularly use a system of 'bookdown' at local stores to purchase goods on credit during the period between social security payments. Another important form of local 'micro-credit' is the cash 'advances' made available by Centrelink and CDEP organisations. These loans are then repaid out of the individual's future welfare or CDEP income. Over half the Kuranda respondents had received a Centrelink advance in the 12 months prior to the interview.

These factors, in combination, lead to a situation where many individuals recycle through the social security system over their lifetime, and where a number of families manifest inter-generational dependency on social security. In both communities, welfare dependency is therefore applicable not only to individuals, but to entire families and their households.

But the research results also suggests the need for important qualifiers about the nature of that welfare dependence. The dependence being experienced by families is quantitatively different from that experienced by other Australian families. It is also qualitatively different. Family members fall back upon culturally-based values, their own system of shared child-care, and networks of economic support and demand sharing. This Indigenous system of support is a form of risk-pooling that keeps many families financially afloat. It constitutes precisely the kind of 'social participation' and 'social capital' identified by the McClure Report (2000) as the very basis of strong families and communities (see also

Hunter 2000). As such, they should be supported by government policy, especially given the enormous strains placed on support networks by wider community problems. Respondents identified health and substance abuse, domestic violence, inexperienced young parents, bored and uncontrollable youth, and lack of employment opportunities as major problems in their communities. They consistently pointed to the need for housing—especially for young families—and for local employment other than CDEP, and recreational programs and youth-workers.

Another important qualifier raised by the research is that families and their households can not simply be described as 'welfare dependent'. Rather, they are dependent on a mixed domestic economy of low, often erratic incomes of which social security payments are but one, albeit an important component. In both communities a typical household has members receiving not only welfare payments, but also CDEP income, ABSTUDY monies, irregular income from art and craft production, occasional royalty receipts (in the case of Yuendumu) and some wages income. Only three of 102 adults in Kuranda, and 18 out of 182 in Yuendumu, received a non-CDEP wage income. Given the extent of kin relatedness in both communities, and the constant redistribution of cash within families and between households, it is analytically unsound to separate welfare dependence from people's dependence on other sources of 'welfare-equivalent' income and other public transfers.

The policy and the personal reality for the families surveyed in both communities is that receipt of income support is both a form of entrenched dependence related to poverty entrapment, and a citizenship entitlement that provides a valued base-level income without which many would not survive. Furthermore, while government welfare reform focuses on attempting to move Indigenous Australians off income support, and out of the CDEP scheme into mainstream employment, the survey research suggests that some people are still unaware of their basic welfare entitlements.

Welfare dependence, work and mutual obligation: Policy conclusions

If welfare dependence is to be constructively addressed, we need to think differently about the way the social security system is delivered to Indigenous Australians. The question is how this can be done without undermining the existing strengths of many family structures, and without the exercise degenerating into social engineering. There is a need for an enabling policy framework in which Indigenous people can exercise both their personal and cultural autonomy, and their social and cultural responsibilities.

The community-level research highlights the fact that Indigenous social security recipients have specific characteristics and needs that are not always congruent with those of their mainstream counterparts. A 'one-size-fits-all' policy and service delivery model will fail to adequately represent the diversity of Indigenous realities on the ground, will impact negatively on families and will, as a consequence, provide less effective outcomes. Reforms that focus on encouraging the transition of Indigenous people from welfare to mainstream employment will need to address this diversity.

The research also indicates that Indigenous welfare dependence is a complex phenomenon which cannot be treated in isolation from other social, economic and cultural problems. Government policy will need to be applied in ways that are culturally and economically informed about these local realities if the circumstances of Indigenous people are to improve. Reform must necessarily happen down at the level of community economies, and must address families, not just individuals.

The research conclusions highlight the need for government to:

- formulate an Indigenous Welfare Policy and an Indigenous Mutual Obligation Strategy to reflect the underlying common characteristics as well as the diversity of circumstances, of Indigenous social security recipients;

- provide early intervention assistance and training to youth, young parents and sole parent families immediately upon their entry into the social security system;

- develop strategies to address the growing demands placed upon service delivery by Indigenous young parents, and by youth and children at risk of inter-generational welfare dependence;

- develop a revitalised role for the CDEP scheme and its organisations in providing mentoring, training and early intervention to a wider range of Indigenous welfare recipients, and in negotiating locally-relevant mutual obligation frameworks; and

- develop working partnerships between Centrelink, DFACS, Indigenous communities and their organisations, to ensure more culturally-informed and coordinated service delivery for Indigenous social security recipients.

If it is going to have practical benefit, a policy framework for mutual obligation for Indigenous social security recipients must:

- be flexibly defined to accommodate cultural, family and economic realities;

- be realistically applied in respect to any activity test, and include exemptions;

- accord value to voluntary, culturally-based and community development work;

- accommodate the intricate conjunctions between individuals, their families and the wider community;

- recognise the CDEP scheme as already fulfilling any mutual obligation test;

- specify the 'obligations' that fall on government and the private sector; and importantly,

- be linked to enhanced government investment in education, training, and employment opportunities for Indigenous social security recipients.

Earlier research analysis of NATSIS and comparative ABS survey data indicates that Indigenous Australians undertake voluntary work at a national rate of 27 per cent, compared to 19 per cent for the total population (see Hunter 2000; Smith & Roach 1996). The most common types of voluntary work undertaken by Indigenous Australians involve community and sporting organisations, working with school and youth groups, working on committees, and caring for sick and aged relatives. Over half of those persons who reported that they carried out voluntary work also stated that they received government social security payments as their main source of income (Smith & Roach 1996: 71). It would seem that a number of Indigenous people are already fulfilling the mutual obligation criterion by carrying out voluntary work in their own communities.

For Indigenous Australians, improving the delivery and administration of the social security system will not be a sufficient answer in itself. It must go hand in hand with a significant improvement in their access to, and take up, of meaningful paid employment and vocational training in their own communities. However, an underlying premise of the welfare reform agenda seems to be that Indigenous Australians have access to viable labour markets and paid employment, and that training is available to them in the communities where they reside. In fact, the 1994 NATSIS survey reported that a substantial proportion of unemployed Indigenous men and women (42 per cent and 33 per cent respectively), and especially those in remote, rural, and 'other urban' areas, cited the fact that there were 'no jobs at all' and 'no jobs in the local area' as their main difficulty in finding work (ABS–CAEPR 1996: 57–8).

Research by Taylor and Hunter (1998) indicates that substantial government investment in training and job creation would be needed to achieve employment equity. More recent research suggests that even with additional investment, if participation in education and vocational training (perhaps as requirements of mutual obligation), is going to assist in reducing welfare dependence, then it will have to take account of the local demand for skills, and locational constraints on labour markets (Daly 2000; Gregory & Martin 2000).

The future implementation of mutual obligation, if it is insensitive to the circumstances of Indigenous people, could translate into a form of welfare enterprise-bargaining in which Indigenous income support recipients would be at a disadvantage, and their rights potentially jeopardised. An element of discretion will be necessary simply in order to make feasible the requirements of mutual obligation (Keating 2000: 27; Smith 2000: 112–15, 126–9). These concerns might be addressed partly through a revitalised role for the CDEP scheme in which local CDEP organisations develop realistic guidelines and facilitate outcomes for social security recipients, and their families and communities.

Reforming welfare: A revitalised role for the CDEP scheme?

In Yuendumu, the CDEP scheme offers the only sustained employment opportunities to the majority of adults. This is also true in Kuranda, which appeared to have a reasonably thriving tourist-based local economy. For many families, the employment exit from the social security system is likely to continue to be via the local 'community development' labour market, of which the CDEP scheme constitutes the major component.

Government policy which attempts to transform the scheme into a labour market program, to secure increased transitions to mainstream employment, will fail in locations where there are no such labour market opportunities. This is the case in the majority of the 172 remote

CDEP communities. The practical reality of the scheme is that CDEP organisations operate on the 'front-line' of the social security system, at the family and household level, where they are often called upon to address a wide range of social and economic problems. Furthermore, recent legislative changes mean such organisations can accept a wider range of social security recipients as participants, including sole parents, the aged, and the disabled. The welfare-related roles and responsibilities of CDEP organisations could be widened accordingly.

It seems there is potential for CDEP organisations to play an enhanced role in assisting the development of regional and community-wide frameworks for the implementation of mutual obligation; in negotiating customised mutual obligation agreements for individual welfare recipients; and in providing mentoring, work experience, and training to sole parents and young parents on income support. But such expanded responsibilities raise concerns about the overall effectiveness of CDEP organisations, the adequacy of their funding base (see Bartlett, Ch. 20, this volume), and the availability of local training and employment opportunities for participants.

It goes without saying that some CDEP organisations are not operating effectively, or are operating in locations where opportunities for enterprise and employment generation are extremely limited. But equally, there are also CDEP organisations which are establishing viable employment projects, generating additional income, developing enterprises and small businesses, and assisting participants to become work-ready and to take up employment within and outside the scheme.

CAEPR case studies carried out with CDEP organisations (see Gray & Thacker 2000, and Ch. 15, this volume; Madden 2000, and Ch. 18, this volume; Smith 1994, 1995, 1996) suggest that the successful ones generally share a mix, or all, of the following characteristics:

- a competent, stable governing body with the capacity to systematically formulate and enforce policy guidelines;

- competent management and staff capable of operating consistently and fairly;

- a stable organisational structure;

- a separation of local politics from the daily business and decision-making of the CDEP scheme;

- transparent decision-making, and procedures for dealing with conflict of interest and appeals;

- financial accountability, and financial management policies and systems;

- active networks which feed into the wider community economy and local businesses;

- ongoing assessment of training needs, and an in-house training coordinator;

- the capacity to provide intensive case management and mentoring of participants (both within the scheme and during the transition to other forms of employment);

- a match between cultural and commercial objectives that allows successful participation in the 'real' economic world facing the organisation and its participants;

- cultural authority and community support; and importantly,

- a stable source of recurrent block funding sufficient to undertake their administrative, economic, employment and training, and governing roles.

Where CDEP organisations do not exhibit these characteristics, or are insufficiently funded to develop them, they are unable to develop the capacities needed to generate local economic opportunities, and to assist people to move off welfare. They tend instead to replicate the conditions and experience of welfare for their participants. If such CDEP organisations were to undertake a wider role in assisting welfare recipients in their communities, they would need an enhanced level of funding for training, governance and the capacity building of staff and participants.

Lessons from an overseas welfare initiative

While there has been consideration by Australian policy makers and academics of overseas initiatives in welfare reform, there has been relatively little discussion of how those reform processes are being carried out with Indigenous groups. This concluding section briefly describes an important initiative in welfare delivery being made with Native American people—US Federal government's progressive move towards the devolution of service delivery jurisdictions to Native American tribes.

In October 2000, the US media reported the signing by the Navajo Tribe of a proclamation establishing the largest Indian-operated reformed welfare program in the country. With the US Department of Health and Human Services supplying US$31.2 million and another US$1 million from the State of New Mexico for office construction, the Federal government and the State governments of Arizona, New Mexico and Utah will turn over to the Navajo the various welfare payments and service delivery system known as the TANF Program. The State governments will keep operating from their current offices for six months while the Navajo Tribe hires and trains staff and sets up offices to deliver the TANF program to an estimated 27 000 Navajo people.

The Navajo TANF program is just the latest of 30 tribal-run welfare programs encompassing 155 tribes that have been set up since 1996, when President Clinton signed the welfare reform law known as the *Personal Responsibility and Work Opportunity Reconciliation Act*. Thus, in the process of implementing reforms which look very much like those now being considered in Australia, the US Federal government has also been progressively handing over service delivery jurisdictions to Indian tribes.

Passed with bipartisan support, the legislation established a comprehensive welfare reform program that was designed to move welfare recipients into work, replaced existing national welfare programs with TANF, and enabled not only State governments, but federally recognised Indian tribes and consortia of tribes, to apply for block federal funding to directly operate their own TANF programs.

The legislation gives approved tribes the authority to use Federal government welfare funds in any manner that is reasonably calculated to accomplish the purposes of its welfare agenda. The Federal government redirects to the tribe an amount equal to that which would have been provided to the State for welfare services to all Indian families residing in the proposed service area. Tribes can administer the program themselves, or outsource program delivery to the State or to a private provider.

Federal approval is based on a tribe's submission of a Tribal TANF Plan covering a three to four year period which identifies its service area and population; sets out its welfare policies, guidelines and penalty regimes, and the welfare services and programs to be provided; and provides an economic development plan to enhance access to local employment opportunities. A Tribal TANF Plan must obtain Federal government approval. To qualify, a tribe must have a governing body to administer the program, and a mandate from their constituents. Importantly, implementation of the program is subject to statutory national regulations, and the same data collection and reporting requirements as State government programs.

There are important areas of flexibility for tribes in the formulation of TANF policies and guidelines, including the capacity to:

*   determine programs and eligibility criteria;

*   decide what social security benefits are appropriate for their population;

*   define participation and work requirements, and work standards that must be met in order to receive benefits;

*   establish timeframes for the receipt of benefits;

*   define work as including culturally relevant work, job search, subsidised employment, community service, vocational training and education; and

*   define their own concept of 'family' and 'needy family'.

Tribal TANF programs also have regulated flexibility to provide 'assistance' in a variety of forms including cash payments, vouchers (e.g. for food), clothing, shelter, utilities, household goods, personal care items, child care, and transportation to work. Native American people participating in a TANF program for at least two years are required, under regulations, to participate in work activities. If the service population has more than 50 per cent unemployment, federally established welfare time limits need not apply.

Conclusion

In some ways the USA's Tribal TANF program is very similar to the CDEP scheme. Participants must perform some work for the receipt of their welfare-equivalent incomes and such work can be locally defined and culturally relevant. But there are obvious major differences. Under TANF, tribes may elect to provide assistance other than cash to their clients; all recipients of social security within a designated region may participate; the governing body must carry out a comprehensive assessment of regional economic conditions and demand for skills; and substantial policy formulation responsibilities have been handed over in conjunction with service delivery.

But most importantly, the tribes have accepted responsibility for administering an entire component of welfare service delivery in a devolved jurisdiction. They have done so after carrying out comprehensive planning, after establishing a representative governing body and administrative structure for their identified region, after having consulted widely with their constituents, and after having obtained a mandate to operate the program. In other words, in the phase leading up to the jurisdictional devolution of service delivery, tribes have undertaken substantial work in governance, institution and capacity building. The program is still in its infancy and has not been without establishment difficulties, but is apparently making important inroads into welfare dependence and job creation in rural and remote Native American communities.

Jurisdictional devolution of welfare services has considerable potential to be an enabling framework for Indigenous welfare reform in Australia. However, it would require both governments and Indigenous Australians to think differently about how welfare is delivered in this country. Substantial added investments would be required from government for Indigenous education, and local training and job creation, and Indigenous people and their leaders would have to develop, as a matter of priority, stable and depoliticised governing institutions, and the capacities needed to administer such a devolved responsibility.

Notes

1. Kuranda is a small hinterland town with a population of 600 people, about half an hour's drive from the urban and tourist centre of Cairns in North Queensland. Yuendumu is a discrete, remote and predominantly Aboriginal town of nearly people located about 300 kilometers north-west of Alice Springs (see also Musharbash, Ch. 16, this volume).

2. I would like to thank Anne Daly, Julie Finlayson, Yasmine Musharbash and Tony Auld for their contributions to the research reported in this paper.

3. In 1998–99, this specifically meant Parenting Payments and Family Allowance delivered by the Federal government. Parenting Payment includes both sole parent and couple parents with children, and recognises a person's responsibility for caring for children irrespective of their marital status. Family Allowance is a payment to help all parents raise their children and is paid to the parent caring for the child. In 2000 these payments have been replaced by the Family Benefits Tax Package.

4. The second stage of follow-up interviews have been conducted in both communities (in Yuendumu by Yasmine Musharbash, and in Kuranda by Rosita Henry and Anne Daly) and published results are found in Musharbash (2001) and Henry and Daly (2001).

References

Aboriginal and Torres Strait Islander Commission (ATSIC) 2000. *Annual Report 1999–2000*, ATSIC, Canberra.

Altman, J.C. and Hunter, B. 1998. 'Indigenous poverty', in R. Fincher and J. Nieuwenhuysen (eds), *Australian Poverty: Then and Now*, Melbourne University Press, Melbourne.

—— and Sanders, W. 1995. 'From exclusion to dependence: Aborigines and the welfare state in Australia', in J. Dixon and R. Scheurell (eds), *Social Welfare for Indigenous Populations*, Routledge, London.

Australian Bureau of Statistics and Centre for Aboriginal Economic Policy Research (ABS–CAEPR) 1996. *1994 National Aboriginal and Torres Strait Islander Survey: Employment Outcomes for Indigenous Australians*, Cat. no. 4199.0, ABS, Canberra.

Brown, J., Hirschfeld, R., and Smith, D.E. 1974. *Aboriginals and Islanders in Brisbane*, Commission of Inquiry into Poverty, AGPS, Canberra.

Commonwealth of Australia 2001. 'Welfare reform: A stronger, fairer Australia', Commonwealth government statement on welfare reform, DFACS, Canberra.

Daly. A.E. 2000. 'The winner's curse? Indigenous Australians in the welfare system', *The Australian Economic Review*, 33 (4): 349–54.

—— and Smith, D.E. 1999. 'Indigenous household demography and socio-economic status: The policy implications of 1996 Census data', *CAEPR Discussion Paper No. 181*, CAEPR, ANU, Canberra.

Fisk, E.K. 1985. *The Aboriginal Economy in Town and Country*, George Allen & Unwin, Sydney.

Gray, M.C. and Thacker, E. 2000. 'A case study of the Bungala CDEP: Economic and social impacts', *CAEPR Discussion Paper No. 208*, CAEPR, ANU, Canberra.

Gregory, R.G. and Martin, Y.M. 2000. 'Macro employment policies and the economic wellbeing of female Indigenous sole parents in Australia and the United States', *The Australian Economic Review*, 33 (4): 369–76.

Henderson, R.F. (Chair) 1975. *Commission of Inquiry into Poverty: Poverty in Australia, First Main Report*, AGPS, Canberra.

Henry, R, and Daly, A. 2001. 'Indigenous families and the welfare system: The Kuranda community case study, Stage Two', *CAEPR Discussion Paper No. 216*, CAEPR, ANU, Canberra.

Hunter, B.H. 2000. 'Social exclusion, social participation, and Indigenous Australians: Measuring the social costs of unemployment', *CAEPR Discussion Paper No. 204*, CAEPR, ANU, Canberra.

—— and Smith, D.E. 2000. 'Surveying mobile populations: Lessons from recent longitudinal surveys of Indigenous Australians', *CAEPR Discussion Paper No. 203*, CAEPR, ANU, Canberra.

Keating, M. 2000. 'Welfare reform: From exclusion to participation', *CDEA Bulletin*, October 2000: 24–7.

McClure, P. (Chair) 2000. Participation Support for a More Equitable Society: Final Report of the Reference Group on Welfare Reform, July 2000 [the McClure Report], DFACS, Canberra.

Madden, R. 2000. '"If it wasn't for CDEP": A case study of Worn Gunditj CDEP, Victoria', *CAEPR Discussion Paper No. 210*, CAEPR, ANU, Canberra.

Musharbash, Y. 2001. 'Indigenous families and the welfare system: The Yuendumu community case study, Year Two', *CAEPR Discussion Paper No. 217*, CAEPR, ANU, Canberra.

Newman, J. 1999. 'The challenge of welfare dependency in the 21st century', Discussion Paper by Senator The Hon. J. Newman, Minister for Family and Community Services, Commonwealth of Australia, Canberra.

Ross, K. 1999. *Occasional Paper: Population Issues, Indigenous Australians*, Cat. no. 4708.0, ABS, Canberra.

Smith, D.E. 1994. '"Working for CDEP": A case study of the Community Development Employment Projects scheme in Port Lincoln, South Australia', *CAEPR Discussion Paper No. 75*, CAEPR, ANU, Canberra.

—— 1995. 'Redfern works: The policy and community challenges of an urban CDEP scheme', *CAEPR Discussion Paper No. 99*, CAEPR, ANU, Canberra.

—— 1996. 'CDEP as urban enterprise: The case of Yarnteen Aboriginal and Torres Strait Islanders Corporation', *CAEPR Discussion Paper No. 114*, CAEPR, ANU, Canberra.

—— (ed.) 2000. *Indigenous Families and the Welfare System: Two Community Case Studies*, CAEPR Research Monograph No. 17, CAEPR, ANU, Canberra.

—— and Roach, L.M. 1996. 'Indigenous voluntary work: NATSIS empirical evidence, policy relevance, and future data issues', in J.C. Altman and J. Taylor (eds), *The 1994 National Aboriginal and Torres Strait Islander Survey: Findings and Future Prospects*, CAEPR Research Monograph No. 11, CAEPR, ANU, Canberra.

Taylor, J. and Hunter, B.H. 1998. *The Job Still Ahead: Economic Costs of Continuing Indigenous Employment Disparity*, Office of Public Affairs, ATSIC, Canberra.

Tesfaghiorghis, H. and Gray, A. 1991. 'The demographic structure and location of the Aboriginal population: Employment implications', in J.C. Altman (ed.), *Aboriginal Employment Equity by the Year 2000*, CAEPR Research Monograph No. 2, CAEPR, ANU, Canberra.

8. The Indigenous Employment Policy: A preliminary evaluation

Peter Shergold

The Indigenous Employment Policy (IEP) was introduced by Minister Peter Reith in 1999 as a result of decisions made in the 1998 Budget. It has been administered by DEWRSB. The IEP is a significant development: there had not been a major Commonwealth government initiative in the area of Indigenous employment since the mid 1980s. Indeed it is fair to say that before responsibility for employment became part of DEWRSB as part of a machinery of government change following the last election, the issue of Indigenous employment had not had a high priority. There had been a reasonable expectation that the radical new creation, Job Network, which replaced the old Commonwealth Employment Service (CES) and Employment Services Regulatory Agency (ESRA) would provide equity to Indigenous Australians—equity not only in terms of equitable access to labour market programs but equality in employment outcomes.

However, it soon became clear that although Job Network is working increasingly well, delivering better employment outcomes at significantly lower cost, Indigenous Australians are the group who are least able to make effective use of its services. The rate of Indigenous unemployment continues to be unacceptably high. DEWRSB estimates that 40 per cent of Indigenous people are unemployed, if those on CDEP are included in the count. Estimates from other sources are even higher. It was necessary to introduce a policy framework and program initiatives to complement Job Network.

A matter of even greater concern is that very few of those Indigenous people who are employed are at work in the private sector. The great majority are on CDEP, or have jobs in Commonwealth, State and Territory public services, or have jobs in local government or are working for community controlled Indigenous organisations which are largely publicly funded. Private sector employment remains the great challenge. If there is one key emphasis to the new IEP, it is to make more headway in accessing private sector jobs and getting them filled by Indigenous Australians.

In instituting Job Network we moved from 300 CES offices operating as a government monopoly to a new system delivered by a range of public, private, and voluntary welfare organisations offering a range of employment services. They deliver job-matching, the old 'swing-of-the-door' placement service; intensive assistance to those clients most at risk of welfare dependency; job search training; the New Enterprise Incentive Scheme (NEIS) to support unemployed people in establishing small businesses; and project contracting for harvest work. Employment services costing $1 billion a year are outsourced under contract by DEWRSB and delivered by a competitive market of 200 providers from some 2000 sites. The good news is that, as a consequence, many Indigenous Australians who previously had no access to a CES office now have a Job Network member near them. Often they are able to choose between providers. Unfortunately that does not mean that the services that are being provided are necessarily appropriate.

We face a challenge. Job Network is not performing as well as it should for Indigenous Australians. That is why the Government has introduced the IEP. But I do want to emphasise that Job Network is not nearly such a failure as some of the criticisms that I hear suggest.

If you examine Job Network, particularly the intensive assistance that is provided to the most disadvantaged job seekers, you will find that in terms of *registrations* Indigenous Australians represent just over 5 per cent of the client base. Perhaps it should be as high as 7 per cent, but it is still not too bad an achievement. In terms of *referrals*—the point at which clients are referred from Centrelink to the Job Network member to provide employment services—that is running at about 6 per cent. Then occurs the first major problem. From the time Indigenous Australians are referred from Centrelink to a Job Network member, to become a *commencement*, there is a drop-off, from Indigenous people representing 6 per cent of those referred, to representing only 5 per cent of those actually beginning with a Job Network member. People are falling through the cracks in the system before they even arrive at a Job Network member. And then, if you look at the *outcomes* (people who after intensive assistance are placed into employment for at least 13 or 26 weeks), although Indigenous people are 5 per cent of commencements, they represent just under 4 per cent of outcomes. For each criterion—registrations, referrals, commencements, outcomes—Indigenous jobseekers are slightly under-represented. The cumulative impact is significant. It is not a disastrous picture, but it nevertheless indicates that Indigenous people are not doing as well as other groups in terms of assistance.

My department has the responsibility of evaluating outcomes through post-program monitoring. After people have received assistance, we look at what has happened to them. We can assess outcomes in two ways: how many of those who get assistance end up in unsubsidised employment or go back into education. Both are defined as positive outcomes. Across all job seekers we are presently achieving positive outcomes of around 40 per cent. That is a very good result. The evidence suggests that in terms of the outcomes being recorded and the cost at which they are being achieved, the present Job Network is working more effectively than the old CES system. Some groups are doing remarkably well. Sole parents, for example, who come into the Job Network achieve relatively high outcomes. People from non-English-speaking backgrounds are also doing slightly better than the average in terms of outcomes. The lowest outcomes are for Aboriginal people and Torres Strait Islanders. So that is the challenge that had to be addressed.

That is why IEP was launched last year. It includes the IEP, a small-business fund, and a number of measures which are designed to improve the operation of Job Network. The aim is to do two things concurrently: improve the operation of the Job Network providers from the perspective of Indigenous clients and at the same time introduce a complementary program that will help to counter inequities in accessing Job Network and in making use of the services that are provided.

The IEP itself has a number of crucial elements. It includes wage assistance, which in effect provides a subsidy to employers for taking on Indigenous job seekers for periods of 26 weeks. Indigenous Australians are now the only group in Australia to get that wage assistance. It also includes a CDEP placement incentive fee, to which I will return; a Corporate Leaders for Indigenous Employment initiative, encouraging private sector business corporations to sign up to an employment strategy for Indigenous Australians; Structured Training and Employment Projects (STEP) to provide outcome-focused training; a Voluntary Service Foundation to match community needs with the skills and commitment of volunteer workers; and cadetships for Indigenous Australians at universities.

Now what I want to do—and this [the conference] is the first time I have had a public opportunity to do this—is evaluate the initiatives: to look at what is working in this program and what is not. We have now had between 12 and 15 months' experience. Is the IEP actually making a difference?

In terms of wage assistance, the answer is categorically 'yes'. An employer taking on an Indigenous job seeker can get a payment of up to $4400 if they employ that person for 26 weeks. In the first year 1600 Indigenous Australians were taken on in this way. We are running now between 200 and 250 people being placed each month. Crucial, from our point of view, is that wage assistance is starting to break through the most difficult barriers to employment—some 83 per cent of the placements are in the private sector. Better still, about half of the jobseekers are still at work three months after the completion of the subsidy, which by labour market program standards is a very good outcome. It does seem to be working.

The STEP projects also seem to be having a significant positive impact. We have tried to make these training programs far more flexible than has usually been the case. STEP now provides assistance to employers willing to train five or more Indigenous Australians. There are at present 180 projects, providing almost three-and-a-half thousand placements over the life of the projects. Again the important feature is that 60 per cent of the placements under STEP are with the private sector. This is a quite extraordinary achievement.

These successes reflect a different approach than in the past. When I think back to former times I recognise how demoralising it was when unemployed Indigenous people were sent on a short-term training program, followed by a bit more time on the dole, before being sent on another training program with never a job in prospect. We have got some of the most trained Australians without jobs in the country. What we have done now is to fund training projects with employment outcomes in mind. Before we support structured training we need to know that there is actually a good chance of a job placement at its end. So although STEP has become much more flexible in delivery, it has also become much more outcome focused. We are trying to get away from training programs that led to nowhere except cynicism and despair.

The Corporate Leaders for Indigenous Employment initiative is also significant. I can remember when I was in ATSIC, and used to get a bit frustrated sometimes with DEET and DEETYA—and I'm sure the feelings were often reciprocated—because of their heavily articulated and relatively rigid training. Well-intentioned public servants would sit around in Canberra, providing advice to government and designing very clever training programs to attract the private sector. Then hapless bureaucrats would be sent out to private sector employers around the country, touting the latest design models: 'Do you want to sign up to this? If you do you will be eligible for government funds.' Not surprisingly, very few private sector employers, particularly the big ones, wanted to get involved on that basis.

What we have tried to do on this occasion is to place ownership with the companies. We have said to the 40 companies that have signed up: 'Look, you design your strategy. You decide on your approach. What we want to see is that in one way or another you're going to provide work experience, pre-training, education, training, apprenticeships and employment for Indigenous Australians.' But we do not start from the basis that what Ansett will want to do is necessarily what Coles Myer will want to do, or that the approach of Lactos cheesemakers will be the same as for Rio Tinto mining. They have different markets, different products, different regions within which they work and different labour forces. The aim is to persuade committed corporate leaders to design their own strategies, to encourage them to develop their individual approaches in consultation with communities, and then for DEWRSB to provide financial and/or administrative support and (if it is requested) advice.

With respect to the cadetship program aimed at Indigenous Australians at university, this year we have almost doubled the number of cadetships to 92, of which 34 are in the private sector. This is a program that is designed to create role models: it is intended to identify Indigenous people coming through university and place them in companies in fields as diverse as accountancy, information technology and engineering.

Thus far I have extolled the modest successes of the IEP. For me it generates cautious optimism. Where is the failure? The biggest disappointment is undoubtedly in the area of CDEP. A CDEP placement initiative has been established so that if a participant moves off benefits there is a payment made of $2000 to the CDEP. The objective is to encourage CDEPs to support participants in progressing to mainstream employment. How successful has it been? It has been an abysmal failure. This is the part of the IEP that has not worked so far. It is the part that we need to address. We have only had 180 placements move from CDEPs to employment until now, out of some 34 000 CDEP participants (see contributions in this volume which respond to this point: Bartlett, Ch. 20; Lewis, Ch. 30; Loomes, Ch. 31).

There are other things we need to do in terms of the IEP. We need to place a much stronger emphasis on employment retention. That means we have to put greater resources into mentoring support for Indigenous recruits and cross-cultural training for management and employees in those companies that are taking on Indigenous workers. It is one thing to fill jobs. If those recruitments are not converted into retained employees we are failing. We have also got to increase the emphasis on program flexibility, to meet the needs both of employers and of communities. And, importantly, we need to take a whole-of-government approach to providing the extraordinary range of support—health, education, community capacity building—that is required to achieve sustained employment outcomes.

The biggest single issue, however, is the relationship between the IEP, for which DEWRSB has responsibility, and CDEP, for which ATSIC has—and must keep—responsibility. At this stage only 6000 of the CDEP participants are registered with Centrelink. As I have just noted, over a 12-month period only 180 participants, a grand total of 0.5 per cent of CDEP workers, appear to have moved from CDEP into paid employment. Statistically a person has a worse chance of getting a paid job if they are on CDEP than if they are off it. It is true that many of these CDEPs are operating in areas remote from an effective labour market, where the CDEP must necessarily remain a community enterprise. But ATSIC is starting to argue, and DEWRSB is in full agreement, that where possible CDEPs have to be designed in such a way as to become a stepping stone—through training and work experience programs—into paid employment. Too often, even where a metropolitan or regional labour market exists, CDEP is presently a dead end.

At the moment, the balance of incentives and disincentives is all wrong. A CDEP naturally wants to retain its best workers; that is what makes the CDEP function well. Unfortunately, those workers are precisely the people who are most likely to have an opportunity to gain entry to mainstream employment if they are encouraged and supported. The incentives for CDEP need rethinking.

There are several options that could be considered. Perhaps CDEPs should be paid greater up-front fees, in order for them to help some of their participants into the wider labour market? Where there exist labour market opportunities, perhaps government should be willing to fund CDEPs to run training or mentoring programs? In this way CDEPs might receive money at the start, but the continuation of that funding would depend upon achievement of agreed outcomes: for instance, a negotiated outcome with a CDEP might be based on an agreement that at the end of a CDEP-provided training program three, or six, or ten participants will come off CDEP. They could then be funded for the cost of the training that is going to be required for the first year. If the program is successful in terms of its outcomes, then funding the following year to continue the program would be assured. That might be a better way of increasing the financial incentives to a CDEP to focus on moving its job-ready participants off community-based welfare support into paid employment.

Perhaps the incentives being paid to the CDEP should be increased? It might possibly make a difference if the incentive payment was increased to $3000 or $4000. However, this by itself might not be an effective strategy, since very few placement fees at $2000 have been claimed so far, and many of these placements may have been fortuitous. It is not clear that simply raising the fee would drive cultural changes in CDEPs.

Another option is to establish joint arrangements between DEWRSB, ATSIC and Job Network members so that, for example, if a Job Network member is working with a CDEP and gets a successful outcome, the CDEP and the Job Network member share the financial benefits from the outcome. Or perhaps CDEPs need financial incentives to enter into formal partnership arrangements with Job Network members?

It is not yet determined whether any or all of these options are feasible. It is apparent, however, that these crucial issues must be addressed in the short term, to strengthen what appears to be the weakest link in this new IEP. The majority of CDEPs, located in remote Australia, will remain important vehicles for community enterprise and self governance. But there are a significant minority of CDEPs with access to stronger labour markets who could be attracted by incentives to transform their role and become facilitators of employment. Trying to find a new approach to winning their support is the key challenge for the government and DEWRSB in the months ahead.

Postscript (June 2001)

The forum of the CAEPR conference offered the earliest opportunity to float for (vigorous) discussion ideas on how policy might be re-designed in such a way as to attract some CDEPs to a greater focus on achieving employment outcomes. It is now apparent that the presentation represented the first stage of an ongoing process of change, the directions of which are clearly defined.

The performance of the IEP has, as I had hoped, continued to improve. In the first nine months of 2000–01, 1866 Indigenous Australians were supported to gain employment through wage assistance, an increase of 48 per cent since the corresponding period in 1999–2000. Some 2750 Aboriginal and Torres Strait Islanders commenced in 174 STEP projects, 66 per cent greater than in the previous nine months. Fifty companies now participate in the Corporate Leaders for Indigenous Employment initiative, and have committed to providing over 1600 employment opportunities.

In part because of these complementary programs, and in part because of a greater focus by providers, the ability of Job Network to serve Indigenous clients has also risen. In the nine months since 1 July 2000, 7530 job placements have been made and 1942 intensive assistance interim outcomes achieved, representing increases of 35 per cent and 29 per cent respectively on the same period in 1999–2000. A year ago Indigenous clients represented only 5 per cent of intensive assistance commencements: today they are almost 7 per cent.

Perhaps most importantly the need to increase the potential of CDEPs as stepping stones to employment has been addressed. A pilot has recently been established with eight CDEPs in Brisbane, Port Augusta, Shepparton, Canberra–Queanbeyan, Broome, Geraldton, Sydney and Newcastle. The trial, for a 12-month period, requires the participating CDEP to provide an agreed number of their participants with work preparation training, assistance into sustainable employment and pre- and post-placement support. Participating CDEPs may receive up to $6600 for each trial participant who achieves 26 consecutive weeks of employment. In other words, a CDEP funded for 25 participants may receive up to $165 000 if they are able to achieve employment outcomes for the entire group.

This trial, and its evaluation, will inform the new Budget initiative included as part of the *Australians Working Together* welfare reform package announced in May 2001. From February 2002, in areas where job opportunities exist, selected CDEP organisations will take on the additional role of Indigenous Employment Centres (IECs). The IECs will be funded to offer work experience, job search support, access to training and support and mentoring assistance to Indigenous jobseekers. They will work in partnership with local employers and Job Network members to find their participants work and help them keep it. They will be paid a management fee and receive a bonus for achieving lasting job outcomes for participants. The Budget provides for total spending of $48 million over four years ($31m in new funding) to assist up to 10 000 participants make the transition from CDEP work experience into paid employment.

The CAEPR conference provided a very useful environment for public servants, academics and community workers to debate public policy. It contributed to the new initiatives recently announced. I have no doubt that the outcomes from this bold new program will serve to focus discussion at a future CAEPR forum!

9. Reforming the CDEP scheme

Terry Whitby

The importance of CDEP to Indigenous people

I begin this paper with some facts which are indisputable. CDEP continues to be Australia's largest employer of Indigenous people, with over 270 projects involving over 33 000 participants. Of these projects, 95 per cent are located in regional and remote Australia, in places with limited access to viable labour markets. Unemployment trends will deepen unless Australians invest in collaborative, holistic programs.

CDEP is one of the most important programs for Indigenous people. It continues to provide an important focus for communities to undertake a wide range of activities which support the operation of the community, maintain services, and build upon and strengthen Indigenous culture. Most importantly, CDEP is community driven.

ATSIC's commitment to the further development of the scheme could not be stronger. The ATSIC Board considers that the scheme is one of the most important avenues of opportunity for Indigenous people to work in their communities and to gain skills which may lead to further employment or to developing the capacity of their communities. While the CDEP continues to demonstrate successful social, economic, and community development outcomes, the ATSIC Board does not see it as a substitute for real employment.

The ATSIC Board believes that CDEP should continue to play a major role in the creation of employment and training for participants, and should form the basis for creating enterprises in economically sustainable activities, to strengthen the capacity of their communities. CDEP is something which we can all be proud of, but ATSIC and the CDEP projects must work together, and with other government agencies and the private sector, to continue to develop the scheme into the future.

The Spicer Review and its aftermath

In 1997 the CDEP scheme was the focus of a major review by Ian Spicer (Spicer 1997). The recommendations from that review have served to shape and influence the development of the scheme since that time. The ATSIC Board endorsed the broad recommendations of the Spicer Review, and in particular lent support to three key elements of suggested reform. These are:

- a refocusing of the objectives of CDEP to the provision of 'work' and skill acquisition, as reflected in the new objective of the scheme to 'provide work for unemployed indigenous persons in community managed activities which assist the individual in acquiring skills which benefit the community, develop business enterprises and/or lead to unsubsidised employment' (Spicer 1997);

- a recognition that the development of economic independence for Indigenous people is firmly based in providing opportunities for income generation and enterprise development within CDEP, and in securing resources to develop commercial opportunities for CDEP; and

- improving the linkages between CDEP and other programs to improve outcomes for CDEP participants, including access to other income support benefits made available by the 1998 CDEP budget initiative, improved access to training and employment opportunities through initiatives such as Job Network, the Indigenous Employment Program, DETYA's Numeracy and Literacy Programs, and DFACS's Families and Disability Support Programs.

Since the Spicer Review the government has continued to seek an improved focus on outcomes from CDEP, particularly in regard to employment and training outcomes. ATSIC has identified an agreed number of outputs in relation to the effective delivery of CDEP, on which it will have to report to government. These include:

- increased employment;

- increased training opportunities;

- enhanced community development;

- expanded economic activities;

- maintenance of culture; and

- enhanced social cohesion.

In implementing this new framework there are a number of issues that need to be considered:

- how ATSIC is to effectively obtain reporting information from CDEP projects so that they can in turn report to government on these outputs;

- how ATSIC is to measure and report back to government on achievements relating to the social and cultural outputs of the scheme (e.g. enhanced social cohesion and maintenance of culture);

- the question of whether priority should be given to these types of outputs and whether ATSIC should set specific reporting targets against these outputs; and

- whether reporting measures should be framed in terms of the number of participants who find full-time work outside the scheme.

ATSIC is considering initiatives like these to ensure that CDEPs situated in reasonable labour markets produce employment outcomes for participants in the private or public sectors. ATSIC needs to demonstrate that CDEP already successfully delivers these outcomes, and that the additional investment of resources by government will provide the opportunity to further enhance the capacity of the CDEP scheme to deliver them. The government has invested in the Job Network to deliver employment outcomes for the Indigenous unemployed (see Shergold, Ch. 8, this volume). This investment should also be applied to CDEPs if they are to be expected to deliver enhanced employment outcomes.

Who represents CDEP?

At first glance, there are many possible answers to the question: 'Who represents CDEP?' This answer might be the ATSIC Commissioners who hold the brief for CDEP, the ATSIC Board, the ATSIC Regional Councils, the Community Councils, the communities, the local CDEP coordinators, the project officers, the participants themselves, or even in some respects all levels of government, or industry. The real answer is that all these players have a role in representing and supporting CDEP.

Wider economic forces have an integral part to play in determining the employment situation in Australia today. However, within those constraints the disadvantaged must be listened to, and their cause advocated, if the gap between the 'haves' and the 'have nots' is not to widen further. The Australian community as a whole, through its elected representatives and government agencies, must take some responsibility for helping the disadvantaged, many of whom are to be found in Indigenous communities.

I see it as my role, as portfolio Commissioner, to broadcast the message, wherever and whenever I can, that CDEP remains an important program for Indigenous peoples and communities. We must not lose sight of the fact that the CDEP has been developed by Aboriginal and Torres Strait Islander communities, and that the scheme, as a community and participant driven program, is meant to respond to their needs.

In its recent restructuring, ATSIC created Policy and Support Units at all levels of the organisation. These reflect directly the core values of the organisation, and are intended to strengthen its advocacy role in reflecting the concerns of Indigenous people. The decision to reprioritise resources and to establish these units reflects a fundamental shift in focus to policy and advocacy, and recognises a greatly increased interest in effecting change through externally directed argument, persuasion, and influence. The Board of Commissioners endorsed the restructure and it is now the task of the elected and administrative arms to deliver outcomes. It is encouraging that these extra resources are now available at all levels within the organisation to advocate the needs of CDEP projects and Indigenous people in general.

It is important, therefore, for all our voices to be heard in support of the CDEP scheme and particular CDEP projects. There is also a mutual obligation requirement on governments to deliver. For too long the role of the CDEP projects in delivering essential services to communities has gone unacknowledged (see contributions to this volume by Bartlett, Ch. 20; Kean, Ch. 21; Dukakis, Ch. 27: Nalliah, Ch. 28). If this service delivery continues, then those CDEP workers must be properly remunerated for the work they do. Governments have an obligation, at the very minimum, to deliver essential services to communities.

The use of labour market programs like the 'work for the dole' is one strategy adopted by this government to address its objective of mutual obligation. There should be consistency in funding between Indigenous and 'work for the dole' organisations. Over the last 25 years, Indigenous communities and individuals have been meeting their mutual obligations, and they will continue to do so. CDEPs are under-resourced, an it is hoped that greater advocacy will influence the government to appreciate and recognise the benefits of the program, and resource it appropriately.

Industry needs also to be responsible in meeting its social obligations with respect to the Indigenous employment situation. It can achieve this through developing partnerships with ATSIC at national, State, and regional levels, and by creating real employment opportunities which include a commitment to employing Indigenous trainees after their training subsidy has run its course. Industry will be the beneficiary if it realises the potential of the skills base that the CDEP scheme has produced.

Reconciliation is currently a salient issue in Australia, and now is the time to capture some of the momentum and turn it into real outcomes for Indigenous people. If this opportunity is allowed to slip away, Indigenous people will remain sceptical, cynical, and marginalised.

Government and community investment

Australian governments continually commit to the principle of improving the delivery of programs and services to Indigenous Australians. Many Indigenous Australians are sceptical about these professions of good will, viewing them as lip-service that does not become manifest in policy, resources, or programs. The gap between rhetoric and delivery has lead to cynicism in the Indigenous community. ATSIC's adoption of a greater advocacy role at all levels will go some way to addressing this cynicism, but advocacy alone will not implement real change.

ATSIC needs to put forward workable frameworks that monitor CDEP performance against other labour market programs, and that engage all levels of government, industry, and the community in general to consult and develop effective policy and programs. Some outcomes of such frameworks could be joint policy development, bilateral agreements at State and local levels, community service agreements, and commitments by CDEPs in turn to achieve improved outcomes for CDEP participants.

Government has indicated that it intends to review the outputs that it gets from ATSIC in terms of the dollars funded into its budget, and has also recently undertaken a review of CDEP on-cost funding. For CDEP the implication is that government wants to look at what it costs to obtain employment, training, economic activities, and community development outcomes through CDEP.

We need to demonstrate to government that it receives many cost-effective outcomes from funding the CDEP scheme, and that it would gain greater outcomes through a further investment of funds. We need to demonstrate that further government investment will allow:

- the strengthening of pre-vocational skills and on-the-job and accredited training through better linkages with other agencies;

- increased employment outcomes for participants through more effective utilisation of the Indigenous Employment Program and Job Network; and

- further development of CDEP communities to deliver a wide range of social, cultural, and community-based outcomes for participants.

For too long, and in too many places, CDEP has been expected to provide a broad range of services and to support Indigenous Australians without appropriate funding to support the expected outcomes. CDEP needs the support of and the goodwill that will come from partnerships with governments, the private sector, and the wider community. These partners must first understand the issues of disadvantage, and then work hand in hand with CDEP to deliver a better future for Indigenous Australians—a future which will continue to be community driven, outcomes focused, and one of which we can all be proud.

References

Spicer, I. 1997. *Independent Review of the Community Development Employment Projects (CDEP) Scheme* [The Spicer Review], Office of Public Affairs, ATSIC, Canberra.

10. Myth-making and the delivery of banking and financial services to Indigenous Australians in regional and remote Australia

Neil Westbury

Introduction

This paper summarises the major findings of two case studies that examined Aboriginal people's access to banking and financial services in central Australia and north-west New South Wales, and some of the assertions that are commonly made about the delivery of banking and financial services to Indigenous Australians.[1] It then identifies some comparative best practice from overseas, drawing on developments in the delivery of banking services to indigenous peoples and low- and moderate-income earners in North America. It concludes that many of the assertions regularly employed in Australia by banks and others to justify the withdrawal or current lack of provision of banking services to Indigenous peoples are either based on myths or, at a minimum, deserve to be severely tested.

Before addressing the two case studies it will be helpful first to describe some of the underlying factors which directly impact on Indigenous people's access to the delivery of banking and financial services in Australia.

Underlying factors

The three factors I will briefly describe are:

- the current level of Indigenous people's social and economic disadvantage which shapes their interaction with the cash economy;

- demographic and locational issues; and

- the impact of the deregulation of banking and financial services in regional areas.

Indigenous Australians are both relatively and absolutely socio-economically disadvantaged when compared to other Australians (Council for Aboriginal Reconciliation 2000). In practical terms, this means that most low-income Indigenous households are without financial savings and often pay more than other households for financial services. These charges include for example cheque-cashing fees, bank account keeping fees and 'book down' interest charged by stores (Westbury 1999, 2000).

Families that do not maintain financial savings often have poor or non-existent credit ratings or debt to income ratios that exclude them from mainstream forms of credit. Such households have no financial margin for safety; even temporary disruptions in family earnings or unforeseen expenditures can create serious hardship.

The demographic spread and location of Indigenous Australians compared to the wider community also affects their access to banking services. The Indigenous share of total usual resident population is shown in Table 10.1 for each census since 1981 in respect of an area which includes the Far West and North Western Statistical Divisions (SDs) in New South Wales; the South West, Central West, North West and Far North SDs in Queensland; the Eyre and Northern SDs in South Australia; the South Eastern, Central, Pilbara and Kimberley SDs in Western Australia; and Northern Territory Balance SD.[2] This roughly corresponds to the area popularly termed 'the outback'.

Table 10.1   Indigenous share of the outback population, 1981–1996[a]

Census year	Indigenous population[b]	Non-Indigenous population	Indigenous share of total population (%)
1981	77 372	531 050	12.7
1986	93 681	565 729	14.2
1991	102 205	563 645	15.4
1996	121 580	560 768	17.8

Notes: (a) Based on usual residence counts.
         (b) Aboriginal and Torres Strait Islander status 'not stated' in each SD is pro-rated according to the revealed usual resident share in each census year and added to the Indigenous count.

Source: ABS Census of Population and Housing.

Table 10.1 demonstrates that the Indigenous share of the total outback population has grown from 13 per cent in 1981 to 18 per cent in 1996. This represents an overall growth over the period of some 23 per cent (Taylor 2000). Preliminary projections indicate that the Indigenous share of the outback population should rise from 18 to 20 per cent by the 2001 Census (Taylor 2000; and see Taylor & Hunter, Ch. 11, this volume).

This growth is occurring due both to a net reduction in the non-Indigenous population, and to higher population growth amongst Indigenous families. At a time when reference to meeting the needs of people living in regional Australia has become a constant political catchphrase it should not be overlooked that a significant and growing proportion of that population is, in fact, Indigenous.

The third related factor that is impacting on Indigenous people's access to banking and financial services in Australia is the deregulation of the banking and financial services sector. One of the major impacts of deregulation is the rapid adoption of new technology occurring concurrently with major increases in consumer banking fees (Takac 1997; Westbury 2000). For example, in 1991 the major banks charged zero for account keeping fees. As at October 2000 this fee had risen to $6.00 per month (Westbury 2000). Similarly, over-the-counter withdrawals have risen from $0.50 to $2.50 per withdrawal (Westbury 2000). The continuing hike in bank fees acts as a strong disincentive for poor people to maintain a bank savings account (Stegman 1999).

Arguably the most important impact of deregulation has been the withdrawal and closure of branch and agency services in rural and remote areas (Ralston & Beal 1997a, 1997b). At a time when some of the major banks are foreshadowing hundreds more branch closures, they have also been announcing successive record profits. In the two years up to December 1999, the Reserve Bank *Bulletin* reported 763 branch closures Australia-wide, with 311 of these occurring in rural and remote regions. In regional New South Wales alone, over the same two-year period branches have been closing at a rate of five per month (Westbury 2000).

What we are looking at is a massive and continued withdrawal of banking and financial services in rural and remote areas. These changes have hit hard in regional Australia and have hit Aboriginal communities even harder (Commonwealth of Australia 1999). Not only have many Aboriginal communities lost agency or branch services, but also, in other locations, the historical legacy of a lack of any appropriate banking services looks set to continue (Westbury 1999).

Major findings: The case studies

Central Australia

The first case study was conducted in central Australia for ATSIC and Centrelink. It focused on the relationship between Aboriginal people's lack of access to banking and financial services and the continued payment of social assistance by cheque. While most Australians receive their Centrelink payments electronically, as at May 1999, 30 000 people Australia-wide were still paid by cheque (Westbury 1999). Just under 47 per cent of these cheque payments are made in northern Australia, comprising nearly 42 per cent of the total amount paid by this method. Of these welfare recipients 90 per cent are Indigenous, and Indigenous people are therefore highly dependent on payment by cheque (Westbury 1999).

The retention of welfare payment by cheque reflects the harsh reality of Indigenous people's lack of access to banking and financial services. The Commonwealth Ombudsman has concluded that this practice has led Indigenous people to be dependent on third parties such as storekeepers and taxi drivers to cash cheques and fill out complex correspondence. The result is that many people are caught in exploitative situations and are captive to exorbitant fees (Westbury 2000). In remote communities the result can contribute to a vicious circle where families have difficulty maintaining a cash flow to purchase foodstuffs over the fortnightly period between welfare cheques. Even in Alice Springs, where all the major banks are represented, Aboriginal people are experiencing major difficulties in adapting to electronic banking. They tend to rely on the goodwill of the banks to keep pass books in safe custody, or rely on third parties to cash cheques (Westbury 1999).

The case study found that in direct response to these problems a number of Aboriginal communities in the Top End of the Northern Territory banded together to establish the Traditional Credit Union (TCU), which now boasts over 5000 members. It operates six branches, five of which are supervised by an Indigenous staff member. Of its 32 staff, 25 are Indigenous.

In remote communities, TCU branches are the only financial institution providing over-the-counter banking services. Staff at community branches also speak the language of community members, many of whom have English as a second language. The TCU also has a loans scheme with a maximum loan of $5000 allowed to members, repayable over five years. A significant proportion of loan recipients are women. A member must save a specified amount on a regular basis over a three-month period to be eligible for a loan. This loan program has worked well to date, with only one loan written off, and arrears are subject to a personal one-on-one follow up by TCU staff or directors. The TCU reports that 70 per cent of loans are being repaid in advance. The evidence suggests that these loans have made a significant contribution to improving people's standard of living (e.g. by making possible the purchase of refrigerators to store food, and washing machines and furniture and fittings for housing), with repayments reflecting people's level of income and capacity to repay (Westbury 2000).

Murdi Paaki Region

The second case study was conducted in five country towns in north-west New South Wales. It was commissioned by ATSIC, and its purpose was to examine a proposed joint venture between the Murdi Paaki Regional Council and five local shires to establish a credit union. In contrast to central Australia, the vast majority of Aboriginal people in the region receive their welfare and CDEP wages payments electronically into accounts held with the major banks. But despite the fact that people have made the transition to utilising electronic services, the research highlighted a number of obstacles that effectively worked against their ability to equitably access banking and financial services.

Because of the comparatively low incomes of Indigenous people, the high levels of bank charges have had a disproportionate impact and serve as a disincentive to maintaining bank savings accounts. Also, Aboriginal people consistently complained about their inability to access small-scale loan finance via the banks, despite having long-term employment histories under CDEP or as salaried employees. This allegedly often resulted in subsequent referral to private finance companies who charge exorbitant interest rates.

As a result of these charges and the withdrawal or refusal of services, a number of Aboriginal CDEP organisations provide de facto banking services. These range from Christmas Club Savings accounts and payroll deduction services to meet water and electricity payments, to the provision of wage advances to meet family emergencies (this was further highlighted by the fact that in north-west New South Wales, as in central Australia, approximately 90 per cent of welfare recipients utilise the annually available $500 Centrelink advance to meet emergency needs).

Aboriginal people place high value on being able to access face-to-face banking services. People strongly objected to the lack of privacy and the embarrassment associated with accessing services through agencies such as newsagents. These services often serve as a replacement for bank branches that have been withdrawn or closed down.

CDEP organisations constitute at least one of, or sometimes the major employer in many country towns in north-west New South Wales, but the management of these organisations argued that they nevertheless found it difficult to access commercial loan funds from the banks. Similarly, citing a lack of local bank competition, CDEP organisations asserted they were unable to secure bank fee concessions despite their collective annual multi-million dollar budgets (Westbury 2000).

Both research reports made a number of short and longer-term recommendations, including those listed below.

- That Centrelink pay welfare benefits weekly rather than fortnightly as a direct incentive to those recipients who transfer to electronic payments.

- That the Rural Transactions Program be enhanced so it can respond to regionally based applications for assistance. This program currently focuses on individual community applications rather than on those that are regionally based. This operates as a disincentive to Indigenous communities, which invariably lack the infrastructure to support stand-alone banking services. The lack of Indigenous representation on the Advisory Board that advises the relevant Minister on applications also hinders the operation of the program.

- That an investigation be conducted into the feasibility of supporting the expansion of the TCU's services in remote communities. The TCU has saved the Commonwealth hundreds of thousands of dollars by enabling cheque recipients in six remote Aboriginal Top End communities to receive their payments electronically.

- That the banks develop best practice policy approaches in service delivery, employment, and education that specifically address the needs of Indigenous customers.

- That ATSIC should co-operate with other major Indigenous organisations in combining their financial muscle to leverage a beneficial commercial agreement with one of the major banks that would include initiatives aimed at improving the availability of financial services to Indigenous Australians.

- Finally, that a pilot project be conducted in Alice Springs with the objective of assisting existing welfare recipients to transfer to electronic payments.

As a result of these recommendations a pilot project has commenced through a partnership involving the Tangentyere Council in partnership with Westpac and the DFACS. This project has the objective of assisting current welfare cheque recipients to transfer to electronic accounts, with appropriate financial and budgeting education. Westpac has also recently joined the Commonwealth Governments Corporate Leaders for Indigenous Employment Project (see Shergold, Ch. 8, this volume).

Common assertions

The two case studies and other research (McDonnell and Westbury 2001) undertaken on these issues have highlighted a number of justifications commonly employed by the banks, government and some economic commentators for the withdrawal of or inability to deliver banking and financial services to Indigenous communities. Among these are:

- that because of deregulation of the industry and greater competition the continued provision, let alone the establishment of new branches, in regional and remote areas by the major banks, is no longer commercially viable;

- that Indigenous customers are high risk because of their general lack of credit histories, comparatively low incomes and limited collateral to secure personal or housing loans;

- that communities resident on Aboriginal lands or reserves are necessarily precluded from access to individual housing or commercial loans, because Commonwealth and State laws prevent use of Indigenous land as collateral; and

- that a bank's first obligation is to secure maximum profit returns for their shareholders. This precludes the exercise of any wide ranging obligation to provide a community service.

Some international comparisons in best practice

What might a future ideal situation look like, in which Indigenous communities secure fair and equitable access to banking and financial services? It might be that one of Australia's major banks recognises that there are very real commercial opportunities in pursuing a business plan to corner the Indigenous money market. It then:

- pursues a strategy involving the establishment of a series of branches which provide face-to-face services in Indigenous communities;

- actively employs and trains Indigenous people in its workforce;

- develops housing loans accessible to individual families resident on Aboriginal reserves;

- provides financial and budget management training to its customers;

- funds scholarships for Indigenous people to gain tertiary qualifications; and

- takes loan applications from individuals over the fax machine.

And of course it makes a sound commercial return on its investments.

Concurrently, government regulators recognise that any long-term success in reducing welfare dependence is directly linked to facilitating equitable access to banking services for low-income earners, and providing incentives to build assets. Government institutes regulations and provides direct incentives to the banks to provide loan funds and services to low-income earners.

We might say that such a scenario is merely a fantasy. The bad news is that in Australia, at present, it is a fantasy; the good news is that in Canada and the USA it is not.

The Bank of Montreal

When visiting Toronto in 2000 I met with Ron Jamieson, a Mohawk man, who is Vice President of Aboriginal Banking at the Bank of Montreal, and previously chaired the Royal Commission on Economic Matters Affecting Aboriginal People in Canada. When Jamieson joined the bank in October 1992 the value of its commercial loan business with aboriginal communities amounted to C$10 million. Today, some eight years later that same commercial loan business has grown to C$1 billion, with the bank holding a further C$1 billion in trust for First Nations communities. The bank has, over the same period, increased from 121 to 600 the number of its indigenous employees, opened 16 Aboriginal Banking centres, and established an alliance with Canada Post that has resulted in first time access to banking services for 20 remote communities (Bank of Montreal 1999).

The Bank of Montreal has also concluded innovative On Reserve Housing Loan Program agreements with 12 First Nations communities, enabling member families to borrow funds for the construction, renovation and purchase of owner-occupied housing. The default repayment rates for its First Nations customers are below those for its wider community customers (Bank of Montreal 1999).

This bank is not a lone player. Other major Canadian banks are actively chasing the indigenous dollar. They are also designing and delivering financial education and training courses for First Nations communities and funding scholarships for indigenous students. The banks believe these investments are essential in order to build long-term trust and credibility (Royal Bank Financial Group 2000).

The Canadian Bankers Association

Both the Canadian Bankers Association and the Canadian Federal government have also assumed important leadership positions in promoting equitable access to banking services for First Nations. For example governments, business and First Nations are active in creatively utilising existing tax incentives to promote economic and business opportunities on indigenous lands. This has resulted in the development and wide distribution of a comprehensive guide, *Frequently Asked Questions: Understanding the Regulatory Environment for On-Reserve Lending* (Minister of Public Works and Government Services Canada 1999) developed jointly by the banks, the First Nations and the Canadian Government.

All these initiatives contrast markedly with the Australian trend. In Canada, the banks are actively employing and training more indigenous people, opening up more branches (including in remote communities) and making a commercial return.

Welfare reform and banking services

In the USA, there is recognition that achieving reductions in welfare dependence, and designing initiatives aimed at encouraging asset accumulation amongst the poor, are inextricably linked to people's ability to access banking and financial services (Gensler 2000; Stegman 2000; Summers 2000). Key government agencies such as the US Treasury and regulators such as the Federal and State Reserves play a central role in ensuring low- and moderate-income earners have equitable access to affordable credit and appropriate services (Stegman 2000; Summers 2000). Driven partly by the phenomenal growth from the 1980s in 'fringe banking' services, such as commercial cheque-cashing outlets and pawnshops, which charge exorbitant fees (Caskey 1996), the Federal government has sought to strengthen the provisions of the *Community Reinvestment Act 1977* (CRA) and provide direct savings incentives to low- and moderate-income earners.

This policy has also been reflected in the decision of the US Treasury to provide significant resources to community-based groups to educate low-income earners about the benefits of having a bank account, managing household finances, and building assets (US Department of the Treasury 2000a). In order to assist welfare recipients to make the transition from cheque to electronic payments, the US Treasury has also negotiated arrangements with the banks that have led to the establishment of low-fee-paying accounts for low-income earners and has directly funded an expansion in access to automatic teller machines (ATMs) in poorly serviced areas (Summers 2000).

The Community Development Financial Institutions Fund

Another important initiative of the US Treasury has been to establish the Community Development Financial Institutions Fund (CDFI). The CDFI is a statutory corporation wholly owned by the US Treasury. It was created in 1994 under a bipartisan US Congress initiative to expand the availability of credit, investment capital and financial services in distressed urban, rural and Native American communities.

The CDFI seeks to stimulate the creation and expansion of community development financial institutions and to provide incentives to traditional banks and credit unions to invest in CDFIs (US Department of the Treasury 2000b). Since 1994 the fund has certified over 406 funds across the USA, including 22 that specifically service Native American, Alaskan and Hawaiian communities. CDFIs include community development banks, credit unions, venture capital funds and micro-enterprise loan funds (US Department of the Treasury 2000b).

CDFIs are defined as specialised financial institutions that work in market niches that provide a wide range of financial products and services to low-income earners, for needs ranging from community facilities to business loans and housing renovations. In addition these institutions provide services to help ensure credit is used effectively, including counselling and financial budget training. The CDFI fund provides small infusions of capital to institutions that serve distressed communities and low-income individuals. It also conducts a Bank Enterprise Award to encourage major banks by way of incentives to increase their lending and provision of services to low-income communities. These incentives to the private sector, amounting to a combined total of US$90 million, have leveraged more than US$1.8 billion of investment and lending by banks to projects in low-income communities—a ratio of 20 to 1 (US Department of the Treasury 1999).

The *Community Reinvestment Act*

These initiatives are centrally linked to the Federal CRA which awards the banks credits based on their performance on lending, investment and the provision of services to low- and moderate-income earners. Banks must have at least a satisfactory credit rating to gain regulatory approval to merge, or to acquire another depository institution, or to open or close a branch (Litan et al. 2000). The CRA's regulations were strengthened under the Clinton administration in 1993 and were retained in the context of the Federal *Financial Services Modernisation Act 1999*. This legislation prohibits banks from commencing newly authorised activities, such as expanding into securities and insurance, without a satisfactory CRA rating (Litan et al. 2000).

A practical example of the impact of the CRA occurred on the Navajo Reservation in Arizona in 1998. Citibank was in the process of selling its branch network to the Norwest Bank. The Navajo complained to the Federal government that Citibank had failed to fulfil their CRA obligations to service the geographic areas surrounding its Arizona branches. At the time there were only two ATMs anywhere in the entire Navajo Nation area, with many residents having to drive up to 160 kilometers to cash or deposit a cheque.

In response to this complaint, the relevant regulatory authority blocked the Norwest acquisition until it agreed to build four additional branches and install two extra ATMs on Navajo land. Norwest agreed. The location of the new branches, and the training of Navajo staff to run them, occurred with the full co-operation and involvement of the local Tribal government (US Department of the Treasury 2000c).

A recent independent evaluation of the impact of the CRA prepared for the US Treasury concluded that in 1998, mortgage lending to low-income earners by CRA-regulated institutions stood at $135 billion, up from $75 billion in 1993—an 80 per cent increase. This increase is also reflected in other loans approved over the same period to borrowers, which have risen in total number by over 45 per cent (Litan et al. 2000).

The Native American Lending Study

Congress has also required the US Department of the Treasury, through the CDFI, to investigate and make recommendations to Congress and the President on the elimination of barriers to private sector lending and investment on Native American reservations. This study has been conducted through a series of 13 workshops covering ten regions throughout the USA. It brought together Native American Tribal governments, and private and public sector representatives to jointly identify barriers to financing and lending, and strategies to overcome them (US Department of the Treasury 2000c).

In addition to the workshops, over 1000 financial institutions and Tribal governments have been surveyed via a detailed questionnaire. Both these exercises have identified a number of misconceptions and misunderstandings between financial institutions and Tribal governments, and have resulted in locally based initiatives built around developing mutual understanding and strong relationships. In practical terms they include partnerships to develop and deliver financial literacy programs, on-reserve home lending programs, and increased awareness of the CRA provisions. The findings of the study and recommendations of this report will be submitted to Congress and the President during 2001.

Individual Development Accounts

One of the best-kept secrets of welfare reform in the USA has been the widespread adoption of measures to allow savings and asset-building by the poor (Sherraden et al. 2000; Stegman 1999). The most innovative development involves the provision of Individual Development Accounts (IDAs). A key feature of IDAs is that a community group, foundation or government matches every dollar saved by an individual. Participation is conditional upon the saver's completion of a financial education program.

Withdrawals from IDAs are limited to specific purposes, including deposits for housing purchase, self education, buying a business, and buying or repairing a car for work or for family emergencies. These programs have mushroomed throughout the USA, in tandem with welfare reform. Detailed evaluations have confirmed that IDAs are being effectively taken up by low-income earners, and particularly by women (Sherraden et al. 2000). Specific Youth IDAs have also been established that provide up to a three-to-one dollar match for similar purposes (Stegman 1999).

The Federal government's decision to devolve responsibility for the Temporary Assistance for Needy Families (TANF) program to Tribal governments has also included provisions that enable Indian Tribal governments to apply these monies as matching IDA funds, therefore encouraging the active accumulation of savings (US Department of the Treasury 2000b).

Conclusion

These overseas developments hold important lessons for Australia. At the very least they severely test some of the myths about the supposed inability of Australian banks to maintain social and community obligations whilst generating corporate profit for shareholders. Not only does this Australian banking myth run contrary to the commercial experience of some of their overseas counterparts, its net effect runs counter to the spirit and intent of banking regulatory frameworks that apply in that true bastion of the free market—the USA. I am not arguing that all the initiatives identified in this paper are immediately transferable to Australia. However they do, at the very least, raise serious questions about many of the readily cited justifications for continuing inequities in the delivery of financial and baking services to Indigenous Australians in regional and remote areas.

Overseas experience also points to a need for governments, financial institutions, and Indigenous interests to seriously examine and consider new and innovative methods of ensuring that commercial loan and capital funds can be made available to Indigenous communities. Options developed overseas include using community block grants as collateral, community councils acting as guarantors and setting aside community investment or royalty funds as collateral, and the use of tax incentives to encourage economic activities in remote communities. Consideration should also be given to how tax and other incentives could be applied to facilitate improvements in financial literacy and individual asset accumulation. The McClure Report on welfare reform (McClure 2000) remained strangely quiet on these issues, especially given the North American experience in welfare reform where the role of financial institutions and IDAs are seen as critical factors in promoting asset accumulation for low and moderate income earners.

In the USA and Canada connecting poor people in poor communities with the financial mainstream is a key plank of government policy, as are the provision of funds for financial education, and tax incentives to promote savings. In Australia, we are yet to translate those clear connections into the necessary regulatory, policy, and program incentives needed to help deliver real and sustainable reductions in welfare dependency.

In the light of highly restricted (and worsening) Indigenous access to banking services in Australia, and given these overseas initiatives and best practice, a number of practical steps could be taken in this country.

- It is recommended that the Commonwealth government examine the impact and relevance of the US *Community Reinvestment Act 1977* to Australia, with a view to ensuring equitable access to credit and appropriate financial services for all Australians, especially those on low and moderate incomes.

- Consideration should be given to the conduct of an Indigenous lending study in Australia, modelled on the one commissioned by the US Congress and undertaken in the USA. The study should investigate and make recommendations aimed at eliminating barriers to and developing incentives for private sector lending, investment and provision of banking services on Indigenous lands and other lands held in trust for Indigenous Australians.

- The Commonwealth government should give active consideration to the potential relevance of IDAs as a key element of any policies aimed at reducing welfare dependence.

- Finally, a comprehensive program of financial education needs to be promoted and supported by the Federal government in partnership with Australia's banks and ATSIC.

Notes

1. The research for this paper was undertaken when the author was a Visiting Fellow at CAEPR.

2. The Cairns Statistical Sub-Division (SSD) and Darwin Rural Areas SSD are excluded.

References

Bank of Montreal 2000. 'Aboriginal Banking Services Bankwide', Information papers (various), Bank of Montreal, Toronto, Canada.

Caskey, J.P. 1996. *Fringe Banking, Check-Cashing Outlets, Pawnshops, and the Poor*, The Russell Sage Foundation, New York.

Commonwealth of Australia 1999. *Regional Banking Services: Money Too Far Away, Report of the House of Representatives Committee on Economics, Finance, Public Administration, and Regional Banking Services*, Parliament of the Commonwealth of Australia, Canberra.

Council for Aboriginal Reconciliation (CAR) 2000. *Overcoming Disadvantage*, CAR, Canberra.

Gensler, G. 2000. 'Treasury under Secretary Gary Gensler', Submission to US Congress House Committee on Banking and Financial Institutions June 27 2000, Washington, DC.

Litan, R.E., Retsinas, N.P., Belsky, E.S. and Haag, S.W. 2000. *The Community Reinvestment Act After Financial Modernization: A Baseline Report*, US Department of the Treasury, Washington, DC.

McClure, P. (Chair) 2000. Participation Support for a More Equitable Society: Final Report of the Reference Group on Welfare Reform, July 2000 [the McClure Report], DFACS, Canberra.

McDonnell, S. and Westbury, N. 2001. 'Giving credit where it's due: A study of the delivery of banking and financial services to Indigenous Australians in rural and remote Australia, *CAEPR Discussion Paper No. 218*, CAEPR, ANU, Canberra.

Minister of Public Works and Government Services Canada 1999. *Frequently Asked Questions: Understanding the Regulatory Environment for On-Reserve Lending*, Canadian Government, Ottawa.

Ralston, D. and Beal, D. 1997a. 'Bank branch closures in rural communities', *The Australian Banker*, 4: 126–9.

—— and —— 1997b. Economic and Social Impacts of the Closure of the Only Bank Branch in Rural Communities: A Report Prepared for Credit Care, Centre for Financial Institutions, University of Queensland, St Lucia, Qld.

Ross, K. and Taylor, J. 2000, 'Comparative Socio-Economic Profile of the Indigenous Population of Bourke, Brewarrina and Walgett', *CAEPR Working Paper No. 8*, CAEPR, ANU, Canberra [available at http://www.anu.edu au/caepr/].

Royal Bank Financial Group 2000. 'Aboriginal banking initiatives', Information paper, Calgary, Canada.

Sherraden, M., Johnson, L., Clancy, M., Sondra, B., Schreiber, M., Zhan, M. and Curley, J. 2000. *Savings Patterns in IDA Programs*, Center for Social Development, George Warren Brown School of Social Work, Washington University in St Louis, St Louis, WA.

Stegman, M.A. 1999. *Savings for the Poor: The Hidden Benefits of Electronic Banking*, The Brookings Institute, Washington, DC.

—— 2000. 'Statement of Professor Michael A. Stegman before The House Committee on Banking and Financial Services, on House of Representatives 4490, *First Accounts Act* of 2000, June 27 2000', The Frank Hawkins Kenan Institute of Private Enterprise, University of North Carolina, Chapel Hill, NC.

Summers, L.H. 2000. 'Remarks of Treasury Secretary Lawrence H. Summers to the Consumer Bankers Association, Washington, DC, May 2000', Department of the US Treasury, Washington, DC.

Takac, P. 1997. 'The electronic bank: Taking value without taking over', *The Australian Banker*, 4: 136–8.

Taylor, J. 2000. 'Transformations of the Indigenous population: Recent and future trends', *CAEPR Discussion Paper No. 194*, CAEPR, ANU, Canberra.

United States (US) Department of the Treasury 1999. *Building Partnerships: Putting Capital to Work, Community Development Financial Institutions Fund, Fiscal Year 1999, Annual Report*, US Department of the Treasury, Washington, DC.

—— 2000a. 'The *First Accounts Act* of 2000: Bringing the "unbanked" into the financial mainstream', Information paper, US Department of the Treasury, Washington, DC.

—— 2000b. *Overview of the Community Development Financial Institutions Fund*, US Department of the Treasury, Washington, DC.

—— 2000c. *Native American Lending Study/Action Plan Regional Report, Proceedings of Round Table Workshop January 13–14, 2000 Washington, DC*, US Department of the Treasury, Washington, DC.

Westbury, N. 1999. 'Feast, famine and fraud: Considerations in the delivery of banking and financial services to remote Indigenous communities', *CAEPR Discussion Paper No. 187*, ANU, Canberra.

—— 2000. 'What's in it for Koories? Barwon Darling Alliance Credit Union and the delivery of banking services in north-west New South Wales', *CAEPR Working Paper No. 7*, CAEPR, ANU, Canberra [available at http://www.anu.edu.au/caepr/].

11. Demographic challenges to the future of CDEP

John Taylor and Boyd Hunter

Introduction

Increasingly over the past three decades, the scale and the nature of initiatives aimed at achieving social justice for Indigenous Australians have been guided by information about the size, composition, and changing location of the officially identified Indigenous population. The data drawn from five-yearly censuses and, progressively, from other surveys and administrative collections have aided in determining the global quantum of Indigenous need for government services. More recently, there has been a growing recognition that an understanding of the dynamics of demographic change is important for the formulation of policies that are based on some estimation of anticipated requirements, and not solely on current or historic assessment of government obligations (Taylor 2001).

The age structure and related growth of the Indigenous population differs markedly from that of other Australians, and this has consequences for the direction of public policy. For example, Indigenous Australians are on average much younger than the rest of the population and will continue to be so for decades to come (their median age is 19 years compared to 35 years for the general population). As a consequence, the focus of population expansion in the years ahead among Indigenous Australians will be among those of working age (15–64), especially in the school-to-work transition years, whereas for the rest of the Australian population the focus of growth will be amongst the aged (over 55 years). These are opposite ends of the social policy spectrum and point to quite different needs. Such is the momentum for growth built into the Indigenous age distribution that it is estimated that the population aged 15–64 will be 16 per cent greater by 2006 (285 000 compared to 245 000 in 2000). This is the figure adopted for the use in the present analysis.

It should be noted, however, that this estimate of the future size of the Indigenous working-age population is conservative. The Indigenous population is enumerated by self reporting, and consequently there is a major methodological difficulty in projection, deriving from the absence of a rigorous model for capturing change in the propensity of individuals to identify as Indigenous. Different assumptions regarding this propensity can produce widely differing population estimates (ABS 1998). Thus, the low series ABS projection, as used above, assumes no further growth due to increased identification as Indigenous. On the evidence of past census counts this seems an unreasonable expectation and so higher projections, based on varying assumptions about increased propensity to identify, are also provided. Of these, the published high series assumes a continuation of the rate of new identification observed over the most recent inter-censal period. This yields an Indigenous working-age population of 650 000 by 2006.

Despite a 44 per cent increase in Indigenous employment between 1991 and 1996, the underlying rate of employment was little altered, with only 26 per cent of the adult population engaged in mainstream work (Taylor & Bell 1998). There were two reasons for this anomaly. First, much of the recorded employment growth was due to increased participation in the CDEP scheme. By 1996, as much as one-fifth of the Indigenous workforce was employed by the scheme. Another contributory factor was an increase in wage-subsidised employment and training under the Federal government's *Working Nation* initiatives. Against these government-sponsored labour market interventions, growth in mainstream work was negligible. The second reason, as might be expected, was demographic—quite simply, growth in jobs, especially mainstream jobs, failed to keep up with growth in the Indigenous working-age population.

A number of studies have analysed the consequences for labour force status of the persistently youthful Indigenous age profile (Altman & Gaminiratne 1994; Gray & Tesfaghiorghis 1991; Taylor & Altman 1997; Taylor & Hunter 1998). The most recent of these estimated that over the 10-year period from 1996 to 2006 an extra 25 000 Indigenous people would need to be employed just to maintain the Indigenous labour force status at its 1996 level (an employment rate of 39 per cent and an unemployment rate of 26 per cent). The anticipated crisis for public policy that this figure signalled was based on an estimation that only 21 000 additional jobs were likely to be created over this period, leading to worsening labour force status.

Significant changes have occurred in labour market conditions for Indigenous people since 1996, especially in regard to the supply of CDEP work. It is timely, therefore, to review these estimates. Accordingly, this paper has four aims: to estimate the future supply of CDEP scheme positions against the background of population growth and growth in non-CDEP jobs; to assess this against anticipated demand for CDEP; to estimate the consequences of these parameters for future Indigenous labour force status; and to examine the consequences of projected employment and population growth for the achievement of parity in labour force status.

New estimates of employment outcomes

To estimate future numbers of Indigenous jobs, separate calculations are made for mainstream (non-CDEP scheme employment) and CDEP-scheme employment.[1] Previous estimation of mainstream employment growth was based on an assumption that this would continue at the rate observed between 1991 and 1996, of 1.3 per cent per annum (Taylor & Hunter 1998: 17). Historically, this is a relatively high annual rate of Indigenous employment growth and it incorporates the impact of government-sponsored *Working Nation* job programs in boosting the numbers counted as employed. Since 1996, a number of significant changes have occurred in the labour market. This assumed growth rate is therefore in need of review, although this can only be undertaken by inference because reliable inter-censal estimates of Indigenous employment are absent from sources such as the monthly Labour Force Survey (LFS) (Hunter & Taylor 2001).

The first important change was the dismantling of *Working Nation* programs in 1996 and the second was the subsequent privatisation of employment services. Indigenous people were over-represented in *Working Nation* programs (Taylor & Hunter 1996) and the new Job Network has generally failed in servicing the needs of Indigenous people (Commonwealth Grants Commission (CGC) 2000), so the assumption is made here that these developments served to deflate the original estimate of mainstream employment growth. On the other hand, in 1999, the government launched the Indigenous Employment Policy (IEP), which restored, for Indigenous job seekers, many of the features of *Working Nation* programs including wage subsidies for eligible employers (see Shergold, Ch. 8, this volume). In addition, since 1996, employment growth overall in the labour market has been buoyant, with a concomitant substantial decline in the rate of unemployment. In turn, these developments may be assumed to have boosted the employment prospects of Indigenous job seekers. Thus, balancing all these factors leads to the conclusion that the original assumption of 1.3 per cent per annum growth in Indigenous mainstream employment should be retained.

Greater certainty surrounds the future scale of CDEP employment. The broad level of participation in the scheme is controlled by agreement between ATSIC and government at a national policy level, while the actual allocation of places stems from administrative procedures enacted by ATSIC Regional Councils. Thus, planned participant numbers provided by ATSIC provide a basis for estimation. As for demand, less is understood about why communities and individuals seek to participate in CDEP, but the proven capacity for rapid expansion of the scheme suggests that many more would if they could (Sanders 1993).

Previous estimates of growth in CDEP employment were constructed from a composite of assumptions informed by analysis of the administrative procedures for new participant places. For example, given the intermittent nature of CDEP scheme work in 1996 and the fact that non-working spouses of participants could be included in participant totals, the percentage of scheme participants who could be counted as employed (according to ABS criteria) was set at 60 per cent in remote areas and 80 per cent in the rest of the country. Following the review of the scheme in 1997 (Spicer 1997) and implementation of reforms to focus more on equipping participants for mainstream work, these ratios were assumed to rise to 80 per cent and 90 per cent respectively. This effected a jump in estimated participant numbers from 21 228 in 1998 to 27 028 in 1999, with numbers increasing thereafter by 550 per annum in line with government provision for the expansion of existing schemes (Taylor & Hunter 1998: 17).

Subsequent administrative developments require that these assumptions be revised. First of all, the recommendations of the Spicer Review, in emphasising the importance of the scheme as an employment program, coincided with the movement off the scheme of non-working participants to become clients of the social security system (see Sanders, Ch. 6, this volume). As a consequence, ATSIC now advises that all registered participants should be classified as employed. Initially, it was assumed that this push towards a more work-focused scheme would put off the need for expansion since CDEP could 'expand' internally by re-classifying non-working participants, thereby increasing the proportion of participants who were working. However, provision for an additional 1500 places was announced in the 2000–01 Federal Budget and this is factored in to revised estimates of future CDEP employment, along with provision for 580 additional places annually to accommodate natural growth.

The impact of these revisions on projected employment estimates is shown in Table 11.1. As indicated, mainstream employment estimates remain unaltered but CDEP employment is raised markedly, commencing in 1999. The overall effect is that by the end of the projection period (in 2006), the number of the Indigenous employed is expected to be around 6700 higher than previously estimated.[2]

Table 11.1   Revised Indigenous employment estimates, 1996–2006

Year	Mainstream jobs	Original estimate: CDEP jobs[a]	Revised estimate: CDEP jobs	Original estimate: Total jobs	Revised estimate: Total jobs
1996	71 556	18 656	18,656	90,212	90,212
1997	72 486	19 974	19 974	92 460	92 460
1998	73 429	21 228	21 228	94 657	94 657
1999	74 383	27 028	31 650	101 411	106 033
2000	75 350	27 486	32 220	102 836	107 570
2001	76 330	27 944	34 175	104 274	110 505
2002	77 322	28 402	34 725	105 724	112 047
2003	78 327	28 860	35 275	107 187	113 602
2004	79,345	29,318	35 825	108 663	115 170
2005	80,377	29 776	36 375	110 153	116 752
2006	81,422	30 234	36 925	111 656	118 347

Note: (a) Based on figures of Agreed Participant Growth provided by ATSIC.

It is interesting to consider the impact of this revision on previous estimates of future job needs developed using ABS experimental projections of working-age population (Taylor & Hunter 1998: 10–12). This is shown in Table 11.2. With an estimated 25 000 additional jobs required just to maintain an employment rate of 38.9 per cent, the original anticipated jobs growth of 21 400 was clearly insufficient: it led to a projected jobs deficit of 3600 against this target. The revised calculations, which take into account the changes to CDEP, estimate that by 2006 a total of 28 100 extra jobs would have been created. This leads to a job surplus against the target of maintaining the status quo and translates into an employment rate by 2006 of 40 per cent—a positive outcome, but still way below the national average.[3] If the aim is to achieve employment equality, then the task remains enormous, with an additional 49 000 jobs still required.

Table 11.2   Revised estimates of Indigenous employment growth required to maintain the status quo (A) or to achieve employment equality (B), 1996–2006

Employment/ population ratio	Base employment 1996[a]	Total jobs required by 2006	New jobs required by 2006	New jobs projected by 2006	Projected jobs deficit by 2006
Original estimates					
(A) 38.9[b]	90 212	115 307	25 059	21 444	3651
(B) 56.4[c]	90 212	167 181	76 969	21444	55 525
Revised estimates					
(A) 38.9[b]	90 212	115 307	25 059	28 135	-3076
(B) 56.4[c]	90 212	167 181	76 969	28 135	48 834

Notes: (a) The estimated number of Indigenous Australians in employment in 1996.
(b) The estimated employment/population ratio for Indigenous Australians based on 1996 population estimates.
(c) The employment/population ratio for non-Indigenous Australians from the 1996 Census.

Implications of demographic trends for Indigenous unemployment

Indigenous unemployment rates in the 1996 Census were between two-and-a-half and five times the national average depending upon whether participation in the CDEP scheme counts as being unemployed (Taylor & Hunter 1998). If CDEP scheme participants are counted as unemployed, Indigenous unemployment will become even greater over time as large numbers of Indigenous youth enter the workforce. Fig. 11.1 shows that if the CDEP scheme did not exist, the overall unemployment rate among Indigenous people would increase steadily from just over 41 per cent to about 48 per cent between 1996 and 2006. Detailed projections are found in Table 11.3. However, the CDEP scheme does exist and it substantially reduces the official unemployment rate. If CDEP scheme jobs are treated as employment, the Indigenous unemployment rates falls by over one-third.

The recent expansion of the CDEP scheme resulting from changes to the CDEP administration and the renewed spending push in ATSIC has not only contained the growth in Indigenous unemployment but has even led to a small reduction in Indigenous unemployment rates. However, on current projections such gains will be eroded by the large increase in the numbers of Indigenous people entering prime labour force age. The Indigenous unemployment rate falls from just over 25 per cent in 1996 to a low point of 20 per cent in 2001 (coincidentally the census year), before it increases under the current policy settings to about 25 per cent in 2006.

The CDEP seems to be keeping total Indigenous unemployment in some sort of holding pattern. We now seek to address the question of what are the numbers of jobs required for Indigenous people to achieve equity, in terms of unemployment rates, with the rest of the Australian population.

Figure 11.1   Projected trends in Indigenous unemployment rates, 1996–2006

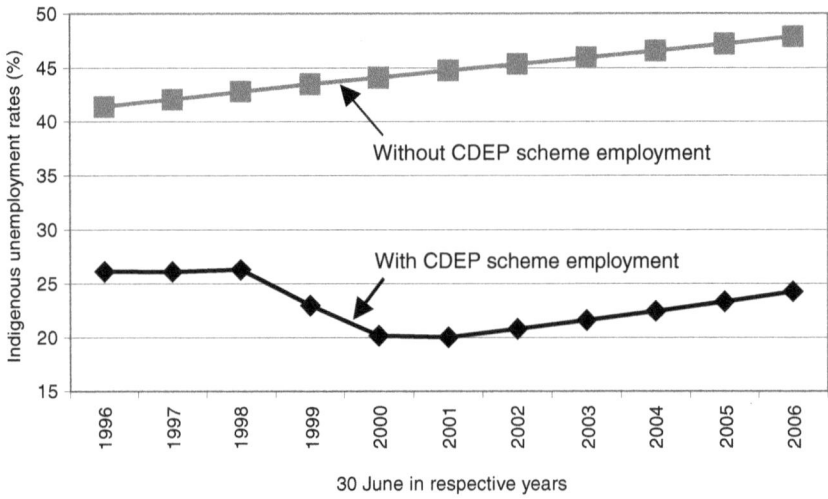

Source: Table 11.3.

In July 2000, the overall Australian unemployment rate was 6.2 per cent. Fig. 11.2 describes the number of jobs required to reduce the Indigenous unemployment rate to this level. It follows the same basic pattern as Fig. 11.1, showing a substantial fall in the number of jobs required to June 2001. Unfortunately without further supplementation of the number of CDEP scheme places, the number of jobs required increases consistently after that point.

Figure 11.2   Jobs required to achieve equity in unemployment rates, 1996–2006

Source: Table 11.3.

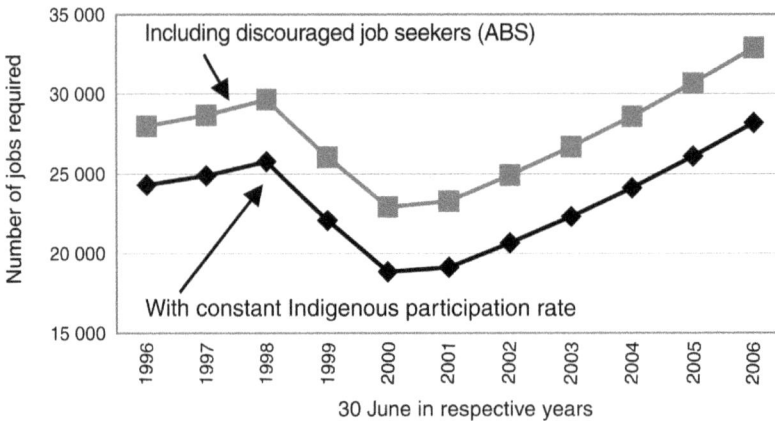

Table 11.3   Estimates of Indigenous employment need, 1996–2006

| Year | Indigenous unemployment rates (%) | | | Additional jobs required | |
	Without CDEP scheme employment	With CDEP scheme employment	Including discouraged workers[a] as unemployed	Indigenous labour force held at 1996 levels [b]	Including discouraged workers [c]
1996	41.4	26.1	29.2	24 303	27 992
1997	42.1	26.1	29.2	24 885	28 665
1998	42.8	26.3	29.4	25 763	29 643
1999	43.5	23.0	26.2	22 065	26 044
2000	44.1	20.2	23.6	18 834	22 906
2001	44.8	20.0	23.4	19 106	23 282
2002	45.3	20.8	24.2	20 644	24 919
2003	45.9	21.6	24.9	22 307	26 685
2004	46.6	22.4	25.7	24 101	28 588
2005	47.2	23.3	26.6	26 081	30 683
2006	47.9	24.2	27.5	28 181	32 902

Notes: (a) Discouraged workers according to ABS definition.
(b) Calculated using the national unemployment rate in 2000 of 6.2 per cent.
(c) The unemployment rates used in this column are adjusted by adding the number of discouraged workers to both the numerator and denominator (ABS 2001).

These estimates are conservative—or low—because they are based on Indigenous labour force in 1996, which excludes many people who want to work. For example, workers who have become discouraged by prolonged exposure to poor labour market conditions (or, indeed, who have experienced persistent discrimination) may re-enter the labour force when job prospects pick up (or we enter a brave new world without racism) (see Hussmanns, Mehran & Verma 1990: 107 for the precise International Labour Organisation [ILO] definition). The potential labour force, which includes all those currently in work as well as those who are discouraged from looking for work, can be substantially greater than the existing labour force (Hunter & Gray 1999).

Being discouraged from looking for work is an inherently subjective phenomenon. The conventional ABS definition of a discouraged job seeker in the LFS uses the reasons for not looking for work to classify whether or not a person is a discouraged worker. For example, job seekers are deemed to be discouraged if employers' attitudes or behaviours dissuade them from looking for work. Individuals who are not looking for work for personal reasons but state that they want to work are not classified as being discouraged workers. Given that many respondents (especially Indigenous people with a history of experiencing discrimination) may not be able to abstract their personal circumstances from the labour market situation, this definition is probably too circumscribed.

The 1994 National Aboriginal and Torres Strait Islander Survey (NATSIS) provides the only reliable data on the extent of the discouraged Indigenous workforce. Unfortunately, it is not possible to achieve the correspondence between the NATSIS and LFS categories that would allow a direct comparison between Indigenous and non-Indigenous peoples' reasons for not looking for work. However, it is possible to observe that personal reasons also dominate those given in the LFS survey (ABS 1994). Almost three-quarters of LFS respondents who are not in the labour force and want to work indicate they were not looking for work for personal reasons (especially to do with child care or attending an educational institution).

The predominance of personal reasons for not looking for work among both the Indigenous and non-Indigenous populations indicates how potentially sensitive the results might be of an analysis of Indigenous labour force status based narrowly on the ABS definition of discouraged worker. The theoretical literature on the discouraged worker emphasises the relative productivity of family members in both market and non-market work, and the level of welfare entitlements, and as a result the official definition can easily be challenged (Hunter & Gray 1999). Nevertheless, the ABS definition should provide a conservative benchmark for the extent of discouraged workforce.

That there are many Indigenous discouraged workers is highlighted by the fact that the ATSIC regions with the highest employment rates (often because of substantial numbers of CDEP scheme places in such areas) also have the highest labour force participation rates. For example, the Cooktown region has the highest Indigenous male labour force participation rate of any ATSIC region, presumably because of the relatively large numbers of CDEP scheme participants in the area (Hunter 2000). The Cooktown rates can be contrasted to those in nearby Cairns which, despite a larger and more buoyant labour market, has substantially lower Indigenous labour force participation rates because of relatively small number of CDEP scheme places in that region.

What happens to the estimates if one includes all of these discouraged job seekers in the projections of Indigenous job need? In an attempt to be consistent with the ABS definition, only NATSIS respondents who nominated 'economic' reasons for not looking for work are counted here as discouraged: thus a person is counted as a discouraged job seeker if they want to work but are not looking for work because of the lack of suitable jobs in the local area, or in the economy at large.

As noted above, it is not possible to compare directly the proportion of discouraged workers in NATSIS with that in other ABS collections because of the lack of concordance in the reasons given for not looking for work. For example, potential workers who have given up looking for work because of their low levels of skill cannot be identified through NATSIS, further reinforcing the conservatism of the definition adopted in this paper. However, another problem arising from using a standard definition is that the formal ABS definition requires that discouraged job seekers be available to start work within four weeks (ABS 1994). Since the NATSIS unit record file does not include information on availability of job seekers, the operational definition may tend in this respect to overstate the numbers of Indigenous discouraged job seekers. These competing biases will thus tend to balance out, and the estimates which follow thus provide a reasonable basis for approximating the potential Indigenous workforce.

According to the 1994 NATSIS, only one-sixth of people who want jobs but are not currently in the labour force indicated they were not looking for work because of the lack of availability of suitable jobs. If such discouraged workers are included as unemployed then the number of jobs required to reduce Indigenous unemployment to that of other Australians is lifted by another 4000–5000 (Fig. 11.2). This adjustment does not substantially change the pattern in the trend of the number of jobs required; it merely shifts it up. The upshot is that by 2006, about 33 000 jobs are required nationwide to achieve equity with the non-Indigenous unemployment rates.

The reinforcement of CDEP scheme employment is clearly a vital strategy for expanding Indigenous labour force participation. Even so, producing incremental improvements in Indigenous employment is just tinkering around the edges of an enormous, and growing, problem. Estimates of job need are conservative because they focus on the low series projection of the Indigenous population, and the estimates of the number of discouraged workers are very low, based as they are on the official ABS definition. If all the Indigenous people who want to work are counted as unemployed, then policy makers need to find work for another 30 000 or so people.

The bulk of growth in the Indigenous population is occurring in urban Australia. If CDEP growth only occurs outside the capital cities, then Indigenous unemployment rates in the cities are liable to remain high and participation rates low. This is not to say that there is no room for growth of CDEP schemes in rural and remote Australia. Clearly the population growth in such areas means many new jobs are required. However, an unbalanced approach to CDEP funding which ignores the urban areas may result in a greater inclusion of discouraged workers, and hence an increase in the Indigenous labour force, in non-urban areas relative to urban areas. This raises the question of horizontal equity in labour force status among Indigenous Australians.

Finally, the excess demand for CDEP scheme places is of a similar size to the current number of participant places (see e.g. Dukakis, Ch. 27, this volume). That is, the number of CDEP scheme places would have to double to reduce the Indigenous unemployment rate to that of other Australians. If all people who want to work are included in the Indigenous labour force, then the number of CDEP places would have to treble. This calculation is designed to illustrate the magnitude of Indigenous employment need: it is probably not feasible to expect that the scheme will absorb all Indigenous people who want a job. Clearly, it will be necessary to augment the demand for Indigenous labour by other means as well (for example, through education and training).[4]

Conclusion

The McClure Report (2000) has reinvigorated the debate about mutual obligation, both of the unemployed and of the state, encouraging a re-examination of relationships between labour force participation, unemployment outcomes and the social security system. In the Indigenous employment context, the CGC's ongoing Indigenous Funding Inquiry provides one important impetus for re-evaluation of such relationships and consequent implications for future Indigenous employment requirements (Hunter 2000). The need for employment can be defined in two ways: in terms of the utility it brings to individuals in giving them command over resources (money income), or through the non-pecuniary benefits that flow from work, including psychological connection to the community and wider society.

Notwithstanding that CDEP scheme employment meets the ILO definition of employment, a perennial problem for defining Indigenous labour force status is whether to treat CDEP scheme jobs as work or welfare. In reality, the scheme contains elements of both (Sanders 1997). In terms of employment need, the CDEP scheme fulfils both aspects of the defining features of need: it provides a psychological link to society and also provides some discretionary financial income in addition to social security entitlements (although the amount involved may be quite small, see Altman & Gray 2000; ATSICOEA 1997). Therefore, if one gives precedence to non-pecuniary aspects of CDEP work, then it should be considered as employment.[5] In many non-urban areas, the scheme is the only source of employment and, in the absence of mass migration to more developed labour markets, there is little alternative for increasing the economic activity of local Indigenous residents (see Scott, Ch. 24, this volume). Frequently, CDEP schemes are also development programs delivering goods and services to local communities which, in many cases, would not be provided by the mainstream economy (see Kean, Ch. 21 and Nalliah, Ch. 28, this volume).

The CGC's Indigenous Funding Inquiry highlights the importance of taking into account demographic factors, employment demand, the treatment of the CDEP scheme and the large numbers of Indigenous people not included in the Indigenous workforce (i.e. discouraged workers) in establishing employment requirements. Indeed, the CGC's preliminary indicator of Indigenous employment need in the 36 ATSIC regions (the proportion of the labour force receiving income support) would be substantially revised if CDEP scheme were classified as employment, as it is by the ABS.[6] There would be further revisions if discouraged job seekers were included in the Indigenous labour force. Such revisions tend to increase the measured level of employment need in urban areas where there are few CDEP places. For example, Hunter (2000) shows that official participation rates are highest in remote areas with large numbers of CDEP scheme places, presumably because more of the potential labour force (i.e. discouraged job seekers and the official labour force) are included in statistics. The larger labour force in such areas means, all else being equal, that Indigenous employment need is greater there than in other (usually urban) areas.

A previous analysis of the relationship of Indigenous population growth and employment outcomes concluded that to prevent Indigenous labour force status from slipping further behind it would be necessary to maintain a commitment to special employment programs as well as ensuring that Indigenous people continued to find jobs in the mainstream labour market (Taylor & Hunter 1998). The estimates that were put forward indicated that just maintaining the status quo was going to be difficult, given the policy settings of the day. The idea of moving beyond this and achieving an improvement in labour force statistics was seen to require, in the face of demographic pressure, a quantum leap in the scale of policy intervention.

It appears that the recent adjustments to CDEP administration and the announcement of additional CDEP places have created such a shift. The revised estimates presented in this paper show that inroads can be made into changing official levels of employment and unemployment. However, they also demonstrate that if such interventions are not sustained then the situation can very quickly deteriorate once more.

Notes

1. These estimates are not developed from a formal labour market forecasting model; they are more in the nature of a plausible scenario.

2. The year 2006 is used because this is the limit of currently available Indigenous population projections from the ABS.

3. The projected deficit of −3076 jobs by 2006 (see Table 11.2) is, of course, a surplus of 3076 jobs over that required to maintain the employment to population ratio at 1996 levels.

4. Recent ABS estimates of Indigenous labour force status are consistent with the projected decline in unemployment rates predicted in this paper for the late 1990s (ABS 2000). Indeed, there is no significant difference between the unemployment rates calculated in this paper and those calculated using the latest LFS data (Hunter & Taylor 2001). Notwithstanding legitimate questions about the reliability of Indigenous data from the LFS, one can be confident that the analysis above provides a reasonably accurate estimate of excess supply of Indigenous labour in the near future.

5. In this respect, the 'work for the dole' scheme should also be considered as a form of work. However, the official ABS definition of employment excludes 'work for the dole' schemes because there is no employer–employee relationship. Since CDEP scheme work does involve such a relationship, it is easy to rationalise the treatment of CDEP jobs as genuine work.

6. See Table 10-5 in CGC (2000).

References

Aboriginal and Torres Strait Islander Commission Office of Evaluation and Audit (ATSICOEA) 1997. *Evaluation of the Community Development Employment Projects Program: Final Report, September 1997*, ATSIC, Canberra.

Altman, J.C. and Gaminiratne, K.H.W. 1994. 'Employment implications of the growth of the Indigenous Australian working-age population to 2001', *Australian Bulletin of Labour*, 20 (1): 29–44.

—— and Gray, M.C. 2000. 'The effects of the CDEP scheme on the economic status of Indigenous Australians: Some analyses using the 1996 Census', *CAEPR Discussion Paper No. 195*, CAEPR, ANU, Canberra.

Australian Bureau of Statistics (ABS) 1994. *Persons not in the Labour Force, Australia*, Cat. no. 6220.0, ABS, Canberra.

—— 1998. *Experimental Estimates of the Aboriginal and Torres Strait Islander Population*, Cat. no. 3231.0, ABS, Canberra.

—— 2000. *Labour Force Characteristics of Aboriginal and Torres Strait Islander Australians: Experimental Estimates from the Labour Force Survey*, Cat. no. 6287.0, ABS, Canberra.

—— 2001. *Persons not in the Labour Force, Australia*, Cat. no. 6220.0, ABS, Canberra.

Commonwealth Grants Commission (CGC) 2000. Draft Report of the Indigenous Funding Inquiry, *Discussion Paper IFI 2000/2*, CGC, Canberra.

Gray, A. and Tesfaghiorghis, H. 1991. 'Social indicators of the Aboriginal population of Australia', *CAEPR Discussion Paper No. 18*, CAEPR, ANU, Canberra.

Hunter, B.H. 2000. 'A perspective on defining and measuring Indigenous employment need', submission to the CGC's Indigenous Funding Inquiry, ANU, Canberra.

—— and Gray, M.C. 1999. 'Further investigations into Indigenous labour supply: What discourages discouraged workers?' *CAEPR Working Paper No. 2*, CAEPR, ANU, Canberra [available at http://www.anu.edu.au/caepr/].

—— and Taylor, J. 2001. 'The reliability of Indigenous employment estimates', *Agenda*, 8 (2): 113–28.

Hussmanns, R., Mehran, F. and Verma, V. 1990. *Surveys of Economically Active Population, Employment, Unemployment and Underemployment*, ILO, Geneva.

McClure, P. (Chair) 2000. Participation Support for a More Equitable Society: Final Report of the Reference Group on Welfare Reform, July 2000 [the McClure Report], DFACS, Canberra.

Sanders, W. 1993. 'The rise and rise of the CDEP scheme: An Aboriginal "workfare" program in times of persistent unemployment', *CAEPR Discussion Paper No. 54*, CAEPR, ANU, Canberra.

—— 1997. 'How does (and should) DSS treat CDEP participants? (What are these allegations of racial discrimination?)', *CAEPR Discussion Paper No. 149*, CAEPR, ANU, Canberra.

Spicer, I. 1997. *Independent Review of the Community Development Employment Projects (CDEP) Scheme* [the Spicer Review], Office of Public Affairs, ATSIC, Canberra.

Taylor, J. 2001. 'Aboriginal population dynamics and future growth in Uluru-Kata Tjuta National Park', *CAEPR Discussion Paper No. 211*, CAEPR, ANU, Canberra.

—— and Altman, J.C. 1997. *The Job Ahead: Escalating Economic Costs of Indigenous Employment Disparity*, Office of Public Affairs, ATSIC, Canberra.

—— and Bell, M. 1998. 'Estimating intercensal Indigenous employment change, 1991–96', *CAEPR Discussion Paper No. 155*, ANU, Canberra.

——and Hunter, B. 1996. 'Indigenous participation in labour market and training programs', *CAEPR Discussion Paper No. 108*, CAEPR, ANU, Canberra.

—— and —— 1998. *The Job Still Ahead: Economic Costs of Continuing Indigenous Employment Disparity*, Office of Public Affairs, ATSIC, Canberra.

12. Training by doing: Pathways through CDEP

Shirley Campbell and Jerry Schwab

Introduction

Indigenous Australians often say that their traditional forms of education involved 'learning by doing'—a hands-on and practical approach that fitted with the immediate needs and interests of individuals and communities. This particular approach is certainly not unique to Indigenous education and is a strategy deployed at every level of education today, from preschools to postgraduate studies. At the vocational level 'training by doing' is the heart of effective skill and knowledge acquisition, making this level of education particularly amenable to Indigenous students (Aboriginal and Torres Strait Islander Peoples Training Advisory Council (ATSIPTAC) 1997, 1998, 1999b, n.d.; Australian National Training Authority Research Advisory Council (ANTARAC) 1998; Schwab 1997; Teasdale & Teasdale 1996). Many who have lived or worked in and with Indigenous communities will be familiar with stories of failed training programs based on decontextualised classroom lectures and abstract book-work. On the other hand, stories of practical success abound, telling of Indigenous students who have gained and refined their understanding of a new skill or process 'in the field' with their hands on tools. Clearly, a desirable means of providing education and training opportunities looks to the practical acquisition and application of skills with an immediate use value. If ever there was an avenue leading to the development of new skills and knowledge for Indigenous Australians, it is CDEP—a program that allows Indigenous people to work in and for their own communities. Yet training, as part of the CDEP scheme, is problematic.

It has been said on many occasions at the national level (Deloitte Touche Tohmatsu 1993; Spicer 1997), that CDEP is the single biggest employer of Indigenous people in the country. This is particularly pronounced for young Indigenous people, with CDEP employment accounting for around 40 per cent of employment among 15–19 year-olds. Given its prominence in so many Indigenous Australians' lives, one might expect that CDEP would be a significant pathway to other forms of employment, yet, as so much research has shown, that is not the case (Altman & Gray 2000; Saunders 1993; Spicer 1997). Few CDEP workers go on to take up jobs in any other sector, despite government initiatives to facilitate this process.

Of equal concern is the fact that too few CDEP workers accumulate skills or knowledge that is transferable to other community contexts, let alone to outside employment opportunities (ATSIC 1999; ATSIPTAC 1999b; ANTARAC 1998; Commonwealth Grants Commission (CGC) 2000). While there are countless reasons for this, the poor articulation between CDEP and training is one of the most significant. For those intimately engaged with issues concerning CDEP training and employment readiness, this is not news. Both policy makers and communities have wanted for a long time to find ways to underpin CDEP more effectively through the provision of appropriate education and training. This was noted most prominently in the Spicer Review (1997) and more recently by ATSIPTAC. Drawing out the key issues from Spicer, ATSIPTAC has recommended a 'three-pronged approach' to increase the articulation between CDEP and vocational education and training. ATSIPTAC recommends a nationally consistent approach involving coordination at the national, State and Territory, and regional and local levels, nationally consistent accredited vocational education and training (based on the Australian Qualifications Framework), and flexible delivery options (ATSIPTAC 1999b). This is in accordance with the national strategy set out by the Australian National Training Authority (ANTA) for vocational education and training in Australia (ANTA 1998).

While reviews are conducted and a plethora of position papers are drafted and discussed, CDEP goes on in nearly every corner of this country with CDEP managers, boards and workers having to contend, as best they can, with a system which too often fails to meet their training needs. This paper arose out of a desire to contribute to discussions on the future shape of CDEP by drawing out relevant vocational education and training issues 'on the ground', which are experienced today within CDEP programs across the country. The goal has been to better understand how training is being managed within the current constraints affecting CDEP, at a time when vocational education and training is undergoing considerable re-shaping at the national level. This paper focuses both on the obstacles and opportunities that CDEP programs encounter, and on the strategies some employ to work through (and sometimes around) the obstacles as they struggle to find pathways to improve the training content of CDEP programs and to meet the needs of the workers who seek employment and training experience through them.

Methodology

We had neither the time nor resources to carry out a major investigation involving significant field research, but that was never our intention. Our research design and methodology were intended to produce an exploratory study; we make no claim to have exhaustively surveyed or even randomly sampled from the 300 or so CDEP schemes across the country. Our aim was to gauge the current state of affairs 'on the ground', to establish the critical issues surrounding training needs in a sample of different CDEP schemes which represent the diversity of programs currently in operation.

We began by drawing up a list of research questions which focused on current opportunities available through vocational education and training, the types of training being carried out, and the strategies individual CDEP schemes employed to identify funding and conduct such training. ATSIC's CDEP office in Canberra then assisted us to locate a range of sites which might be appropriate for exploring these questions. ATSIC contacted their regional offices, calling for suggestions of programs that fitted a range of specific criteria. The response was quick and extremely useful. We subsequently contacted many of these State and regional ATSIC officers, who have direct knowledge of the programs within their areas. We discussed our research with them in more detail and sought further advice on appropriate programs to contact directly. Our sample included large and small programs, some rural, some remote, and some urban. Several of the programs were newly established, while others had been in existence for a number of years. Ultimately, we were able to conduct in-depth telephone interviews with 11 managers of CDEP programs across the country. In addition, a few managers responded in writing to our formal interview questionnaire. This paper is a presentation of our findings, taking up the concerns raised by those we spoke to and in the materials sent to us.

The ability of CDEP programs to meet their training needs

Overview of key issues

As we analysed the responses of the various people involved with CDEPs, four broad indicators emerged as significant in the sourcing of training. First, there was a clear relationship between location and access to adequate training. Programs in capital cities have a range of training providers at their disposal. Programs in rural areas, on the other hand, have far fewer choices, while programs in remote areas sometimes found it nearly impossible to obtain training of the nature they required. However, the urban–rural–remote differentiation is not so neatly predictive of a CDEP's ability to obtain training. While there may be more options for the provision of training available in urban areas, there is also greater competition for training places, access to training dollars, and employment placements.

There appears to be a 'critical mass' in terms of program size that correlates with the ability to secure appropriate and recurrent training. Large CDEP programs have larger budgets from which it is possible to draw funds to purchase training, while a small program with few participants has little if any fiscal flexibility. Once a program attains a critical mass, staff numbers grow and staff time may be allocated to develop applications for funded training, or, in some cases, to undertake the extensive and time-consuming process involved in qualifying the CDEP as a Registered Training Organisation (RTO), able to deliver its own training.

Other significant factors are the individual skills and knowledge of CDEP managers. 'Learning the ropes' takes time and it is clear from our research that experienced managers are better able to negotiate the difficult terrain of securing training than are new managers unfamiliar with the various policies, rules, and procedures. Similarly, securing training can require perseverance, determination and patience that not every CDEP manager or staff member is fortunate to possess or able to sustain. In some cases, individual personality and knowledge of agency networks appears to be a key factor in finding the means to provide the desired training.

Finally, community aspirations play a part. These are hard to measure, but are nonetheless a very real factor. If a community has clear and realistic goals and desires, and if the CDEP program is part of a larger community strategy, it appears easier to locate, obtain or create opportunities for training that can in turn facilitate the attainment of those goals.

Conversations with those CDEP people involved in the articulation between vocational education and training and employment opportunities raised a number of issues. Many of these pointed to shared difficulties experienced by a diverse range of CDEPs, and others reflected unique local circumstances. However, all fell broadly within four areas of concern: socio-economic disadvantage, relevance of training, resources, and access. In what follows, these four problem areas provide the basis from which to examine a range of pertinent key issues. In order to respect the anonymity of the CDEPs in the survey, the illustrative material used to highlight those issues that are of major concern to the respondents will not be attributed to individual CDEPs.

Socio-economic disadvantage

The socio-economic disadvantage experienced by Indigenous Australians in relation to the wider Australian population can hardly be disputed. In the context of CDEPs and their ability to provide training opportunities, this disadvantage is implicated in nearly every attempt to incorporate training into CDEP programs. Indeed, the policy discourse from which CDEPs arose was based in part upon a recognition of the socio-economic disadvantage of Indigenous Australians, particularly those living in remote locations (Altman & Sanders 1991; Altman & Smith 1993; Sanders 1988).

A prevailing message recurring in all interviews, regardless of any other indicators, was the continuing low level of skills that are transferrable to 'mainstream' training and employment opportunities. Although CDEP participants in some communities may have considerable skills in looking after country, maintaining cultural continuity and managing family connections, these do not lead to recognisable skills outside an Indigenous cultural context.

Low levels of numeracy and English literacy are a significant impediment to commencing training, regardless of whether it leads to employment. Generally, the most basic expectation for competency in both non-accredited and accredited training is that students are able to read and write, and that they have the ability to perform basic numeracy tasks. The relatively low rates of numeracy and competence in English literacy among Indigenous Australians have implications for the cost of training, and significantly affect the kind of training that is reasonably possible. All training must include basic numeracy and literacy, and has implications in terms of the length of time required to complete the training. Finally, the cost of training may be affected: the trainer may need qualifications to deliver appropriate numeracy and literacy, over and above the qualifications needed to deliver the specific training protocol.

Low educational achievement has a flow-on effect, particularly when CDEP participants are competing for jobs with non-Indigenous people. Securing employment becomes more challenging without basic skills, and a lack of them also restricts people's ability to undertake further training for career development. This was an issue for some of the larger CDEP organisations located in areas where job opportunities existed outside of the CDEP, but where the competition for these jobs was open to the majority—that is non-Indigenous people with basic numeracy and literacy skills. This situation was considered to be one of the major problems militating against gaining further training through employment. One CDEP considered registering for RTO status just so that they could access funding to provide basic courses in numeracy and literacy and give their clients a better competitive edge.

Many organisations highlighted the difficulty of placing CDEP participants in outside employment because of the problem of low skill levels. To overcome this, some CDEPs have adopted enterprise development as a strategy to assist their participants to become 'job-ready' by giving them basic, 'hands-on' skills. In so doing, they feel they will be in a better position to place their job-ready participants in outside employment, where they can then receive further education and training, and improved access to numeracy and literacy skills. Another solution is to determine what business opportunities exist in the area, develop relevant enterprises to capitalise on these, and thereby create job opportunities for CDEP participants through these enterprises. In this way, the organisations can provide employment and skill development opportunities for their Indigenous clients without their having to compete in the outside employment market.

The relevance of training

The value of training is intrinsically connected to its relevance to the people undertaking the training. However, relevant training is not so easily defined. Several issues emerged when we were trying to determine the relevance of training in any given context. Our research suggests that relevant training is strongly associated with local opportunity (see also ANTARAC 1998).

A recurring frustration evident throughout the interviews was that Indigenous people are 'training saturated', but with few identifiable outcomes. Meaningful vocational education and training enables Indigenous individuals and families to maintain an adequate standard of living, as it does for all Australians. However, for many Indigenous people, maintaining a standard of living includes sustaining and managing social and cultural ties. Indigenous people say that they want to determine their training needs so they can engage in training that prepares them for participation in broader economic activity, when and where available, while also participating in training that enables them to maintain a lifestyle that acknowledges and incorporates their cultural responsibilities.

To date, however, training has largely been developed and sold to Indigenous people with the goal of enabling them to contribute to the wider economic activity of the Australian workforce. There has been too little reference to Indigenous aspirations. For example, if training is provided for people to gain the competencies necessary to weld, a generally anticipated outcome is the ability to secure employment in that line of work, wherever there is a job vacancy. However, motivation for an Indigenous person to undergo training in welding may spring from quite different desires. An Indigenous person may initiate training in welding so that he can repair the water pump in the community whenever it breaks down, and thus meet a social need rather than fulfil an economic one. Although not seeking employment in the wider workforce, an Indigenous welder is able to provide a community service that is of value to the rest of his community, while remaining a part of the social fabric of that community. The question arises, whether those responsible for developing policy for training programs, and for providing the funding that is required for their delivery, want to support training that does not necessarily lead to an individual's participation in the labour market.

Training for training's sake has left a legacy of negative attitudes and low expectations. Participation levels in various training programs may have been significant, but outcomes in terms of completions and employment have been negligible relative to the number of people participating. One CDEP used welding as an example, citing the extraordinary amount of training in welding that had gone on over the years with not one Indigenous person employed as a welder in their area. Yet another CDEP employee told of finding a drawer-full of Ranger Certificates. When he tried to hand these out to the certified rangers, each was rejected with complaints from the would-be rangers that they had worked hard to get the certificates, but had not achieved employment as rangers. This training, while considered a success—in terms of completions—by the non-Indigenous providers, was a disaster for the participants. It had led only to disillusionment. Some CDEPs are finding that these negative experiences have left people unwilling to participate in any further training, and sceptical about any assurances that training will change their lives.

CDEPs are in a dilemma over competing priorities. On the one hand they can resource formal training that gives a variety of training experiences to people, but which may or may not lead to further training and employment opportunities. On the other hand, they can give communities the freedom to specify what training they want in response to their immediate needs, recognising that these may be one-off training experiences which generate little ongoing training and few employment opportunities. While the latter may lead to greater participation and may also achieve outcomes that meet the immediate expectations of the community, such training does not necessarily lead to improved pathways for Indigenous people into the wider economy. There is a further consideration: it is not easy to secure funding without some indication of improved employment outcomes. Too often CDEPs are caught in a training mind-frame that automatically links training to employment, leading them to chase the funds that are tied to employment outcomes outside CDEP. In so doing, they lose sight of those training needs of the community that may have no employment outcomes.

A significant message arising from the interviews was that people are not necessarily interested in accredited training for the sake of getting a qualification. Further, they are even less concerned about qualifications that enable them to pursue a trajectory leading towards a career. For many CDEP recipients, pathways to careers are non-existent, and further accredited training and qualifications are therefore irrelevant. However, this should not be construed as a purely negative point of view.

The point is that people do want training, but they do not necessarily want a qualification at the end of it. This puts Indigenous people's participation in the national vocational education and training system somewhat at odds with the goals of ANTA, the organisation responsible for developing a significantly streamlined, nationally articulated, and qualifications focused system. For Indigenous people, however, the issue is the relevance of the training to what people are doing rather than the qualifications gained. Some CDEPs are able to make the training context relevant by developing training environments that include skills acquisition by hands-on training. These training environments are often part of the enterprise development in which the CDEP is engaged, so that the training has an employment outcome within the CDEP, if not outside it. One very large CDEP on the eastern seaboard has identified a niche market and developed a business, with enterprise support, to supply that market. In so doing, it has created a training environment within which CDEP participants can get industry specific training in the anticipation of future employment prospects within that business.

Those CDEPs that are less able to build relevant enterprise within their structure, or which are not located within an economic environment where enterprise development can be sustained, are less able to provide a focus for training. In one such case, the organisation encourages the community to determine its training objectives, leaving the CDEP to broker the training. This training is more often than not unaccredited, one-off, and short term, raising a range of other concerns to do with identifying funding avenues and locating appropriate and willing trainers. This approach also attracts criticism from some training providers who argue that this kind of 'dead end' opportunistic training does not provide transferable skills and qualifications. However, from the perspective of many Indigenous people there is value in this approach, which gives them greater ownership of the objectives and the process. In this particular case, the result has been a high degree of interest and participation in the training, together with a greater sense of accomplishment and corresponding value to the community.

Accredited training may lead to the acquisition of credentials for further career development and portable employment prospects, but Indigenous people's experience is too often that the piece of paper does not change their lives. With one-off training— accredited or not—they are able to get immediate and enduring benefits. Such training puts into their hands the practical skills to build a mechanics' shed, restore a homestead, or to maintain and fix equipment that has lifestyle significance to the community.

Another spin-off of specific, opportunistic training would be that just one person might put their hand up for further training, and their needs could be met within the national training system. The building of intrinsic motivation, together with incremental outcomes that have relevance to the participants, might mean that there is more chance of building a culture of 'life-long learning', which is part of the policy platform developed by ANTA to secure a trained and competitive Australian workforce (ANTA 1998).

Developing training strategies

Many CDEPs are involved in making strategic decisions about the provision of training opportunities. Some CDEPs have been able to develop the infrastructure necessary to support various enterprise initiatives, providing training opportunities and employment (see e.g. in this volume Gray & Thacker, Ch. 15; Humphries, Ch. 32; Madden, Ch. 18; Young, Ch. 29). Such initiatives are possible in areas where opportunities exist, and are dependent upon the support of a critical mass of population, both in terms of the potential workforce and in relation to market demand. However, locational opportunities are not the only factors influencing the ability of a CDEP to develop significant business enterprises. Others in seemingly less amenable locations have managed to identify the available possibilities and to tap into them (see Nicholas, Ch. 25, this volume). One CDEP saw an opportunity to hire out job-ready people, rather than develop their own enterprise operations; the creation of competitive businesses in the area was thought to be too risky, and an unacceptable drain on available CDEP resources. Its approach has been to assist people to become skilled for the specific jobs available, and to hire them out, thereby generating the income needed to keep the scheme going. It was considered better to provide focused skill development relevant to employment possibilities, using non-accredited and accredited training, to help get CDEP recipients into employment and in this way further improve their access to accredited training through other providers.

Yet another CDEP competes with other businesses in the region by tendering for work required by the local council and some private organisations. Another is developing a business in marketing seeds as a subsidiary business to a horticultural farm where CDEP participants work for their CDEP wages and receive training. The strategic decisions made by these CDEPs provide examples where the work and training environment is developed to initiate enterprise opportunity, that in turn generates further training opportunities.

Resources

The securing of adequate resources to facilitate the necessary conditions to promote and deliver vocational education and training is an ongoing concern. In particular, the management of CDEP organisations requires specific skills, yet there is little money to provide the necessary training. Several issues arise out of the need for appropriate resourcing.

We found no cases in which CDEP managers and board members were able to formally access training as part of the CDEP. In part, the problem was a matter of time. A common condition of employment in CDEP management structures is the heavy demand on individuals' time so that finding the opportunity to do training and skill development is nearly impossible (see Lewis, Ch. 30, this volume). The lack of funding to enable the essential training needed to run these organisations keeps the employees under-skilled and the organisations depleted of expertise. One respondent made the poignant observation that they deal with millions of dollars yet there is no money available to train people to manage that money. In a colourful image, he added that they needed to 'suck the money out of the system' in order to provide what little training they could get. Any training that does go on is in-house and opportunistic. If an organisation is fortunate to have a full-time employee within the CDEP who has any skills or job experience whatsoever, these are shared in-house with other employees whenever time permits. Where opportunistic use of employees is not possible, the managers and boards have less success in developing managerial and fiscal strengths within their organisation. One CDEP we surveyed is currently going through another reorganisation with the appointment of a new Chief Executive Officer (CEO). This follows a succession of CEOs who were unable to do the job because of a lack of skills. Nor in this instance did the support staff have sufficient skills and training to assist. Some CDEPs find it difficult to attract trained staff for a variety of reasons including location, services, and living conditions, thus contributing to the continuing circumstances which keep dedicated and highly motivated CDEP employees underskilled.

Active CDEPs that engage in training opportunities invariably have a significant person who acts as 'broker'. As well as managing the payroll for CDEP participants and ensuring that basic services are provided, CDEP staff, if they are to make opportunities available for training, have to act as brokers between potential business interests, potential providers of employment for their job-ready participants, funding agencies, and training providers. Managing the articulation of these interests to enable just one person to gain training and employment represents the workload of more than one dedicated full-time position. Many CDEP organisations operate with less than that. The provision of successful training relies upon securing staff with the ability to broker these opportunities, and keep abreast of funding avenues for the initiatives that become possible through various government agencies. It is a significant asset if a staff member has had experience with one of these other organisations, thus bringing to their job a host of contacts to offer advice or information. The need to attract motivated and experienced staff is a major issue. It might only take one person to make possibilities become realities.

There are substantial costs associated with identifying the possibilities available for training. Our research shows that enterprise development provides significant opportunity for relevant training and employment. However, recognising potential and secure business opportunities is time consuming, and risky at the best of times. Some organisations were able to secure consultants who could identify opportunities for enterprise development, locate funding avenues to support that development, and build short and long-term goals and performance indicators for the CDEP. However, consultants cost money and they do not always have the expertise and experience appropriate to advise Indigenous organisations. Funds to engage consultants are available through the Structured Training and Employment Projects (STEP), administered by DEWRSB (see Shergold, Ch. 8, this volume). STEP can assist employers to develop medium to long-term Indigenous recruitment and career projects. Funding assistance though STEP was being well utilised by some CDEPs while others were unaware of its existence or did not fit the profile for such support. Many CDEPs simply felt they lacked the skills, time, and resources to carry out the necessary research and market analysis to develop relevant and viable enterprise opportunities themselves.

The provision of training and the creation of profitable enterprises do not sit easily together. While on-the-job training seems to have the greatest success in maintaining participation and realising outcomes, it also presents CDEP enterprises with tough decisions. CDEP management must ensure that appropriate training opportunities are available, but they also have to take into consideration various costs of training in relation to the overall viability of the organisation. They cannot divert CDEP money used to support the wages of those CDEP participants who are not involved in CDEP enterprises. Moreover, when training is undertaken, it often takes longer than average for participants to move through the competencies of accredited training. For these reasons, making accredited training as a priority has implications for a business's ability to remain competitive, and to fulfil its wider obligations to the community.

Another issue raised by the respondents was the cost of providing training opportunities, particularly in relation to the New Apprenticeships scheme. One CDEP calculated that it cost the organisation approximately an extra $75.00 per apprentice or trainee per week. This represented the shortfall between paying the apprentice or trainee their CDEP entitlement, and DEWRSB's wage assistance top-up. This shortfall poses a dilemma. The decision to support people in attaining accredited training through employment via the New Apprenticeships scheme militates against the equitable distribution of CDEP wages to all potential recipients. Creaming off dollars in this way means 'robbing Peter to pay Paul'.

Some CDEPs raised the issue that profits accrued through their enterprise activity led to reductions in the CDEP monies made available to them in the following round of CDEP regional funding allocations (and see also Loomes, Ch. 31, this volume). In this sense there is a cost to profit which blocks the reinvestment of CDEP enterprise profits in further training and employment opportunities. There were some instances where profits where being diverted to other parts of the CDEP, for example to set up new enterprises, or to meet the cost of applying for grants, tender submissions, or train other staff. The profit made by CDEP enterprise needs to be available for improving the viability and development of enterprise activity rather than flowing towards the propping up of other CDEP responsibilities usually supported through ATSIC's CDEP funding.

Access

CDEPs and the regional CDEP organisations face difficulties in gaining access to information about the wide range of programs available for vocational education and training and related funding. The complex relationships between Commonwealth, State or Territory, and private organisations which are involved in developing policy, implementing programs, and providing various kinds of funding for vocational education and training is almost impossible to comprehend, even for those working in the various agencies. Navigating one's way through these complex relationships and finding the appropriate vocational education and training programs and funding avenues requires experience, initiative, and human resources. For a CDEP intimately engaged with the day-to-day local issues that challenge its participants, and which also attempts to broker relationships with local businesses, local governments, and schools in its efforts to find available opportunities, the added burden of chasing programs and funding presents almost insurmountable barriers. One CDEP manager had found a 'very helpful person' within his Territory Training Authority whom he could rely on for advice and assistance in getting funding. Finding his 'speck of gold' meant that he was able to accomplish much more. Larger organisations dedicated a specific position within the CDEP to developing ongoing contacts within their State or Territory Training Authorities.

Identified money for training is not a part of the funding formula considered in ATSIC's CDEP allocations. This point was raised by Spicer in his 1997 report on CDEPs. As a result, if CDEPs are going to provide more than 'sit-down money' they have to become creative, and they experience varying degrees of success in brokering training opportunities.

There are currently two labour market initiatives, separated by a chasm. On one side of the divide is the funded support provided by ATSIC for the CDEP, a program created to provide development and employment opportunities for people living in Indigenous communities. On the other side of the divide are funded employment initiatives designed to target improved access for Indigenous people to employment opportunity, most notably through DEWRSB's Indigenous Employment Strategy. However, as noted throughout this discussion, the population targeted for this support has a relatively low education and skill base from which to build specialised, industry-based training. The *extra* training that is required to accomplish something seemingly as simple as training for an outboard motor license, an occupational health and safety certificate, or a Level I certificate in Building Construction attracts little funding. For a CDEP to provide this kind of basic support there is a corresponding need for recurrent funding, specifically directed towards training initiatives that develop basic competencies to enable people to achieve success in their training experiences.

Conclusion: Key findings

This research has investigated a spectrum of activities undertaken by CDEP organisations in their efforts to provide vocational education and training opportunity. Some CDEPs have developed into quite large and complex organisations. They have embarked upon a range of enterprise activities that provide training and employment opportunities, thereby generating profits to feed back to their overall operations. Other CDEPs have successfully tapped into available opportunities, marketing their own resources to employers and businesses in the local area. Still others view a more self sufficient strategy as the best way to provide available choices by arranging one-off, community identified projects that incorporate training. These generally have not led to employment opportunities outside of the CDEP but have provided community focused outcomes. Finally, there are CDEPs that have been less able to identify opportunities, focusing their activities solely on providing essential services. From these varied approaches and experiences, our research highlights a range of critical issues relevant to the provision of vocational education and training through CDEP programs. These are summarised below.

CDEP participants almost invariably have very low education and skill levels. This has implications for all aspects of the training spectrum, influencing the planning and implementation of training programs, the funding necessary to accomplish the training, and the length of time needed to complete the training. Remedial programs are needed to overcome the current situation. Intervention programs implemented at the school level may also be necessary to encourage students to remain in school and thereby circumvent this continuing problem. Without basic numeracy and English literacy skills, Indigenous Australians have reduced chances of successfully completing any kind of training, be it accredited or non-accredited.

Securing training is complex, expensive and time consuming. In order to develop enterprise and employment opportunities CDEP organisations must have access to secure, recurrent training money. Providing vocational education and training requires dedicated staff whose only responsibility is to identify training needs, locate the funds, and find the appropriate trainers. Some CDEPs side-step the administrative burden of training by brokering external employment opportunities through which CDEP recipients can access accredited training. Still other CDEPs plan to enter into complex arrangements to become RTOs so as to attract funding specifically to provide relevant training. CDEPs which had become registered, however, often found that they received no benefit. As a result they preferred to let their RTO status lapse and to continue their activities in less formal ways. Clearly, whatever strategy is employed, there needs to be explicit, recurrent funded training components in the CDEP scheme. While this money may not originate from the ATSIC budget, it should be channelled through ATSIC in order to simplify, for individual programs, the process of accessing available funding.

CDEP workers, managers and board members tend to have few if any managerial skills and, consequently, training of workers, managers and boards is essential. The kinds of skills brought to the managerial operations of CDEPs have a direct impact upon the ability of organisations to become more than conduits for CDEP wages. The capacities of full-time support staff, the managers and the board to oversee the budgets they receive so as to ensure that the organisations are viable, enduring, and able to nurture opportunity, is dependent upon their access to appropriate training and career development.

Building education and training capacity is essential for the success of CDEP programs. There should be greater latitude allowed to organisations in identifying their own needs and setting goals for vocational education and training outcomes that are realistic within the context of the organisation and the community. In many cases CDEPs may need some funding assistance to secure the advice and expertise of relevant consultants in order to identify these needs and set goals. In addition, CDEP programs should be allowed to invest in their own ability to provide training or purchase training from other providers; where profits have been generated by individual programs, they should be available for reinvestment in the program and must not, as happens now, result in what is effectively a financial penalty when an equivalent amount is sliced from the CDEP funding allocation for the following year. This practice can too easily result in the eventual strangulation of the very enterprises that achieved the profit.

Enterprise development should be promoted as one of the most effective means of providing relevant training-by-doing for CDEP participants. Small businesses developed by CDEPs are a significant avenue for the provision of training and employment opportunities, and some CDEPs have found that enterprises contribute to keeping children in school, providing them with work experience and meaningful education. In the face of persistent low levels of school retention among Indigenous youth and their consequent poor employment prospects, this represents a significant community benefit.

Finally, our research revealed a wealth of experience and knowledge among CDEP programs spread across the country. Directly sharing that knowledge between programs has until now been virtually impossible. There would be enormous benefit in establishing some form of national association of CDEP schemes in order to facilitate the exchange of information among members about funding options and opportunities, training approaches, strategic development and so on. This could be facilitated on-line, as well as through the various other channels. In addition, our research suggests the need for some type of 'one-stop shop' for information on vocational education and training. This would greatly improve the ability of CDEPs to access and make use of all government and non-government programs available to them. We suggest that relevant agencies investigate a means of facilitating a model for disseminating this information.

References

Aboriginal and Torres Strait Islander Commission (ATSIC) 1999. 'Submission to the Senate Inquiry into Indigenous Education', July 1999, ATSIC, Canberra.

Aboriginal and Torres Strait Islander Peoples Training Advisory Council (ATSIPTAC) 1997. *Community Development through Skills Development: New Apprenticeship and Traineeship Opportunities for Aboriginal and Torres Strait Islander Peoples*, ATSIPTAC, Melbourne.

—— 1998. *Building Pathways: School–Industry Workplace Learning for Aboriginal and Torres Strait Islander Peoples*, ATSIPTAC, Melbourne.

—— 1999a. *Making I.T. Our Own: Vocational Learning in Information Technology and Multimedia for Australia's Aboriginal and Torres Strait Islander Communities*, ATSIPTAC, Melbourne.

—— 1999b. Partners in a Learning Culture, Draft Report, June 1999, ATSIPTAC, Melbourne.

—— n.d. *Wadu: National Vocational Learning Strategy for Young Indigenous Australians*, ATSIPTAC, Melbourne.

Altman, J.C. and Gray, M.C. 2000. 'The effects of the CDEP scheme on the economic status of Indigenous Australians: Some analyses using the 1996 Census', *CAEPR Discussion Paper No. 195*, CAEPR, ANU, Canberra.

—— and Sanders, W. 1991. 'From exclusion to dependence: Aborigines and the welfare state in Australia', *CAEPR Discussion Paper No. 1*, CAEPR, ANU, Canberra.

—— and Smith, D.E. 1993. 'Compensating Indigenous Australian "losers": A community-oriented approach from the Aboriginal social policy arena', *Social Policy Research Centre Reports and Proceedings*, 112: 1–14.

Australian National Training Authority (ANTA) 1998. *A Bridge to the Future: Australia's National Strategy for Vocational Education and Training 1998–2003*, ANTA, Brisbane.

Australian National Training Authority Research Advisory Council (ANTARAC) 1998. *Djama and Vocational Education and Training: Exploring Partnerships and Practices in the Delivery of Vocational Education and Training in Rural and Remote Aboriginal Communities*, 2 vols, Northern Territory University, Bachelor College, and Training Network NT, Darwin.

Commonwealth Grants Commission (CGC) 2000. Draft Report of the Indigenous Funding Inquiry, *Discussion Paper IFI 2000/2*, October 2000, CGC, Canberra.

Deloitte Touche Tohmatsu 1993. 'No Reverse Gear: A National Review of the Community Development Employment Projects Scheme', Report to the Aboriginal and Torres Strait Islander Commission, May 1993, ATSIC, Canberra.

Sanders, W. 1988. 'The CDEP scheme: Bureaucratic politics, remote community politics and the development of the Aboriginal "workfare" program in times of rising unemployment', *Politics*, 23 (1): 32–47.

—— 1993. 'The rise and rise of the CDEP scheme: An Aboriginal "workfare" program in times of persistent unemployment', *CAEPR Discussion Paper No. 54*, CAEPR, ANU, Canberra.

Schwab, R.G. 1997. 'Post-compulsory education and training for Indigenous Australians', *CAEPR Discussion Paper No. 131*, CAEPR, ANU, Canberra.

Spicer, I. 1997. *Independent Review of the Community Development Projects (CDEP) Scheme* [the Spicer Review], Office of Public Affairs, ATSIC, Canberra.

Teasdale, J. and Teasdale, R. 1996. *Pathways to Where? Aboriginal and Torres Strait Islander Participation in Vocational Education and Training*, National Centre for Vocational Education Research, Adelaide.

PART III

REGIONAL STUDIES

13. 'Mutual obligation', the CDEP scheme, and development: Prospects in remote Australia[1]

Jon Altman

Introduction

Many observers feel that current social policy, and particularly the payment of welfare to the unemployed, needs to be fundamentally rethought. It is notable that advocates of change include both the government-appointed McClure Committee and influential Indigenous spokespersons, most notably Noel Pearson. In their publications *Participation Support for a More Equitable Society* (McClure 2000) and *Our Right to Take Responsibility* (Pearson 2000b) both these parties adopt the language of mutual obligation and, on the face of it, appear to agree with the general principle. The central tenet of mutual obligation in the context of current debates is the problem of how to shift individuals from being 'passive' welfare dependents into active engagement with the 'real' economy. The model is predicated on the forging of new partnerships between governments, business, the community, and the individual.

Both the McClure Committee and Pearson recognise that many Indigenous communities face major structural and systemic barriers to full economic participation, particularly in rural and remote regions. Both only make passing reference to the CDEP scheme that was first established in 1977 as Australia's prototype mutual obligation program. While the wages component of the scheme is covered by notional welfare equivalent payments, additional amounts are also provided with which to administer the scheme and purchase capital equipment. At 1 July 2000, there were nearly 31 000 participants in the scheme across Australia.[2] The CDEP scheme, as a model, meets many of the principles of mutual obligation as ennunciated by McClure and Pearson as well as by academics like Yeatman (1999) and Saunders (see Ch. 3, this volume).[3]

In the discussion that follows, I first define the boundaries of remote Australia, noting that about 70 per cent of the 265 CDEPs that existed at the time of the 1996 Census fall within this jurisdiction. On the basis of joint research with Matthew Gray (Altman & Gray 2000), I then provide a very brief assessment of the economic impact of the CDEP scheme in this region. McClure's and Pearson's prescriptions for facilitating Indigenous engagement with the 'real' economy are then examined and subjected to some reality checks; and finally I set out my own views on how the CDEP scheme, with modification, could be used as an institutional framework for Indigenous economic development.

Defining 'remote' Australia

The remote regions of Australia are those where mainstream economic opportunities are most limited and where the CDEP scheme is most prominent. They constitute what is without doubt the most problematic economic development extreme. In a paper written a decade ago (Altman 1990), remote Indigenous communities were typified as having extremely limited capacity to generate income independent of government. Such communities have come into being historically because of their very remoteness.[4] This in turn is the reason for their current under-development: they have poor resource endowments and poor market linkage. This generalisation has exceptions: major mineral deposits can provide development opportunities based on exploitation of non-renewable resources, and remoteness can be an advantage for tourism enterprises and cultural industries. With globalisation, improved transport links, and electronic communication, remoteness need no longer be a major barrier to effective market linkage.

Official statistics on CDEP scheme participation are rare; indeed it was only in the 1996 Census that the ABS started asking a question specifically about CDEP employment. It so happens that this question was only asked in nominated discrete communities, almost all of which are located in remote areas, although a few exist in, or near, towns and cities. These required specialised enumeration procedures because of their geographic isolation and/or the extent of their cultural or language difference from mainstream Australia.[5]

The 'specialised' enumeration strategy (SES) was used for an Indigenous population of 72 229, or 20 per cent of the total Indigenous population in 1996. There is a high degree of CDEP scheme participation in this statistical region, as shown by Altman and Gray (2000). At the time of the 1996 Census, there were 265 CDEP schemes, and it is estimated that 183 of these (69 per cent) were in Indigenous Local Areas (ILOCs) where the SES was used. All told, the 1996 Census found 10 948 CDEP-employed Indigenous persons in these areas, nearly 60 per cent of the Indigenous people estimated to be employed by CDEP in 1996. In these remote areas, CDEP employment also coincidentally accounted for 60 per cent of all Indigenous employment, with only 7247 Indigenous people employed outside the CDEP scheme.

The analysis here focuses on the 236 (out of 934) ILOCs where the SES was used. The reasons for this focus are that it is only at these ILOCs that data on CDEP participation are readily available. It also happens to be the case that CDEP is the primary form of employment in these areas: these ILOCs are the remotest from markets, at the difficult extreme in terms of engagement with the mainstream economy; and they demonstrate the highest level of cultural continuity, as measured by imprecise variables like 'cultural or language differences'.

Economic impacts of the CDEP scheme

If the CDEP scheme is characterised as a 'mutual obligation' institutional framework, the question can then be posed: how well does it operate in practice? Statistical analysis that can be undertaken for the first time, because of the data in the 1996 Census, indicates that it operates quite well. Some key findings from Altman and Gray (2000) are summarised below.

Effects on personal weekly income

Indications are that the mean income of the CDEP-employed is substantially higher than that of the unemployed or those not in the labour force. For example, CDEP-employed males and females receive a mean income of $186 and $181 per week respectively, compared to $139 and $145 received by unemployed males and females. The income of CDEP-employed people is much lower than the mean income of $298 and $299 received by Indigenous males and females in mainstream employment (Altman & Gray 2000: 8–10).

Effects of CDEP employment on hours worked

The notional CDEP wages component only provides for part-time work, most commonly 18 hours a week. Indications from the 1996 Census are that people who are CDEP-employed are frequently able to supplement these hours, with 17 per cent of males and 16 per cent of females working between 25 and 34 hours per week and a significant minority (26 per cent of males and 18 per cent of females) working more than 35 hours per week, or full-time. These additional hours of work can be accrued in a variety of ways: from 'top-up' hours provided by the CDEP organisation, from extra work generated by enterprises, or by combining CDEP employment with part-time mainstream employment (Altman & Gray 2000: 10).

Effects of CDEP employment on labour force status

By combining ATSIC administrative data with census data, it is possible to compare CDEP with non-CDEP communities in rural and remote areas.[6] The employment to population ratio, at 50 per cent, is higher in CDEP communities than non-CDEP communities, where it is 38 per cent. This is hardly surprising since recruitment to CDEP entails an immediate change of labour force status. However, in addition, it seems that many of the CDEP-employed are drawn from those groups who otherwise would not be in the labour force. The 'not in the labour force' ratio is 44 per cent at CDEP communities, but 50 per cent in non-CDEP communities. The unemployment rate is remarkably similar in CDEP and non-CDEP communities in rural and remote areas, at 10.5 per cent and 13 per cent respectively (Altman & Gray 2000: 13–14). This indicates that passive welfare exists alongside 'active' welfare in CDEP communities.

These statistics indicate that the CDEP scheme is doing some things right: income is increased, extra hours of work are generated, and labour force status is improved. The obvious proviso is that this is being assisted by allocations of operational and capital support from ATSIC. Two important issues arise. Although people who are CDEP-employed are not welfare dependent, they remain dependent nevertheless on a government program. Indeed many individuals have participated in the scheme for over a decade. The second, related, issue is whether participants are moving though the scheme to mainstream employment.

The McClure and Pearson strategies

McClure and Pearson address the need for reform of the Australian social security system in very different ways. McClure has an Australia-wide focus and is greatly influenced by global welfare debates; Pearson is specifically focused on the Aboriginal communities of Cape York Peninsula. Both analyses have significant limitations when it comes to providing practical policy advice about contexts which are largely devoid of economic opportunity.

McClure's discussion of such situations is largely limited to a brief section titled 'Community Economic Development' (2000: 47–8). There is some mention here of a model devised in the UK to generate economic participation opportunities in disadvantaged regions (typically those where industry might have existed historically, but has now departed). McClure notes that 'in the model community development organisations are formed by local communities to provide a range of social and economic activities on a not for profit basis'(2000: 47). The description of such organisations resonates with the image of CDEP organisations, but these are not really discussed in any detail. Elsewhere, it is suggested that Rural Transactions Centres (RTCs) could be established to assist disadvantaged rural communities with access to financial and other services, including 'passive' welfare delivered by Centrelink. There is no doubt that RTCs could be useful, but they represent another new institutional arrangement. Similarly, reference is made to a new program called Regional Solutions that will provide grants 'for community planning, local project implementation, community adjustment initiatives, regionally based enterprise or infrastructure projects and community-based development officers' (McClure 2000: 48). The best-practice case for Indigenous employment comes from rural New South Wales where a partnership has been forged between Commonwealth and local governments and a cotton growers' association.

McClure completely fails to address the question of how new partnerships can be forged between governments, business, the community and the individual in situations where:

- business is non-existent;

- governmental activity is heavily embedded in community organisations;

- government is perceived as reneging on meeting legitimate needs-based support;

- individuals are heavily embedded in wider social networks and participation in those networks is not contingent on economic participation; and

- 'the community' is divided for a range of historical, cultural or political reasons (see Peters-Little, Ch. 19, this volume).

In seeking to address these problems—which go to the core of the reality faced by many Indigenous communities—one might turn to Pearson's strategies for economic development. However, in a 'four point plan for developing a real economy for Aboriginal society on Cape York Peninsula', Pearson too is light on practical, culturally-informed strategies. The key planks of his plan (Pearson 2000a: 83–92) are as follows:

- rejuvenation of the subsistence economy;

- replacement of all welfare programs with reciprocity programs, like the CDEP scheme;

- development of community economies, that is, generating employment for Indigenous people rather than non-Indigenous wherever possible; and

- engagement with the mainstream economy, which he recognises as the most difficult development aim to achieve.

Some comments are offered here in response to Pearson's proposals. The rejuvenation of the subsistence economy has occurred with some success elsewhere in remote Australia, especially on Aboriginal land (see Altman & Taylor 1989). Participation in this informal economy can be extremely important especially in improving diets and health and in generating non-monetary income. But there is, as yet, no evidence that it is associated with movement towards greater economic independence.

Replacement of all welfare programs with so-called reciprocity programs has already been tried in remote communities where, up until the late 1980s, the CDEP scheme was only introduced on an 'all-in' basis. While it is true that it is extremely difficult to operate a reciprocity program effectively alongside a passive welfare regime, again there is no evidence that reciprocity alone led to reduced dependence on government.

The development of community economies is of crucial importance, for if Indigenous people cannot fill locally available and scarce mainstream jobs how can engagement with the 'real' economy occur? But the growing technical and social demands of many service jobs in remote communities are in fact making them less appealing and less accessible to local people. The cultural persistence of distinctly Indigenous kin-based relations of production greatly dilute the rewards—as conventionally valued—of high-pressure employment. To some extent, it could be said that mutual obligation and reciprocity within the Indigenous domain is hampering economic participation.

And finally there is engagement with the mainstream economy outside the community, at regional, national, and international levels. When opportunities arise in mining, tourism, or cultural industries, where Indigenous people may have special leverage based on land rights or native title, or a clear competitive advantage, these should be grasped. But so often such opportunities are forgone because of political complexities at the community level, or an absence of appropriate development agencies, or for the cultural reasons referred to above. There is often a tension between community and individual engagement and a myriad of potential problematic groupings in between these two extremes.

To be fair to Pearson, his policy prescription is regionally focused on Cape York Aboriginal society and makes a great deal of intuitive sense.[7] It is noteworthy, however, that his approach is little different from that advocated some 15 years ago by the Miller Committee of Review of Aboriginal Employment and Training Programs (Miller 1985). It was the Miller Committee in particular that advocated strongly the need for the development of an economic base in remote Indigenous communities, and for 'localisation' of employment opportunities. Second, Pearson does not refer to other situations where this broad four-pronged approach has been vigorously pursued, such as nearby on the northern tip of Cape York Peninsula. There is some evidence there of improved economic status, albeit with limited evidence of reduced dependence on government.

Using the CDEP scheme to engage in the 'real' economy

The key issue to be addressed is how the CDEP scheme can be better structured to meet diverse Indigenous economic development aspirations in a public policy environment that might focus increasingly on mutual obligation. Suggestions here are tailored for the broad circumstances of remote communities participating in the CDEP scheme and may not be suitable to CDEP scheme participants in other urban or rural circumstances.[8]

Program strengths and weaknesses

An overarching strength of the CDEP scheme, as currently constituted, is its flexibility. It is at once an employment, training, community development and enterprise assistance program. At times it is just an income support mechanism, little different from welfare. The popularity of the scheme is evident in its spread across 290 communities Australia-wide, in very diverse circumstances. This flexibility is also a weakness, because while there is statistical evidence of success in employment and income generation, it is unclear how successful the scheme is in community development and training. This is partly because the latter are more difficult to measure, and partly because in many cases appropriate statistics do not exist. Because of the diversity of its program objectives, CDEP scheme performance is hard to measure and its success, where evident, is difficult to demonstrate.

In many situations CDEP organisations try to do too much, especially those that are successful. This is often because other community-based specialist agencies are non-existent, and as a result CDEP support provided by ATSIC sometimes substitutes for the programs that should be provided by other agencies. If CDEP organisations are to do the jobs of other agencies, be they DEWRSB, DETYA, Centrelink, or other Commonwealth or State agencies, it should be on a full cost-recovery basis (see comments in this volume by Bartlett, Ch. 20; Kean, Ch. 21; Nalliah, Ch. 28). Similarly, if CDEP organisations contract to undertake municipal services or operate as outstation resource agencies, this should be done on a commercial basis and be funded accordingly. There are existing best-practice examples of such approaches.

Ultimately, if CDEP organisations are to focus on employment and community economic development in the new social policy environment, it might be appropriate for the scheme's objectives to be amended and negotiated on a case-by-case basis. There are dangers inherent in pursuing too many diverse objectives.

Transforming CDEP organisations into development agencies

As noted above, McClure (2000) provides few recommendations or solutions for the development problems of remote regions, beyond noting options for establishing community development institutions. Rather than establishing new and additional organisations, it would be far better to use an existing institutional model, the CDEP organisation, to deliver development opportunities at the community level. Rather than inventing new institutions from nothing, it would be more cost-effective to resource CDEP organisations to build their capacity to deliver development. Interestingly, Pearson (2000b) does not nominate CDEP organisations as the governance structures to facilitate development, recommending instead larger regional agencies. More recently he has favoured direct relations between agencies and families and individuals (Pearson 2000a). Intermediary community-based organisations will undoubtedly be needed to facilitate development: the question is whether, as is argued here, CDEP organisations are the best placed to become development agencies.

The answer depends in part on resourcing. In some regions, ATSIC has provided organisations with triennial funding on preparation of development plans. This has allowed a degree of capital and operational funding commitment that has greatly assisted planning for development. A danger that some organisations face is that success might reduce discretionary capital funding; it is important that this does not occur and that funding decisions do not become politicised and biased against the successful.

An advantage of the CDEP as a development agency model is that CDEP organisations can be constituted in a way that separates trading activity from ATSIC-supported activity. This in turn means that trading profits—members' rather than public finance—can be invested in high-risk ventures.

To make the transition to their role as development agencies, CDEP organisations will require resourcing for board and member empowerment. In particular, there is a need for an additional injection of funds for training boards and for participatory planning. If CDEP organisations are to change into 'community economic development' organisations it is imperative that their growing complexity does not result in the alienation and disengagement of their members and over-reliance on non-Indigenous management. Such disengagement can result in organisational instability that is not conducive to sound business practice.

Maintaining the nexus with welfare financing, not welfare institutions

There are mismatches between the CDEP scheme and mutual obligation, and a logical tension between welfare and CDEP regimes, especially when they are found in the same community. For example, as a general rule, CDEP combines high activity testing with almost no income testing. Paradoxically, New Start Allowance (unemployment benefit) in remote situations has almost no, or highly modified, activity testing.[9] Because its income test is so much more generous, CDEP provides positive signals to participants to supplement their incomes either in monetised or in non-monetised sectors, in a way that welfare does not.

It will be difficult to counteract the emerging fusion between CDEP and welfare institutions and the mixed signals that ensue. CDEP 'top up' provided by Centrelink to provide equity with the 'work for the dole' program should be provided to CDEP organisations to administer. The administratively-burdensome CDEPManager electronic database, and daily monitoring of CDEP participation (which far exceeds Centrelink monitoring of New Start Allowance clients), should be reconsidered: CDEP organisations should be allowed flexibility in differentiating types of participants and should be allowed use of wages surpluses for top up. Finally, to be effective and to encourage diversion from passive welfare, CDEP organisations should be provided with wages, capital, and operational support budgets that are open-ended, bearing in mind that most cost (76 per cent according to 2000–01 estimates) will be nominally offset by welfare. A discussion of the means to make these funding changes falls outside the scope of this paper. Delivering development in remote Australia will not be cheap, but the utilisation of a scheme that has considerable welfare offset is a relatively cheap option for government.[10]

Conclusion

The CDEP scheme is only one possible instigator of development in remote Indigenous Australia. But it represents an important, already existing framework by which to link strategically the social policy reform focus on 'mutual obligation' with economic development for remote Indigenous communities. If CDEP is to fulfil its potential, it is crucial to provide options to re-jig the scheme so that it can operate more effectively to facilitate 'mainstream' development in situations where participants aspire to such an outcome. To operate as effective development agencies, CDEP organisations also require funding to strengthen their institutions and build capacity.

Any community desire to distance 'active' mutual obligation CDEP from 'passive' welfare should be facilitated by government. The crucial objective of the CDEP scheme must be to incrementally improve the economic status of participants, to move economic indicators, however measured, in a positive direction and in accord with planned growth. The CDEP scheme will not deliver any immediate development solutions, but appropriately revamped it could be a part of a long-term 'mutual obligation' development strategy for many remote Indigenous communities.

Notes

1. I thank Hilary Bek, Melinda Hinkson, Tim Rowse, and John Taylor for their comments on an earlier draft of this paper.

2. ATSIC differentiates funded places, participant ceilings, and actual participant numbers. At 1 July 2000 these were 33 188, 33 557 and 30 749 respectively. Allocations for CDEP in 2000–01 is divided into $324 million for wages and $102 million for operational (capital and on-costs), a total of $426 million. The division of operational funding is decided by ATSIC Regional Councils.

3. In this paper, no real attempt is made to address the issue of what mutual obligation values might mean cross-culturally and what the diverse Indigenous conceptualisations of their relations with the state might be. This is an issue that has been canvassed very briefly elsewhere (Altman 2000).

4. Indigenous communities are notoriously difficult to define especially as they were invariably established in the process of colonisation. Today, communities may be geographic, social, cultural or administrative units, or combinations thereof. The standard view that a community encompasses a group of people who reside in one locality is problematic when applied to Indigenous people because they are highly

regionally mobile and frequently have multiple residential rights and social orientations (Altman 1990: 48).

5. In such situations enumeration was carried out by Indigenous interviewers using specially designed census forms including the Special Indigenous Personal Form (SIPF). Information on participation in the CDEP scheme was extracted from SIPFs (Altman & Gray 2000: 5–6).

6. This discussion of the impact on labour force status uses the standard census rural balance and locality classification rather than the SES jurisdiction used above.

7. Also, Pearson's treatise is largely about how to get passive welfare out of Aboriginal governance and the passive welfare mentality out of individuals. These issues are more in the realm of politics and psychology than economics. My focus here is primarily on the economic, but I recognise obvious linkages to the political and psychological.

8. My own case study research has focused on work with CDEP organisations like the Bawinanga Aboriginal Corporation (see also Manners, Ch. 26, this volume) and the Djabulukgu Association in the Northern Territory. These are also outstation resource agencies.

9. Sanders' (1999) study provides some interesting statistics and discussion of regional variation in breach rates and causes.

10. The opportunity cost of inaction does not constitute a cheap option. This is clearly demonstrated by Taylor and Altman (1997).

References

Altman, J.C. 1990. 'The economic future of remote Aboriginal and Torres Strait Islander communities', *Australian Aboriginal Studies*, 1990 (2): 48–52.

—— 2000. 'Reconciling mutual obligation under the CDEP scheme: Prospects in remote Australia', Unpublished paper presented at the 'Indigenous Think Tank', 23 August 2000, DFACS, Canberra.

—— and Gray, M.C. 2000. 'The effects of the CDEP scheme on the economic status of Indigenous Australians: Some analyses using the 1996 Census', *CAEPR Discussion Paper No. 195*, CAEPR, ANU, Canberra.

—— and Taylor, L. 1989. *The Economic Viability of Aboriginal Outstations and Homelands*, AGPS, Canberra.

McClure, P. (Chair) 2000. Participation Support for a More Equitable Society: Final Report of the Reference Group on Welfare Reform, July 2000 [the McClure Report], DFACS, Canberra.

Miller, M. (Chair) 1985. *The Report of the Committee of Review of Aboriginal Employment and Training Programs*, AGPS, Canberra.

Pearson, N. 2000a. 'Misguided policies a toxic cocktail', *The Australian*, 24 October 2000.

—— 2000b. *Our Right to Take Responsibility*, Noel Pearson and Associates, Cairns, Qld.

Sanders, W. 1999. *Unemployment Payments, the Activity Test and Indigenous Australians: Understanding Breach Rates*, CAEPR Research Monograph No. 15, CAEPR, ANU, Canberra.

Taylor, J. and Altman, J. 1997. *The Job Ahead: Escalating Economic Cost of Indigenous Economic Disparity*, Office of Public Affairs, ATSIC, Canberra.

Yeatman, A. 1999. 'Mutual obligation: What kind of contract is this?' in S. Shaver and P. Saunders (eds), *Social Policy for the 21st Century: Justice and Responsibility*, Vol. 1, SPRC, UNSW, Sydney.

14. CDEP and careers: Some good news and some bad news from Torres Strait

Bill Arthur

Introduction

Having been in place for around 25 years, the CDEP scheme is the longest standing government work program. It would be surprising therefore if people did not have some view of its possible role in their futures. A recent survey in Torres Strait shows that although communities appear to utilise CDEP to create employment and training opportunities young people feel that the scheme has limited potential to further their careers. This paper uses data from the survey to analyse the apparent contradiction between these 'good news' and 'bad news' stories and suggests what the implications may be for the future of the program.

The data are taken from a survey carried out in Torres Strait of 105 young Torres Strait Islanders between the ages of 15 and 24. The major objective of the study is to determine the aspirations of young people and to discover if these coincide with the aims of the government's welfare programs, which are related to the labour market (see Arthur 1999; Arthur & David-Petero 2000a, 2000b, 2000c). Although the study is not centred on CDEP, the survey revealed information about it, as one of the major programs in the area. In Torres Strait, CDEP is managed individually by each island Community Council. At the time of the survey there were 17 of these CDEP schemes with a total of approximately 1700 participants.

Approximately half of those surveyed were males and half were females. Half lived in the regional centre of Thursday Island and half in a small community on an outlying island. People in the survey were employed in the non-CDEP sector, employed in the CDEP sector, unemployed, or still at secondary school. Therefore, the data reflect the opinions of a fairly broad range of young people.

The general pattern of the CDEP

The principal elements of a CDEP scheme in Torres Strait are laid out, in a very general way, in Fig. 14.1. We can think of these elements as forming inputs and outputs. The inputs are the standard CDEP funding, any wage savings the council is able to make, and funds from other funders and employers. Other funders can include the community school, the child-care centre, the council office and health clinic, and the State and Commonwealth governments. These other funders and employers may provide part of a full-time wage for an employee, trainee or apprentice, with the CDEP providing the other part of the wage. Councils tend to see all of these funds as forming a development pot which they can use for various purposes, or outputs. Under a 'no work, no pay' rule, wage savings occur when people decide not to turn up for CDEP. This is easily managed by using a time clock and getting people to clock on and off.[1]

Figure 14.1   A generalised picture of CDEP, Torres Strait, 1999

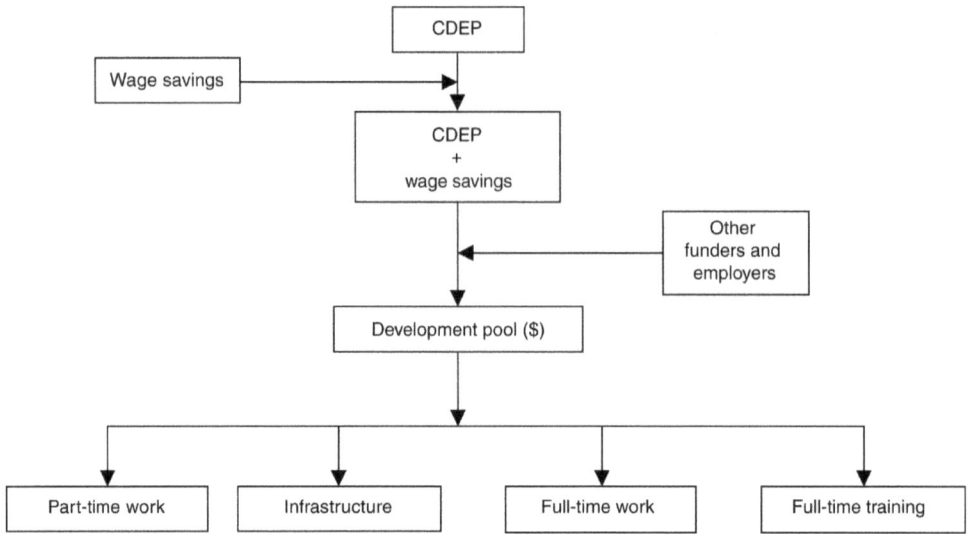

The outputs shown in Fig. 14.1 are the normal or basic CDEP part-time work (the arrangement in Torres Strait is often for participants to work alternate weeks), some infrastructure development, and the full-time employment and training just described. Thus, there are two main kinds of output: part-time work and full-time work and training. The full-time positions are subsidised by the wage savings and by funds from the other employers. Or, looked at another way, the full-time positions are subsidised by the CDEP.

The 'good news' and 'bad news' about CDEP

Data from the survey can be used to examine the role of CDEP in assisting young people to fulfil their aspirations. Fig. 14.2 shows the ways that young people say they have got jobs in the past, and how they plan to look for jobs and opportunities in the future. These are ranked in Fig. 14.2, with most important furthest to the left. The most common strategy that people have used, and would plan to use, is to approach employers directly in person. This includes approaching their CDEP council and in fact all of the young people living on the small island community said that this is a strategy they would use to look for work. In addition, some said that they got their jobs, apprenticeships, or traineeships by looking at the advertisements posted by their council on the council noticeboard. Others said that the council approached them and offered them jobs and training. This often included the full-time training and employment mentioned earlier. Fig. 14.2 also shows that many people get their jobs or opportunities through family contacts and through word of mouth. On the other hand, very few people expected to get jobs through Job Network. Indeed, no one interviewed on the small island community said they would use Job Network, and what is more, many were not sure what Job Network was, or what it provided.

Fig. 14.3 shows where the young people who were interviewed were getting their training, including their full-time traineeships and apprenticeships. Quite a few got their training through the State government. However, the most common way of becoming involved in training was through a CDEP council. Both Fig. 14.2 and Fig. 14.3 show that very few traineeships and apprenticeships were in private industry. Taken together, the results shown in Figs 14.2 and 14.3 suggest that the CDEP community councils are playing a significant role in providing pathways for young people to jobs and training opportunities. This is the 'good news'. However, this has to be balanced against the apparently 'bad news' that young people do not seem to think that CDEP will be much use to them in furthering their careers, as explained below.

Figure 14.2 How young people look for and get jobs or training, Torres Strait, 1999

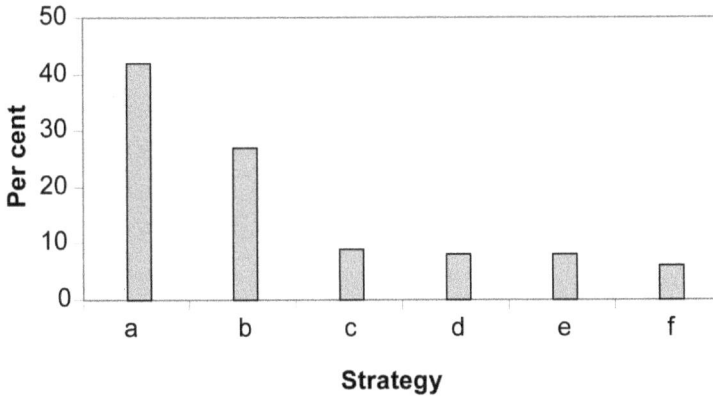

Key: (a) Approach employer or CDEP council   (d) Job Network
      (b) Word of mouth, or family   (e) Approached by employer or CDEP council
      (c) Advertisements or council noticeboard (f) Opportunity arises

Figure 14.3 Training sponsors, Torres Strait, 1999

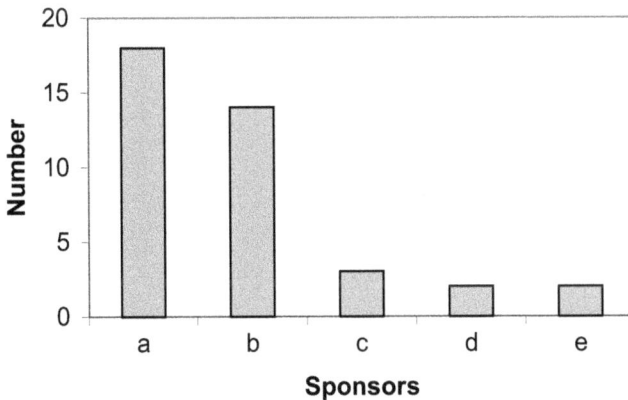

Key: (a) CDEP council   (d) Indigenous organisations
      (b) State government   (e) Private industry
      (c) Commonwealth government

A set of devices that might help people with their careers is given in Fig. 14.4. The young people in the survey were asked to say which of these they thought would be useful to them. Fig. 14.4 shows that they thought that TAFE and their families would be the most helpful. They also thought that university, Job Network, Centrelink and work outside CDEP could help them further their careers. However, it is very noticeable that they did not think CDEP would be much help. This is the 'bad news', and it presents something of a quandary: if, as argued in the previous section, CDEP councils are playing a significant role in presenting young people with opportunities, why do they think that CDEP would not help them with their careers? The answer to this may lie partly in the things that young people say they value in a job—the things that attract them to various jobs and activities. Some of these are described below.

Figure 14.4   Devices thought useful for career, Torres Strait, 1999

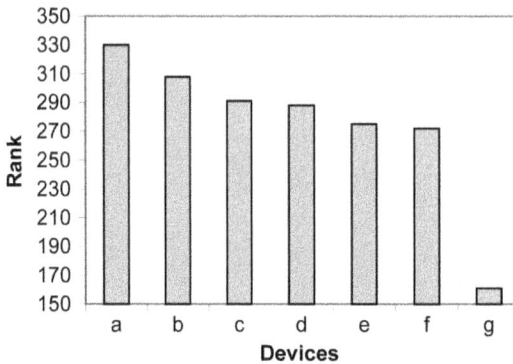

Key: (a) TAFE   (e) Centrelink
        (b) Family   (f) Non-CDEP
        (c) University   (g) CDEP
        (d) Job Network

Note: People were asked to give each item a score of one to four. The rank of an item is
         its total score divided by the number of responses relating to it, multiplied by 100.

The features that people value in work and training

People appear to place a high value on full-time work. Fig. 14.5 shows that almost 90 per cent of all the young people interviewed said that they preferred full-time work to part-time work or to no work at all.

Figs 14.6 and 14.7 show some other qualities that young people say they like in work or training. Fig. 14.6 shows that when young people are asked why they want to take up or like certain work they say that it is because it interests them: they like work that they find interesting. This was a major reason for preferring full-time work: it was thought more interesting than part-time work. Young people also said they liked work that kept them busy all the time. In addition, they liked work and training that they thought would help them achieve their *long-term* goals; and that was getting them somewhere in life. Other qualities that people appear to value in work are some security, reasonable pay, and the opportunity for promotion (see Fig. 14.7). Part-time work is not valued at all highly.

Figure 14.5   Preferred form of work, Torres Strait, 1999

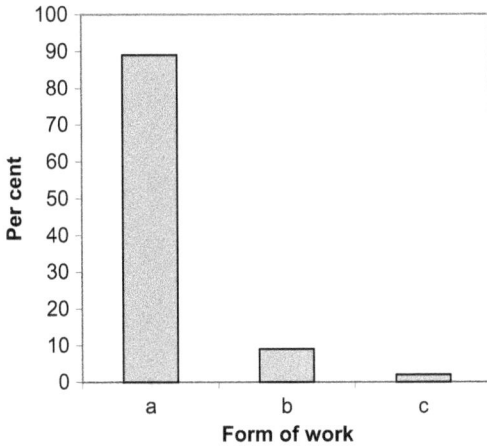

Key: (a) Full-time
        (b) Part-time
        (c) No work

Figure 14.6   Reason for working or training, Torres Strait, 1999

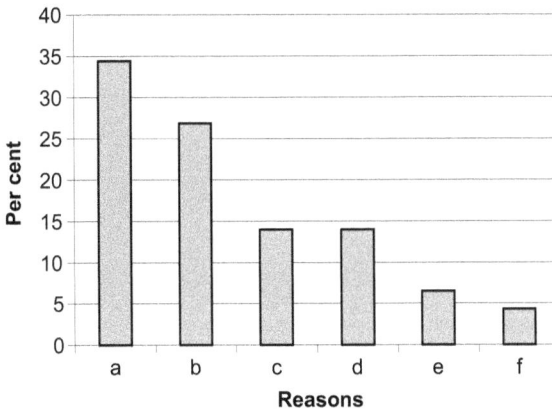

Key: (a) Interest   (d) Family/community
        (b) Achieve goal   (e) Keep busy
        (c) Money   (f) Control

Taking all of these features together it would seem that the ideal job would be interesting, full-time, and reasonably paid; it would afford the chance for some promotion and provide job security. If we compare these features against CDEP employment, we can suggest that it is only the last of these that might apply to it. CDEP work is normally part-time and elsewhere in the survey young people described the work as very boring.

On the other hand, young people found the full-time employment and full-time training that was subsidised by CDEP (shown as one of the outputs in Fig. 14.1) to be extremely enjoyable. Indeed, people aspired to this kind of position. Those that were in this form of

Figure 14.7   Qualities valued in work, Torres Strait, 1999

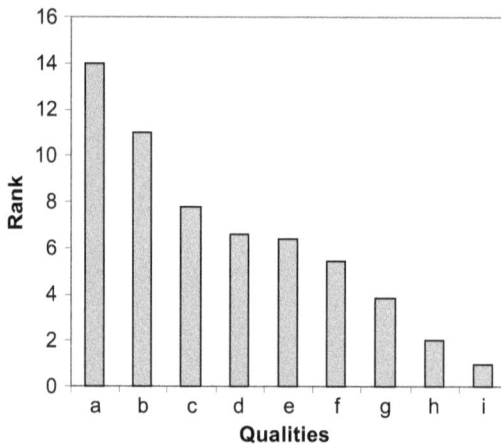

Key: (a) Job security   (f) Working with Indigenous organisations
       (b) Pay level   (g) Being own boss
       (c) Promotion   (h) Making own hours
       (d) Working with friends (i) Working part time
       (e) Having no stress

Note: Respondents were asked to choose from the list the three qualities that they valued most in a job.
       The scores for each were totalled and then ranked, giving the least-mentioned quality (working
       part time) the score of one.

work found it interesting and contrasted it with the part-time CDEP work which they found pointless and boring. Therefore, when young people said that they did not value CDEP and did not think that it would help them with their careers, they were really talking about the normal part-time CDEP work, not about the full-time positions that were facilitated by the scheme.

Policy implications

What, if anything, does all this mean for policy? Making work interesting is hard at the best of times. In some of the marginal economies in remote areas it is doubly hard, and it is a big ask for CDEP councils. Moreover, do young people really want full-time work? In Torres Strait, many fish commercially on their CDEP week off, or leave CDEP to go fishing at short notice. This put into question whether they would really want always to work full-time and have less chance to fish.

Nonetheless, young people do like and aspire to the full-time opportunities created by CDEP councils. These are made available by using CDEP creatively to form arrangements with other employers such as the schools. Councils may also use the wage savings which occur when people elect to come off CDEP for short periods. It is not clear how much these wage savings contributed to creating full-time opportunities for young people. However, it seems that council access to these monies may be reduced with the introduction of the CDEPManager program. This may in turn limit the councils' ability to create the full-time positions that young people appear to value.

Accountability of public monies, such as those in CDEP, is important and the CDEPManager program seems designed with accountability in mind. However, it can also be argued that CDEP is being used by councils as a development program, to create opportunities, and that councils therefore need some leeway regarding how the funds are used. Care needs to be taken to ensure that an overemphasis on accountability does not stifle the ability of CDEP practitioners in the field from using the program to stimulate development.

Notes

1. People may elect not to work on CDEP in order to go commercial fishing.

References

Arthur, W.S. 1999. 'Careers, aspirations and the meaning of work in remote Australia: Torres Strait', *CAEPR Discussion Paper No. 190*, CAEPR, ANU, Canberra.

Arthur W.S. and David-Petero, J. 2000a. 'Career aspirations and orientation to work: Young Torres Strait Islanders, 1999', *CAEPR Discussion Paper No. 206*, CAEPR, ANU, Canberra.

Arthur, W.S. and David-Petero, J. 2000b. 'Education, training and careers: Young Torres Strait Islanders, 1999', *CAEPR Discussion Paper No. 207*, CAEPR, ANU, Canberra.

Arthur W.S. and David-Petero, J. 2000c. 'Job searching and careers: Young Torres Strait Islanders, 1999', *CAEPR Discussion Paper No. 205*, CAEPR, ANU, Canberra.

15. CDEP as a conduit to the 'real' economy? The Port Augusta case

Matthew Gray and Elaine Thacker

Introduction

The role of the CDEP scheme as a stepping stone to employment in the 'mainstream' labour market is receiving a great deal of attention at present. This accords with the emphasis in the current social policy environment on 'mutual obligation'. The CDEP scheme undoubtedly has similarities to the 'work for the dole' program available to all Australians, but its success in acting as a stepping stone to unsubsidised employment is clearly related to the non-CDEP labour market opportunities in particular regions. In remote areas these opportunities are generally much more limited than in rural and urban areas. There has been little research on the success (or otherwise) of the scheme in its role as a stepping stone to unsubsidised employment in regional centres and urban areas. In an attempt to help to fill this gap, we present here the results of a case study of the Bungala Aboriginal Corporation (hereafter Bungala) in Port Augusta, South Australia.[1] The choice of Bungala was influenced by a number of factors. Port Augusta is a regional centre with labour market opportunities, and Bungala has an impressive record of helping its participants to find unsubsidised employment, of placing participants in subsidised employment, and in generating income through its Construction Program.

Port Augusta: The economic and social context

Port Augusta is a regional city located at the top of the Spencer Gulf, in Nukunu traditional country, 300 kilometres north of Adelaide in South Australia. It is a place of significance to Indigenous Australians from a large area, including the Anangu Pitjantjatjara Lands, the Flinders Ranges and the Eyre Peninsula. Within Port Augusta there is a distinct Indigenous community living at the Davenport community. Although this is an important point of reference, the majority of the Indigenous population live in the township of Port Augusta itself. Indigenous people in the region are geographically very mobile, often moving between Port Augusta, Davenport, and remote communities in the far north and north-west of South Australia (see Marika (1995) for a more detailed discussion).[2]

At the time of the 1996 Census there were 14 315 people enumerated as living in Port Augusta, of whom 1917 (or 13 per cent) identified as being of Aboriginal or Torres Strait Islander origin. The Indigenous population is much younger than the non-Indigenous population: their median ages are 21 and 35 years respectively. A combination of a younger population, a higher fertility rate, and a net out-migration of non-Indigenous people means that over the next few decades Indigenous people are likely to comprise an increasing proportion of the Port Augusta population (South Australian Centre for Economic Studies 1998).

The Port Augusta economy has been in decline for a number of years. Between 1991 and 1996 the numbers in employment fell from 6276 to 5114, a fall of 18.5 per cent. Major job losses occurred in the transport and storage, electricity, gas and water supply and manufacturing industries. But the decline is primarily due to cutbacks in public sector employment, with 588 jobs being lost from the Commonwealth government and 275 from the State government. At the same time employment growth in the private sector has been stagnant.

The loss of employment and economic decline is reflected in the labour force statistics for Port Augusta. At the time of the 1996 Census the employment to population ratio among the non-Indigenous population was 60.3 per cent and the unemployment rate was high, at 13.0 per cent. Indigenous people fare even worse, with an employment to population ratio of just 28.1 per cent and an unemployment rate of 33.0 per cent—a level which would be unacceptable in the wider community.[3]

Because of the low levels of Indigenous employment, the low wages and salaries received by those who are employed, and the high levels of dependence on social security payments, Indigenous persons have a median personal income of just $196 per week. This is significantly lower than the median of $259 per week for the non-Indigenous population.

Overview of Bungala

Organisational structure

Bungala Aboriginal Corporation is a corporate CDEP, and the largest CDEP organisation in South Australia. It now has 310 participants, and is the fifth largest employer in Port Augusta. From its administrative centre in Port Augusta it services a number of satellite work sites over a range of 450 kilometres, from Port Pirie in the south to Nepabunna in the northern Flinders Ranges.[4] The satellite schemes are primarily community organisations, responsible for providing a variety of services to their communities.

Bungala has a Board of Management that is responsible for making the major decisions about the overall running of the organisation. The board members are CDEP participants who are elected for a term of one year by their fellow participants. The Board appoints a Chief Executive Officer (CEO) who is responsible for the operation of the scheme and who reports directly to the Board (see Fig. 15.1).

Bungala's work activities are organised into three main work programs: the Construction Program; the Works Program; and the Expansion (satellite scheme) Program. Each of these programs has a full-time manager who reports directly to the CEO. The Office Section, headed by the Office Manager, provides administrative support. There is also a Project Officer responsible for developing new ventures and sources of funding. Bungala hires external accountants to manage its payroll and finances, and to provide financial reporting.

The Works Program provides two days a week of work to participants in Port Augusta. Many of the participants have very limited, if any, non-CDEP employment experience and lack basic work skills. There are a number of work groups undertaking a wide range of work activities including cleaning up yards, firewood collection, arts and crafts production, and the running of a licensed child-care centre. Each work group has a full-time supervisor who is also a CDEP participant. These supervisors tend to be older, long-standing participants, many of whom have employment experience outside CDEP. Their seniority generates respect and provides them with moral authority. The close personal interaction that occurs between participants and the supervisors is an important factor in the development of the participants' work skills and general life skills. As of July 2000 the Works Program had the largest number of personnel, with 132 participants and 11 full-time supervisors.

Figure 15.1   Organisational structure of Bungala CDEP, 2000

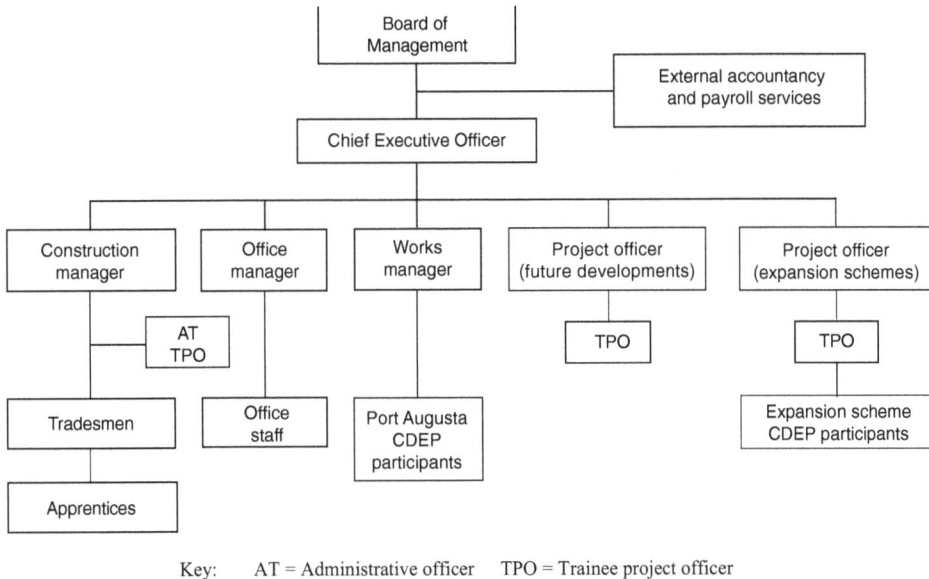

Key: AT = Administrative officer   TPO = Trainee project officer

The Expansion Program provides work activities two days a week for participants in the satellite schemes. The nature of the work activities and the way in which work is managed are primarily determined by the relevant Aboriginal organisation in each community and vary from site to site. In the remote satellite schemes, the opportunities for unsubsidised employment are very limited and therefore the focus is on community development objectives. The work culture in these satellite schemes is much more like that typically found in remote CDEPs (Altman &Taylor 1989). These programs employ a total of 76 participants and one full-time tradesman.

The Construction Program, as its name suggests, undertakes construction work. In general this work is won through competitive tender. Bungala has won contracts to build both residential and commercial buildings as well as for renovations, office refits and a variety of maintenance jobs. There are nine fully qualified tradesmen (who are not CDEP participants) employed in the Construction Program and 19 CDEP participants who are employed full-time and are undertaking apprenticeships. Apprenticeship training leads to a recognised qualification.

In addition to those working in the three work programs and the Office Section, 65 of the CDEP participants are placed with non-CDEP employers. These participants generally work five days a week for the non-CDEP employer, with Bungala contributing the participants' wages allocation (wages for two days a week) to the costs of employing that person. The non-CDEP employer contributes the balance of the participant's earnings. This arrangement is very much like the traditional wage subsidy.

The work culture

Bungala's participants come from a wide range of backgrounds and their experience of employment varies widely. There are also differences in their career aspirations and in what they hope to achieve by participating in CDEP. Of particular relevance to this paper are aspirations about moving to 'mainstream' employment.[5] Almost half of the participants interviewed said that they did not wish to leave CDEP for mainstream employment; the remainder indicated their wish to do so. In general, participants wanted to make the move either to earn more money or because they became bored on those days on which they were not working on CDEP.

For participants in the 'remote' Expansion Program work sites, the question about wanting to move to mainstream employment had little relevance because there is virtually no employment available in their areas. Some of these participants indicated that they would like to move to mainstream employment, but they did not consider it a possibility.

In order to balance the different objectives and the diverse needs of participants each work program has developed a distinct work culture. A feature common to all is the enforcement of a 'no work, no pay' rule for all participants.

In the Works Program, the primary objective is to provide meaningful work and allow participants to develop basic work skills. They work for two days a week in what they perceive as a comfortable work environment. While the no work, no pay rule is enforced, the work culture is sympathetic to the fact that many of the participants employed in this group have very limited work experience or skills.

The Expansion Program also provides work activities for participants for two days per week. The nature of these activities, and the way in which work is managed are mostly determined by the relevant Aboriginal organisation in each community, according to local needs and aspirations. It is more difficult to enforce the no work, no pay rule in this program because of the greater autonomy in determining the work rules, and because it is difficult for staff in Port Augusta to monitor the work efforts of participants in distant locations.

In the Construction Program the culture more closely reflects the mainstream labour market and participants are expected to be more reliable in their work attendance and to work industriously to develop a high level of technical competence. However, as in the Work Program, the work culture allows for some accommodation of family and cultural demands which at times may conflict with the requirements of running a commercial business. Bungala provides a considerable amount of training to participants in the Construction Program.

The clear separation between the different work programs within the organisational structure of Bungala has allowed the different work practices and cultures to develop. Managers can provide a consistent set of rules, and minimise perceptions of unfairness and tensions that might otherwise arise as the result of the application of different work cultures to people who are working side by side.

Commercial activities

The financial context

Bungala's business enterprises are an integral component of its interaction with mainstream economic institutions, but they must first be set in the wider financial context. In the financial year 1999–2000 Bungala had a total income of nearly $5 million (Table 15.1). The source of most of its funding is ATSIC, which provides for participant wages and on-cost funding. The level of participant wages funding is based on the number of participants.[6] On-cost funding includes recurrent funding, which is used for the administration of the scheme, and capital funding for the purchase of capital items. ATSIC participant wages, the largest funding item, contributed $2.6 million in 1999–2000. ATSIC on-cost funding is also important: recurrent funding in the same financial year was $500 000 and capital funding was $295 000. Overall, ATSIC funding in 1999–2000 was $3.4 million, around 68 per cent of Bungala's total income.

Additional funding of $500 000 was obtained from other organisations, including DEWRSB and the South Australian Department of Employment, Education and Training. The remaining income is project-generated, through commercial activities. In 1999–2000 project generated income amounted to $1.1 million.

Table 15.1   Sources of income, Bungala, 1995–96 to 1999–2000

	1995–96	1996–97	1997–98	1998–99	1999–2000
Source	Amount ($)				
Funding: ATSIC recurrent	373 493	329 206	376894	511 723	496 959
Funding: ATSIC capital	213 936	202088	91638	438391	294868
Funding: ATSIC participant wages	1223 663	1 160 765	1 493 441	2 112 385	2 585 943
Funding: Other	398 225	310 893	75 142	339 543	469274
Project generated income	60 524	96 728	234 624	685 884	1 069 457
Interest received	12 921	13 211	10375	20 033	50 848
Total income	2 282 762	2 112 891	2 282 114	4 107 959	4 967 349

Source: Adapted from Compilation Report to Bungala Aboriginal Corporation, 19 July 2000, Inglis & Rowe, Certified Practising Accountants.

Over the period 1995–96 to 1999–2000 there has been an increase in income from $2.23 million to $4.9 million (Table 15.1), largely due to increases in ATSIC wages funding, from $1.2 million to $2.6 million. This reflects the growing number of participants and increases in their rates of pay. Project-generated income has increased dramatically, from $60 524 in 1995–96 to $1 069 457 in 1999–2000.

Commercial viability

Almost all of the project-generated income is produced by the Construction Program through competitively tendered projects. Initially there was doubt among the local non-Indigenous population about Bungala's ability to successfully undertake construction projects. As a result, almost all of the successful tenders were obtained from Indigenous organisations, or the South Australian Housing Trust, for the construction and maintenance of housing for Indigenous people. The successful completion of a number of projects appears to have changed industry perceptions to the extent that Bungala has now successfully completed several very visible jobs for non-Indigenous clients.

Although there was project-generated income of $1.1 million in 1999–2000, the costs of generating this income, excluding CDEP participant wages and administrative support funded by ATSIC and funding received from DEWRSB, was at least as much. When the CDEP participant wages and funding from DEWRSB is added, the amount of money spent in earning this income is greater than the amount of income received. In other words Bungala's commercial activities do not make an accounting profit.

This lack of commercial viability is attributable to the fact that most of the participants come from the ranks of the long-term unemployed, and have never had previous employment. They need intensive graduated training, focusing on basic work skills and routines. This sort of training is very expensive and raises cost structures significantly above that of Bungala's competitors: the Construction Program has 1.6 apprentices for every tradesman, a much higher ratio than that found in the construction industry generally.

Movement to non-CDEP employment

One of the continuing objectives of Bungala is to assist participants to acquire skills that lead to unsubsidised employment. Between 30 and 40 participants leave Bungala each year for such employment (Table 15.2). The number of CDEP participants finding unsubsidised employment any given year is impressive given the extremely low levels of employability of most participants when they enter the scheme and the very low rates of employment of Indigenous people in Port Augusta and surrounding regions. It must be remembered also that around 50 per cent of participants do not wish to leave CDEP for other employment.

Table 15.2   Movements to unsubsidised employment, Bungala, 1996–2000

Year	Participant ceiling	Move to unsubsidised employment
1996–97		33
1997–98	129	68
1998–99	253	39
1999–2000	310	40

Source: Bungala Annual Report (various years), Bungala Aboriginal Corporation, Port Augusta.

The exceptionally large number of participants moving to unsubsidised employment in 1997–98 was primarily due to the Roxby mine expansion, which increased the demand for labour in the region. This shows that when there is strong labour demand in the region, suitably qualified Indigenous people are successful in finding employment.

For participants to find employment two barriers have to be surmounted. First, their work skills need to be developed so that it is profitable to employ them. Second, they need to be able to find an employer who considers them to be employable and is willing to employ them. Bungala is able to address both of these issues directly.

Training

Bungala provides a considerable amount of training to participants in the Construction Program. Much of this is informal, and involves participants gaining basic work skills and routines. In addition, Bungala provides a considerable amount of formal training through traineeships, apprenticeships, and short courses undertaken through TAFE.

The administrative rules of ABSTUDY and CDEP allow participants undertaking CDEP employment two days per week to enrol as part-time students in accredited courses and receive ABSTUDY payments as well as CDEP participant wages. This enables those participants to receive close to a full-time income. A large number of Bungala's participants take advantage of this arrangement.

Bungala has developed an internal labour market that allows participants to be promoted within the scheme. The possibility of promotion is a critical component of the scheme, providing participants with the incentive to work well and enhancing their chances of finding employment outside of CDEP.

Real work opportunities

There is a clear relationship between the commercial activities of Bungala and assisting participants to find unsubsidised employment. There are four main benefits to Bungala and its participants from its business enterprises. First, they allow Bungala to employ skilled tradesmen and supervisors which is essential to the scheme operating well. Second, they enable Bungala to provide a number of participants with full-time, relatively well paid work. This is critical in allowing the scheme to develop an internal labour market and to generate the incentives to motivate participants.

Third, they provide excellent training for participants in the form of traineeships and apprenticeships in areas for which there are employment opportunities in the region. The training environment created by having apprentices and trainees working on real construction sites and with other Indigenous people is one in which they are socially comfortable and likely to succeed. Spicer (1997) in his review of the CDEP scheme arrived at a similar conclusion. The system provides an alternative to the usual classroom-based training environment in which many Indigenous people feel uncomfortable. Yet it still results in a recognised qualification (Schwab 1997, 1998; see also Campbell & Schwab, Ch. 12, this volume).

Finally, the construction work results in a quality finished product which is highly visible. Anecdotal evidence from the local business community suggests that this has improved the public perception of Bungala, and altered the wider community's perceptions of Indigenous people. Public perception of the quality of work is important in helping participants find unsubsidised employment because employers are likely to value and view favourably their work experience with Bungala. The visible success of Bungala's Construction Program gives participants and the wider Indigenous community a sense of pride.

Conclusion

One of the fundamental differences between Indigenous and non-Indigenous people in regional centres experiencing economic decline is that many of the latter will move to areas with better economic prospects, whereas the Indigenous population remains. Thus the Indigenous population comprises an increasing proportion of the total population in many declining regional centres, such as Port Augusta. This raises the problem of how government can provide a framework in which Indigenous people in these areas can have an opportunity to actively participate in the labour market. CDEP provides an avenue to assist people who wish to find unsubsidised employment at the same time as providing meaningful work to people who do not. CDEP organisations in regional centres and urban areas need to maintain a delicate balance between the 'Aboriginalisation' of work and providing work activities that make people employable.

Bungala serves as a model of how CDEP schemes in regional centres and urban areas can meet their multiple objectives of assisting participants to acquire skills which result in unsubsidised employment, developing business enterprises, and providing employment in a community development setting. The study demonstrates that, in Port Augusta, CDEP is an important conduit to the 'real' economy for participants wishing to make this move. But just as importantly it also provides an avenue for participants who do not wish to find non-CDEP employment to undertake useful work in an environment that allows them to balance their cultural and family commitments with the demands of employment. It is possible to provide what from the government's point of view would be considered real and meaningful employment on the CDEP. Not everybody should be encouraged to leave. This is true for perhaps half of Bungala's participants, maybe more.

Not all CDEPs in regions with comparable labour market opportunities are as successful as Bungala in facilitating the movement of Indigenous people into employment, whether it be on CDEP or in the 'mainstream' (Smith 1994, 1995). Several factors have been identified as critical to Bungala's success. These are the development of an internal labour market, the employment of high quality supervisors and tradesmen, the use of the commercial enterprises as a training ground for the participants, and local business perceptions of Bungala and its participants engendered by the high quality of the work they produce.

None of this would be possible without income in addition to ATSIC's funding for participant wages, and capital and recurrent funding. While commercial activities can generate income, they are extremely unlikely, because of the high training component, ever to be profitable in an accounting sense. In the past wages surpluses could be used to provide additional work; this is no longer possible. If the government wishes for CDEPs like Bungala to continue to operate effectively, then it must increase funding, in one way or another.

Notes

1. The analysis presented here is based upon primary data collected during eight days of fieldwork in Port Augusta in July 2000, and secondary data analysis of the 1986, 1991 and 1996 Censuses and ATSIC administrative data. During the fieldwork extensive discussions were held with the management of Bungala, the CEO, and members of the Board of Management. Questionnaires were administered to 35 participants, and a number of the work sites in Port Augusta and many of the satellite schemes were also visited. During these visits discussions were held with work supervisors and participants were interviewed. Discussions were held with other stakeholders, including Inglis and Rowe Certified Practising Accountants (Bungala's accountants), Centrelink's Port Augusta Manager, Job Network providers (Complete Personnel and Mission Australia), Port Augusta City Council City Manager, and the CEO of the Northern Areas Regional Development Board. A follow-up visit was made to Bungala in September 2000 in order to present and discuss the research findings. An expanded version of this paper was published as a CAEPR Discussion Paper (Gray & Thacker 2000).

2. There are many reasons why Indigenous people choose to move between these areas, including attendance at ceremonies, access to services (particularly medical services), and maintenance of relationships with other family members.

3. Estimates are from the 1996 Census.

4. Satellite schemes are located at Davenport, Nepabunna, Iga Warta, Beltana, Port Pirie, and Hawker.

5. The short questionnaire that was administered to 35 participants included questions on why the person was on CDEP, whether or not they wanted to leave CDEP for 'mainstream' employment, and why. In addition there were questions on basic personal

characteristics (such as age, gender and marital status), about previous work experience, and about what the participant was doing immediately before starting CDEP.

6. There are two participant rates. One is for participants in remote areas; the other for participants in non-remote areas. As of 1 July 2000 the remote rate was $194.58 per week and the non-remote rate was $175.24 per week.

References

Aboriginal and Torres Strait Islander Commission (ATSIC) 1999. *Annual Report 1998–99*, ATSIC, Canberra.

Altman, J.C. and Taylor, L. 1989. *The Economic Viability of Aboriginal Outstations and Homelands*, AGPS, Canberra.

Gray, M.C. and Thacker, E. 2000. 'A case study of the Bungala CDEP: Economic and social impacts', *CAEPR Discussion Paper No. 208*, CAEPR, ANU, Canberra.

Marika, M. 1995. 'Davenport community profile 1993: A community report in fulfilment of an ethical position', *Australian Aboriginal Studies*, 2: 49–51.

Schwab, R.G. 1997. 'Post compulsory education and training for Indigenous Australians', *CAEPR Discussion Paper No. 131*, CAEPR, ANU, Canberra.

——— 1998. 'Dollars and sense: Economic and social tensions in Indigenous education', in F. Ferruer and D. Anderson (eds), *Different Drums, One Beat? Economic and Social Goals in Education*, National Centre for Vocational Education Research, Adelaide.

Smith, D.E. 1994. '"Working for CDEP": A case study of the Community Development Employment Projects scheme in Port Lincoln, South Australia', *CAEPR Discussion Paper No. 75*, CAEPR, ANU, Canberra.

———1995. 'Redfern works: The policy and community challenges of an urban CDEP scheme', *CAEPR Discussion Paper No. 99*, CAEPR, ANU, Canberra.

South Australian Centre for Economic Studies 1998. Economic Development from the Regional Perspective: What the Cities Say, A Study of the Six Major Provincial Cities Part B, Unpublished report, South Australian Centre for Economic Studies, Adelaide.

Spicer, I. 1997. *Independent Review of the Community Development Employment Projects (CDEP) Scheme* [the Spicer Review], Office of Public Affairs, ATSIC, Canberra.

16. Yuendumu CDEP: The Warlpiri work ethic and Kardiya staff turnover[1]

Yasmine Musharbash

Introduction

Yuendumu is one of the largest Aboriginal communities in Central Australia: the ABS reported 773 usual residents for the community in 1996.[2] It was set up as a government ration station in 1946 (Meggitt 1962) and is located about 300 kilometres north-west of Alice Springs on the Tanami Track. The main languages spoken are Warlpiri and English.

Yuendumu CDEP started up in March 1997. Fig. 16.1 shows the CDEP participant numbers from the beginning of the program to early in 2001. Until June 1999 the numbers were relatively stable at 140. They then plummeted to about 60 where they remained until June 2000, after which they started rising again. The aim of this paper is to examine the reasons which underlie this rather unusual curve.

The most elementary explanation is suggested by a correlation with the changes in management of the program. Since its beginning in March 1997, Yuendumu CDEP has had three generations of management. Fig. 16.2 shows how changeovers in management seem to be directly related to the fluctuation in participant numbers. The first manager started in March 1997 and resigned some time around July 1999. During this period, the numbers were relatively stable around an average of 140 participants. Just preceding and following this person's resignation there was a steep drop in numbers to about 60 participants. The second manager signed on in September 1999 and left in May or June 2000. During this period, the number of participants was stable at 60. Numbers started rising again with the signing on of the third manager in July 2000.

If the number of participants is taken to be one indicator of the success of a CDEP scheme, and if it can be shown, as in the case of Yuendumu, that the number of CDEP participants and the identity of the manager are directly linked, then an analysis of the relationship between management and participants becomes imperative. It is also significant that in every case the CDEP manager was non-Indigenous. This is also true of management in other Yuendumu organisations (see also Altman, Ch. 13, this volume).[3] An analysis of the relationship between management and participants must therefore include an analysis of cross-cultural relations. The main part of this paper will consist of an examination of some of the attitudes and opinions held by Indigenous and non-Indigenous persons which underlie the status quo. It will be argued that they have a considerable history. More than 20 years ago Fred Myers studied very similar phenomena among Pintupi people (who live just to the south of Warlpiri people) when he examined 'the miscommunication that resulted across the cultural and ethnic boundaries of black and white through expectations and action based on differing cultural premises' (1980a: 311).

Figure 16.1   Participant numbers, Yuendumu CDEP, 1998–2000

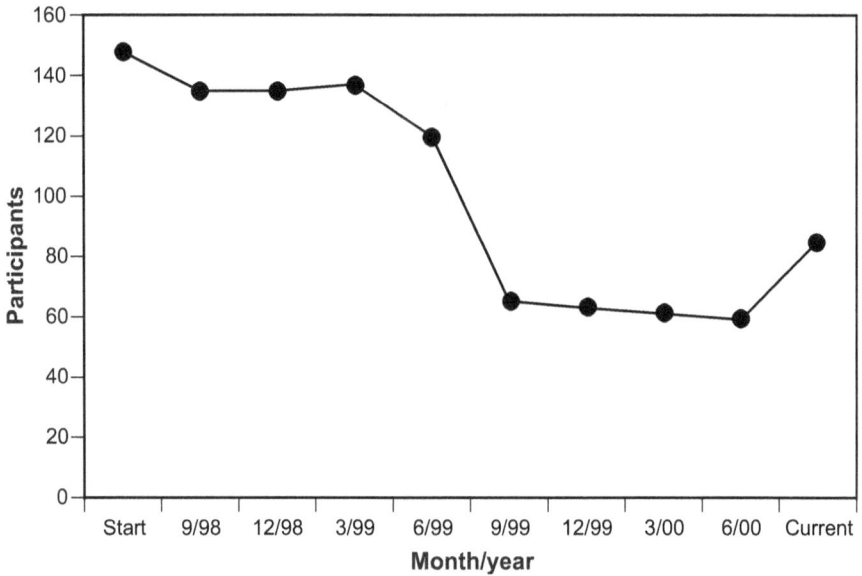

Figure 16.2   Turnover of CDEP managers in relation to participant numbers, Yuendumu CDEP, 1998–2001

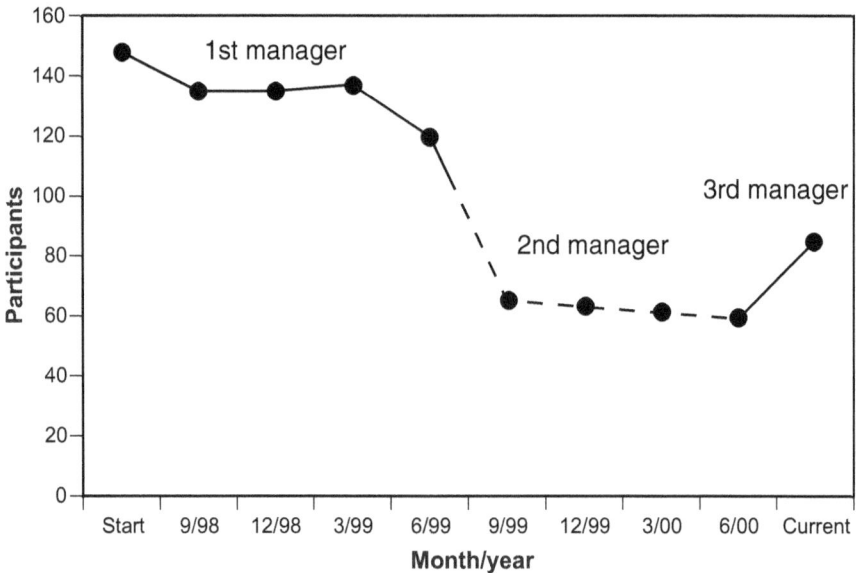

This paper will first provide some general statistical information about Yuendumu as contextual background for the ensuing discussion. It will then look at non-Indigenous perceptions of the work ethic and at Warlpiri ideas of the workplace. The third part of the discussion focuses on Warlpiri perceptions of non-Indigenous staff turnover. In the concluding part of the paper I indicate how the forgoing discussion throws light on the Yuendumu CDEP situation.

Statistical background information

In Yuendumu, as in most parts of the Northern Territory and indeed elsewhere in Australia, people draw clear-cut distinctions between Indigenous and non-Indigenous persons and group them as black or white—Yapa or Kardiya.[4] These distinctions mirror the very different lifestyles and educational backgrounds of Indigenous and non-Indigenous people.[5] In the 1996 Census, of the total Yuendumu population of 773 persons 70 per cent (or 609 persons) identified as Indigenous, and less than one-fifth (or 137 persons) identified as non-Indigenous.[6]

In looking at the qualifications of the Yuendumu population (see Table 16.1), the starkest contrast is in the area of University degrees. Six are held by Indigenous persons and 44 by non-Indigenous persons. Put differently, half of the non-Indigenous population over 15 years old holds a degree, as opposed to 1.3 per cent of the Indigenous population. On the other hand, 78 per cent (324) of Indigenous persons are not qualified at all (this number rises to 92 per cent if the categories 'not stated' and 'inadequately described' are included in the 'Indigenous' category), as opposed to only 32 per cent (29) of non-Indigenous persons.

Table 16.1   Highest educational qualification (15 years and older), Yuendumu, 1996

Qualification	Indigenous (no.)	Non-Indigenous (no.)
Higher degree	0	3
Postgraduate diploma	0	3
Bachelor degree	6	33
Undergraduate diploma	0	5
University degree: total	6	44
Associate diploma	8	3
Skilled vocational	0	8
Basic vocational	0	0
Inadequately described	3	3
Not qualified	324	29
Not stated	76	3
Total	417	90

Source: ABS 1998.

In 1996, only 19 per cent (78 out of 417) of Indigenous persons over 15 years old were employed, as opposed to 84 per cent (76 out of of 90) of non-Indigenous persons (see Table 16.2).[7]

With this background information in mind, I now turn to an investigation of the various, and sometimes clashing, ideas held by individuals in Yuendumu about what 'work' is, and what it should be.

Table 16.2   Occupations of Indigenous and non-Indigenous population, Yuendumu, 1996[a]

Occupation	Indigenous (no.)	Non-Indigenous (no.)
Manager/administrator	0	4
Professional	6	29
Associate professional	3	20
Tradesperson/related worker	3	3
Advanced clerical or service worker	0	3
Intermediate clerical, sales, or service worker	3	4
Intermediate production or transport worker	5	3
Elementary clerical, sales, or service worker	3	4
Labourer/related worker	16	6
Inadequately described	3	0
Not stated	36	0
Total (no.)	78	76
Percentage of population employed (%):	19	84

Note: (a) Excludes persons unemployed, not in the labour force, and under 15 years of age.

Source: ABS 1998.

Non-Indigenous perceptions of the Warlpiri work ethic

There are currently 20 projects and workshops in which CDEP participants at Yuendumu can be involved (not all are operating). In Table 16.3 these have been ranked in descending order according to chances of their leading to unsubsidised employment and likelihood of recurring training.

Apart from the 'cultural' category, all of these projects have a non-Indigenous person in the top managerial, coordination or administrative position. During the course of the research for this project I conducted interviews with a number of these administrators and with other non-Indigenous persons at Yuendumu who employ and work with Indigenous people. Almost all of the interviewees brought up the concept of 'the Warlpiri work ethic' in our conversations, without any prompting from me. Among their comments were:

Table 16.3   CDEP projects at Yuendumu, 2001

Project name/location	Project work and training content
Yuendumu School	Training through Batchelor College; teaching, clerical, school and teaching aides, child care, cleaning
Aged Care	Pick-up service, house cleaning, meals on wheels
Warlpiri Media	Training through Batchelor College; filming, sound recording, editing, broadcasting
Child Care Centre	Training through Batchelor College; child care
CDEP administration	Filing, computer skills, receptionist, payroll, etc.
Yuendumu Revegetation	Training through Centralian College; select, plant and seed stock, prepare soil, plan land use
Yuendumu Store and Mining Store cashier,	Stock control, display, stocking shelves, check out mechanical workshop, tyre repairs
Workshop and yard	Sorting materials, stacking, safe storing
Substance Misuse Program	Fencing, tree planting, waste management at petrol sniffers' outstations
Waste management and wood collection	Truck driving, front loader and bobcat operation
Building	Maintenance work
Warlukurlangu Artists Art Gallery	Database skills, office duties, preparing paints and canvas
Women's Centre and Night Patrol	Cleaning, cooking, night patrol
Housing management finance	Training through Batchelor College; housing and management, office procedures
Steel Furniture	Run in co-operation with Centralian College; welding, design, sales
Small Contracts	Property maintenance
Park, Gardens and Landscaping	Landscaping 'The park', cemetery, ovals and home gardens
Women's sewing	Sewing
Pottery	Pottery
Cultural	Assist in cultural activities, funerals, etc.

They don't know about handling money, the government never educated them, the government handed out rations but never trained or helped Yapa how to handle money, this has an impact on work ethic… Also, sleep deprivation impacts on their work ethic.

They [the new CDEP managers] are up against it: what many people don't realise is that some or most of these people have *never* worked, have no idea about what it means to work for a certain amount of time for a certain amount of money.

We never know when CDEP employees will turn up, they walk off at a moment's notice, we can never depend on anyone, they lack work ethics, I wish I knew how to motivate them.

CDEP as a program: it's good, it works in many communities, the problem here is their work ethic. They come to work, sign on, sign off, maybe stay, maybe not, but make sure to collect their money.

The term 'work ethic' is used in a wide range of meanings in these comments. In the most positive light, non-Indigenous people use it in explaining that few of the Indigenous population have been exposed to the work requirements of mainstream Australian society. They explain in their own words that Warlpiri people have not been working for a very long time at all, that the welfare days and the soup kitchen are a recent memory and that work as paid labour is a newly introduced concept (see also Rowse 1998). In fact, the soup kitchen and the associated 'welfare days' were abolished in the early 1970s. The 'Warlpiri work ethic' is something that is understood within a historical context, and something which the non-Indigenous manager thinks he or she should help to develop and nurture. Others are simply baffled by the perceived lack of interest in work, by people not turning up for work on time or at all, and by people not staying for appropriate hours. In this respect, the 'Warlpiri work ethic' contrasts starkly with non-Indigenous persons' perceptions of their own work ethic: most are very dedicated to their jobs and work long hours, often six or seven days a week.

There are, of course, some Warlpiri people who genuinely enjoy their work and whose work performance correlates with non-Indigenous ideals of the work ethic. However, these come almost exclusively from among the few who have achieved accredited qualifications in areas they are interested in, most often education, child care, and health. They are the ones who get cited as 'proper good workers', and who have considerable autonomy within and control over their own work. Most Indigenous employees, however, are unskilled and incentives to work are few. Warlpiri people do articulate certain incentives for working: to combat boredom, to be with relatives or friends who work at a certain place, and, interestingly, to earn some money. This last reason is significant because often the amount people earn working is less than the payments they would receive when not working. I return to this below in the discussion of the importance of having a 'boss' who looks after one. The concept of 'boss' also comes into play when there is a perceived or real lack of autonomy in the workplace, a topic to which I now turn.

Warlpiri ideas about the workplace

Warlpiri ideas about bosses and the relationship with them stem from Warlpiri concepts of social organisation and land tenure. Country, ceremonies, stories and other things in Warlpiri cosmology are jointly held by kirda and kurdungurlu (see Dussart 2000; Meggitt 1962; Munn 1973). Every person is kirda for some places and ceremonies and kurdungurlu for others, and these positions are acquired in different ways. No ceremony can be performed, no sacred site can be visited by only one or the other. Kirda and kurdungurlu have to operate jointly and are tied to each other by intricate rules of obligations, rights, duties and exchange. When these concepts are translated into Aboriginal English the metaphors employed most often stem from the field of labour. Kirda becomes 'boss' or 'owner' and kurdungurlu becomes 'worker' or 'policeman'.[8] Correspondingly, the Aboriginal English term for ceremony is 'business', as in 'sorry business', 'women's business' and so on.[9]

These metaphors are illuminating for an analysis of contemporary workplace relations at Yuendumu from an Indigenous perspective. Whereas many non-Indigenous persons consider their job done when they have met the requirements of their job, Warlpiri people expect something else beyond the actual work.[10] Ideally, there should be a personal relationship between boss and worker, where both are tied to each other by reciprocal obligations. A boss should look after his or her workers. This issue lies at the heart of many misunderstandings between non-Indigenous and Indigenous people in the workplace. Most CDEP work that Warlpiri do is not satisfying in itself; it is not the work as such which keeps them working (or not, as the case may be) but their relationship to their boss. If there is a personal relationship that involves the boss caring for, looking after and helping the workers then, in return, they feel obliged to turn up for work. They come to work regularly not only because of their 'obligation' to 'help' the boss, but also because they feel part of and included in the workplace.[11] The 'looking after' that a good boss is expected to do covers a wide range of activities and attitudes such as, for example, showing acceptance of and tolerance for cultural obligations of workers (like absences for 'sorry business'), offering seats to workers first when driving to town, assisting with bureaucratic matters, allowing access to office and private resources such as the telephones, and generally 'caring' for workers.[12] A case study will make the point.

> Melissa had been working for a Yuendumu organisation for many years.[13] One day, her 12-year-old son came into the office and asked her for some money to buy lunch. Melissa did not have any money on her and asked her boss, Gertrude, for five dollars. Gertrude answered that the organisation, in compliance with ATSIC directions, had just stopped giving out loans and that she could not help. Melissa left work and did not return for a number of days.

> Both told the story to me. Melissa pointed out that she had worked for the organisation for a long time and that she was owed some respect. She did not ask for a workplace loan but had expected her boss Gertrude to lend her five dollars of her own money—which she would have repaid. The denial of those five dollars by her boss made her feel as though she was not a valued person. Gertrude in turn did not understand why

Melissa, a very reliable worker, did not turn up the next day or the one after. She did not realise that her refusal to lend Melissa the five dollars had deeply hurt her and almost destroyed their relationship.

I have chosen this example to point out that 'looking after' very often entails only little things but that the chances for cultural misunderstandings in everyday interactions are enormous. If a non-Indigenous boss fails to fulfil the perceived obligation of 'looking after', Warlpiri often vote with their feet. This is one issue contributing to the cycles of success and decline that regularly affect most organisations and institutions at Yuendumu. This pattern of rise and decline generates, but is also generated in part by, the rate of non-Indigenous staff turnover.

Warlpiri perceptions of non-Indigenous staff turnover

Much has been written on Aboriginal mobility, particularly in remote areas (see Taylor 1996a, 1996b; Taylor & Bell 1999; Young & Doohan 1989). But while Aboriginal people are highly mobile, their movements are usually confined within a region and have focal points of reference. By comparison, the non-Indigenous population in remote communities is effectively much more transient: individuals move in and out of the region (see Table 16.4). This partly explains the different emphases and viewpoints of Indigenous and non-Indigenous people: whereas non-Indigenous people complain about Warlpiri workers not turning up to work from one day to the next, Warlpiri people complain about non-Indigenous people coming, staying for a year or two, and then leaving forever, and thereby demonstrating a lack of commitment to the people and the place.[14]

Table 16.4   Non-Indigenous managerial turnover at Yuendumu, 1995–2000

Organisation	No. of senior managerial staff, 1995–2000
CDEP office	3
Child Care Centre	3
Clinic	3
Council Clerk	6
Yuendumu Store	3
Mining Store	1
Aged Care program	1
School	3
Warlpiri Media	3
Warlukurlangu Artists	3
Women's Centre	4
Average no. of senior staff per organisation	2.9
Average turnover time (years)	2.1

Table 16.4 shows the turnover of managers or coordinators of some selected organisations at Yuendumu (numbers are potentially higher, as I have no data for the periods I was absent). These indicate that the average stay of a non-Indigenous manager or coordinator at Yuendumu is a fraction over two years. Other non-Indigenous staff turnover is probably even higher.

It is indicative that the non-Indigenous persons who have stayed at Yuendumu longest are those with the fewest complaints about the 'Warlpiri work ethic'. They are the ones who call Yuendumu home, and have meaningful relationships with their Indigenous colleagues and workers. To varying degrees, they have a good understanding of Warlpiri culture and have acquired Warlpiri language skills.

Discussion

The objective of CDEP is:

> to provide work for indigenous persons in community-managed activities which assist the individual in acquiring skills which benefit the community, develop business enterprises and/or lead to unsubsidised employment (Spicer 1997).

Within a remote community context there are some serious obstacles that lie between the objective and its successful realisation. My focus here is not on the question of how successfully Yuendumu CDEP fulfils its objective but rather on what issues pose serious obstacles to the success of CDEP in remote communities like Yuendumu.

First, it seems that Yuendumu CDEP—and this may be true of CDEPs in most remote communities—faces the same challenges in the year 2001 that Myers outlined 20 years ago. The following passage, written of Papunya in the 1970s, could equally have been written of Yuendumu today:

> In Papunya, absenteeism among health workers was common, often to the distress of the white staff when emergencies arose. Sometimes the health workers simply found their medical responsibilities to be in conflict with other obligations—especially obvious when ceremonies were under way. Viewed as 'flexibility,' this is precisely the quality said to be valued or desirable by Aboriginal people. This policy leads to high staff turnover. On the other hand, the most dependable Aboriginal workers appeared to labour out of a personal sense of obligation to a 'boss,' from whom they expected a reciprocal special relationship in turn. In these terms, quitting or taking leave from the job was a personal matter (Myers 1986: 279).

The question for CDEP then becomes: how should Yuendumu CDEP accommodate to Warlpiri ideas about the workplace? To ignore them causes a dramatic decline in participant numbers, whereas to observe them is to foster understandings that would not serve Warlpiri people well in the mainstream workplace. Second, the aim of 'providing unemployed Indigenous persons with activities leading to employment' has to be reconsidered in the light of options available to participants in remote communities.

The quality of work that is currently provided does have an impact on participant staff turnover. Most CDEP jobs are manual, and although their execution 'benefits the community' they do not necessarily provide participants with much job satisfaction. Garbage collection, fence building, road grading, cleaning, the collection of firewood and the fixing of tyres are all essential services within a remote community context. However, these jobs in particular seem to be the ones that participants sign on for occasionally, only to sign off to go back to welfare payments when other events in their lives require their time and attention. Since participants have the choice between doing these jobs on CDEP wages or receiving equal welfare payments it is not hard to understand why there is a lot of participant turnover in this area. It is here, in particular, that a good boss–worker relationship is an incentive for staying in a job, and the absence of such a relationship, as well as boredom and job dissatisfaction, lead to signing off.

Finally, it has to be asked: how realistic is the idea of unsubsidised labour in a remote community context? In communities like Yuendumu, to provide activities which 'develop business enterprises and/or lead to unsubsidised employment' is a distant goal. There are some CDEP jobs that provide and require formal training. These often guarantee the participant a larger degree of autonomy over the actual work and within the workplace. However, they hardly ever lead to unsubsidised labour. Many of the organisations and institutions providing training are financially unable to employ the fully trained CDEP participants. These people remain on their CDEP wages, without the perks they would otherwise have, such as long service leave, better sickness benefits, and superannuation.[15] In fact, many organisations and institutions, like the local school, are dependent upon CDEP-financed labour and could not function without it—thereby creating a vicious circle. Warlpiri people receive training and achieve some job autonomy but do not receive adequate wages (see also Nalliah, Ch. 28, this volume). This reduces job satisfaction and leads to poor levels of attendance.

Both the creation of unsubsidised employment in particular, and the provision of work for unemployed Indigenous persons in general, are challenging and complex issues in a remote community context. Furthermore, the transience of most of the non-Indigenous population in remote communities and the occupation of the most challenging job positions in communities by those persons are crucial structural issues. They need to be debated and resolved before viable and long lasting solutions can be developed. In the end, criticising CDEP for lack of success is like blaming a band-aid for being too small for the wound.

Notes

1. I would like to thank Ruth, Malcolm and James Japangardi Marshall at Yuendumu CDEP for their time, support and generous provision of materials, especially the graph. Thanks also to Valerie Napaljarri Martin and Tristan Ray at Warlpiri Media Association for discussing the first draft of this paper, and to Nicolas Peterson, Jon Altman and Diane Smith for reading and commenting on further drafts. Lastly, big thanks to Ian Bryson and Nicolas Peterson for almost presenting the paper at the conference for me when I had to extend my stay in central Australia.

2. The under-enumeration of Indigenous people has been discussed by Martin and Taylor (1995). In comparison to the relatively stable ABS population numbers the Health Centre Population Screening List gives a number of 930 residents at Yuendumu in October 1997 (Yuendumu Health Profile 1999).

3· In fact, every single organisation or institution operating at Yuendumu has non-Indigenous staff at the top managerial level.

4. At Yuendumu, people of mixed descent are classified as 'Yapa' (Indigenous) by both groups. Elsewhere a third category of 'yellafella' is recognised.

5. The contrast becomes particularly stark in statistical comparisons into health, rates of incarceration and deaths in custody, levels of unemployment, life expectancy, and education.

6. But see Martin and Taylor (1995) on the unreliability of ABS data in remote communities.

7. These ABS statistics were compiled before CDEP started at Yuendumu. There is no comparative data relating to the current situation to show the impact CDEP has had on employment figures. A study I conducted in 1999 (Musharbash 2000) was limited to 30 households (238 people) and caution should be exercised in generalising from these numbers. Of the sample population, 19 per cent of interviewees were on CDEP and 10 per cent were on wages. This suggests that for the 1999 sample population, in comparison to the 1996 total population, employment has risen by 10 per cent, although the increase in CDEP seems to have coincided with a decrease in work for wages. This has dropped by 9 per cent from 19 per cent to 10 per cent.

8. On the translation of the concepts of *kirda* and *kurdungurlu* into English see also Dussart (2000: 28) and Nash (1982).

9. This metaphorical translation seems particularly apt when one considers that ceremonies involve large-scale exchanges on various levels.

10. For a detailed ethnographic account and anthropological analysis of what 'to be boss' and 'to look after' mean, see Myers (1980a, 1980b, 1986, 1988).

11. To give an example cited by Myers: 'the particular conception of reciprocal obligation ultimately was what informed the Pintupi category of "boss" and the appropriate relationship implied by this designation; thus, their view of "work". Men often asked the Community Advisor . . . to drive them to Papunya . . . If he refused, whatever the reason he may have had, most men simply accepted the refusal. Not infrequently, however, men were heard to assert that the "boss" should help them because they worked for him: "I helped you build that fence"' (1980b: 319).

12. At Yuendumu, the only telephones to which most Indigenous people have access are three public telephones: one at the Women's Centre, one in the shop and only available during opening hours, and one often dysfunctional public telephone box in South Camp. Having a 'boss' who looks after one often simply means having access to a telephone when necessary.

13. All names used are pseudonyms.

14. Another constantly levelled accusation is that non-Indigenous people only come to Yuendumu to 'become rich,' that is their stay is seen to be for personal financial gain only.

15. In particular this applies to Warlpiri Media which trains in broadcasting, editing and filming; to the Child Care Centre; to the Old People's Program; and to the school.

References

Australian Bureau of Statistics (ABS) 1998. *1996 Census of Population and Housing: Indigenous Profile, Yuendumu.* Cat. no. 2020.0, ABS, Canberra.

Dussart, F. 2000. *The Politics of Ritual in an Aboriginal Settlement: Kinship, Gender and the Currency of Knowledge,* Smithsonian Press, Washington, DC.

Martin, D. and Taylor, J. 1995. 'Enumerating the Aboriginal population of remote Australia: Methodological and conceptual issues', *CAEPR Discussion Paper No. 91,* CAEPR, ANU, Canberra.

Meggitt, M.J. 1962. *Desert People: A Study of the Walbiri Aborigines of Central Australia,* Angus & Robertson, London.

Munn, N. 1973. *Walbiri Iconography: Graphic Representation and Cultural Symbolism in a Central Australian Society,* Cornell University Press, Ithaca, NY.

Musharbash, Y. 2000. 'The Yuendumu community case study', in D.E. Smith (ed.), *Indigenous Families and the Welfare System: Two Community Case Studies,* CAEPR Research Monograph No. 17, CAEPR, ANU, Canberra.

Myers, F. 1980a. 'A broken code: Pintupi political theory and contemporary social life', *Mankind,* 12: 311–26.

—— 1980b. 'The cultural basis of Pintupi politics', *Mankind,* 12: 197–213.

—— 1986. *Pintupi Country, Pintupi Self: Sentiment, Place, and Politics among Western Desert Aborigines,* University of California Press, Berkeley, CA.

—— 1988. 'Burning the truck and holding the country: Property, time and the negotiation of identity among Pintupi Aborigines', in T. Ingold, D. Riches and J. Woodburn (eds), *Hunters and Gatherers, Vol. 2, Property, Power and Ideology,* Berg, Oxford.

Nash, D. 1982. 'An etymological note on Warlpiri *kurdungurlu*', in J. Heath, F. Merlan and A. Rumsey (eds), *Languages of Kinship in Aboriginal Australia,* Oceania Linguistic Monograph No. 24, University of Sydney, Sydney

Rowse, T. 1998. *White Flour, White Power: From Rations to Citizenship in Central Australia,* Cambridge University Press, Cambridge.

Spicer, I. 1997. *Independent Review of the Community Development Employment Projects (CDEP) Scheme* [The Spicer Review], Office of Public Affairs, ATSIC, Canberra.

Taylor, J. 1996a. 'Short-term Indigenous population mobility and service delivery', *CAEPR Discussion Paper No. 118*, CAEPR, ANU, Canberra.

—— 1996b. 'Surveying mobile populations: Lost opportunity and future needs', in J.C. Altman and J. Taylor (eds), *The 1994 National Aboriginal and Torres Strait Islander Survey: Findings and Future Prospects*, CAEPR Research Monograph No. 11, CAEPR, ANU, Canberra.

—— and Bell, M. 1999. 'Changing places: Indigenous population movement in the 1990s', *CAEPR Discussion Paper No. 189*, CAEPR, ANU, Canberra.

Young, E. and Doohan, K. 1989. *Mobility for Survival: A Process Analysis of Aboriginal Population Movement in Central Australia*, NARU, ANU, Darwin.

Yuendumu Health Profile 1999. Health Profile Database, Unpublished community-based document [updated periodically], Yuendumu, NT.

17. Outstations and CDEP: The Western Arrernte in central Australia[1]

Diane Austin-Broos

Introduction

The issues bearing on remote communities, welfare, and economy are not new. Four of them frame this account of the Western Arrernte outstations and their CDEP schemes.[2] The outstation system is one of the largest in Australia. It developed from Ntaria, the erstwhile Lutheran mission of Hermannsburg that lies due west of Alice Springs and south of the MacDonnell Ranges in an arid but beautiful landscape.

More than a decade ago, Young noted that 'remote communities throughout Australia depend heavily on public subsidies for the provision of services' and, due to public sector employment, for a high proportion of family incomes (1988: 123). More recently, Taylor and Bell have remarked that lack of education, 'policy prescriptions and cultural preference' inhibit the migration of remote Aboriginal people (1997:408). The Western Arrernte are such a group. They have shown a marked reluctance to migrate although there is plenty of intra-regional movement between Ntaria, the outstation system, and Alice Springs. Staying mainly in one place, Western Arrernte people have passed from a situation of mission administered subsidy, through training wages and unemployment benefits (UB), to the current CDEP. This has occurred in the course of 40 years.

To the conditions of public subsidy and cultural reluctance to migrate, a third condition can be added: the corrosive impact of long-term dependency (see Pearson 2000; Sanders 1985, 1993). Today Western Arrernte people do not define themselves simply in terms of kin relations and ritual status. Issues of work role and occupational standing are also part of their identity. Nonetheless these sets of values can conflict. An outstation movement has not meant return to the old way of life, but at the same time, ties to aspects of that life make pursuing new values difficult. An impasse occurs in which people can neither return to the past nor find easy resolutions in the present. Welfare may not be intrinsically corrosive but the impasse it signals is debilitating. It undermines social cohesion, confidence and initiative (Peterson 1998).

The fourth and final pertinent condition is the limited economy of central Australia. Pastoralism was always tenuous and, especially west of the Stuart Highway, clearly a marginal industry even by the time of World War II. There is some mining and extensive natural gas deposits but not enough to constitute a major industrial complex. Alice Springs today is dominated by a variety of service industries to Aborigines, tourists, other residents, and the Pine Gap installation. Linked to these industries is the domain of national parks, land care and the like. These provide only modest employment and income for investment, in comparison with the royalty-rich parts of Arnhem Land. Moreover, these service industries have some notable features. Centralian tourism, like Third World tourism, tends to import its requirements. It does not stimulate local manufacturing or primary production. Like the other service industries, tourism offers employment that requires high levels of literacy and personnel management skills. It is not a mass employer although it does generate demand for repair and maintenance (R&M) of roads, plant and equipment in addition to the R&M required on communities. Service industry in Alice Springs is partially pillarised. While whites work in Aboriginal organisations, most Aboriginal people are confined to Aboriginal service areas. Finally, small business is mainly service, retail or commercial, and based in Alice Springs. There is a notable lack of small business in the rural desert areas. In short, this is a limited economy focused on Alice Springs. Remote communities are very marginal and in general terms there are limited opportunities for Aborigines.

The fourth condition can be linked with the first in order to observe that public subsidy in forms such as CDEP is a prominent part of Western Arrernte life because the region is economically marginal, and would be marginal whoever lived there. By virtue of their history, Aborigines are further disadvantaged. This directs attention to the other two conditions: reluctance to migrate might be reduced by less subsidy but not much. Western Arrernte people remain where they are for reasons of cultural preference strengthened by their sense of a racialised environment beyond their own domain. They are not only different but also peripheralised. Better levels of education might change these preferences but desire for education rests in part on the opportunities it presents. In an economically marginal area, education lacks meaning and this is reflected in the tiny minority of Arrernte over the age of 15 engaged in further study (Papunya Regional Council (PRC) 1999:14).[3] Regrettably, high achievement is required to make the leap into town-based service industry. Overall then, life is hard. Public subsidy in the form of welfare brings low esteem in white society and many Western Arrernte care about this. It accentuates the sense of impasse and causes immense frustration.

My account of the Western Arrernte outstation system and CDEP is framed by these conditions. I focus on what is possible in this circumstance rather than on changing these conditions, some of which are intractable. In particular I am interested in initiatives that Western Arrernte people have taken to address their situation. I give a brief history of the outstations, describe some aspects of CDEP, note some problems, and offer some proposals.

The outstation movement and CDEP

In 1979, after almost 90 years of continuous occupation, the Lutheran mission handed back its government lease to the Western Arrernte. Today, a population of over 900 is distributed between Alice Springs, Ntaria and 40 outstations on the old lease.[4] Roughly half the outstations are within a 25 kilometre radius of Ntaria and, as one Western Arrernte man observed, the outstation movement was more a 'decentralisation' from Ntaria than a 'land rights' movement as such. Nonetheless, there was a significant element of cultural revitalisation in the outstation movement. Rites that had not been performed for many years close to the mission were performed again and with public acknowledgment. The movement responded to initial steps towards self government at Ntaria (then

Hermannsburg) (see Sommerlad 1973). The attempt to revitalise rites was part of a larger concern with how to re-articulate Aboriginal authority in the wake of the mission order.

With growing Federal support in the 1970s, the movement quickened. In 1974 there were nine outstations, then 24 by 1976, and 33 by 1983 when the Tjuwanpa Outstation Resource Centre was established as an Aboriginal corporation. The resource centre was constructed across the Finke River from Ntaria and incorporated under the Federal *Incorporations Act 1983*. This was also the year in which Hermannsburg mission governance was replaced by an autonomous Ntaria council. The council is incorporated under Northern Territory legislation and receives municipal support as a community government. There were five more outstations by 1988, bringing the number to 38 in total. In that year Tjuwanpa and Ntaria both adopted CDEPs.

The original manager and staff of Tjuwanpa were lay Lutherans, the manager staying on at Tjuwanpa for more than a decade after the mission administration withdrew. In an Arrernte sense, he was a 'worker' for the man who many saw as the senior custodian for the country on which Hermannsburg was built. The new Ntaria Council chairman contested this custodian's position though the chairman had neither the support of senior Arrernte nor of their Lutheran brokers. He had gained his council position by virtue of his administrative skills and not through traditional status. The contest has now continued even into the next generation. As a consequence, Tjuwanpa and Ntaria have developed in tandem but with tensions and sometimes open conflict between them.

At the outset the Ntaria CDEP had 140 participants, but even by 1990 the number had declined to around 40 as people progressively transferred from Ntaria to the outstation scheme. Today the Ntaria project still numbers about 40 while the Tjuwanpa-based scheme has more than 300 participants. Ntaria's is a 'community based' project while Tjuwanpa, with its far-flung clientele, is an organisation with both centralised and decentralised aspects.

Tjuwanpa is the hub of the outstation scheme. The centre includes administrative offices, a garage, service station and parts shop, and a steelworks shop. It has a large meeting room, a vehicle compound, and two horticultural sites, the product of terminated projects. A Federal Community Housing and Infrastructure Program (CHIP) grant supports the manager–accountant and a small number of clerical staff. CDEP support pays or contributes funds to the CDEP coordinator, two field officers, the building team staff and road building staff, as well as a senior vehicle mechanic and a land care officer. Further positions in building, mechanics and land care are paid from other sources including profits. A full-time grader operator is retained by the organisation. He bids successfully for regional contract work (see Nicholas, Ch. 25, this volume). In the past, the organisation also employed a full-time welder for the steel shop. The shop was set up a decade ago to make various furniture and fittings for outstation houses. All major housing construction was contracted out from the mid 1990s. Since that time, the Tjuwanpa steel shop has been less active though it still maintains a steady production of fence posts, bed frames, and the like.

Apart from municipal and CDEP management as such, the largest centralised project at Tjuwanpa is the building maintenance team, a DEWRSB Structured Training and Employment Project (STEP) aimed at self sufficiency. A similar STEP project is planned in contract road building and maintenance (see Nicholas, Ch. 25, this volume). The newly established women's centre is developing a meals project for the old and a sewing project to provide outstation curtains. Modest as this latter activity seems, it involves recycling house rental and a subsidy from the Infrastructure and Housing Authority of the Northern Territory to create a market for women's work that moves away from the notion of craft and recreation towards commercial activity.

Tjuwanpa retains about 30 full-time staff of whom eight currently are non-Indigenous. This includes the manager–accountant, two CDEP field officers, the payroll officer, and two mechanics. The CDEP co-ordinator and a number of 'team leaders' in the service station, steel shop, and roads and building maintenance are Aboriginal, including the grader operator. In addition, the Tjuwanpa management committee is entirely Aboriginal. This committee has 20 members who represent the various outstation administrative groupings. The committee oversees both the municipal and CDEP functions of Tjuwanpa. Outstation heads who act as supervisors for their respective outstation projects receive a loading as part of their fortnightly CDEP pay. They propose or delete CDEP participants for their outstations and sign the weekly work sheets.

Outstation activities include mustering and yard maintenance which involves extensive fencing. In the past few years small herds of cattle have been purchased by two outstations. There is more activity in feral animal mustering of brumbies, cattle, and camels. About four outstations are involved in this activity which is influenced by the price of beasts in relation to transport costs. The nearest abattoir at Bond Springs north of Alice Springs is not killing at present, and stock must be trucked across the continent. Horse meat is used for pet food and camel meat holds prospects for an export industry. Two outstations currently maintain commercial art or craft activities. Ironically, in 1992 Tjuwanpa failed to take up the option of managing the Hermannsburg Potters. Although it was feared that the group would be a burden, it is now a successful and internationally acclaimed enterprise. Three outstations in the system house small regional schools and teaching aides are recruited for these from their immediate vicinities. One outstation is involved in building maintenance under the leadership of the outstation head who is a skilled tradesman. One outstation maintains an alcohol rehabilitation program and a few outstations from time to time have been involved in gardening projects, generally not sustained. Most of these activities are intermittent and involve a small minority of those registered for CDEP. The majority of participants are listed for activities concerned with outstation maintenance, land care, or care of the old and young. Much though not all activity on many outstations is notional.

CDEP is the principal source of income for Western Arrernte people. The 1996 Census shows CDEP accounting for 78 per cent of the outstation labour force. Of this labour force, 16 per cent was unemployed, leaving only 6 per cent in other forms of employment (ABS 1998: 112). Most Western Arrernte people receive some royalty payments for Palm Valley gas reserves and/or a natural gas pipeline from Mereenie that travels across Western

Arrernte land. On balance, however, the Western Arrernte are not a royalty-rich group. Income from mining has not been sufficient to prompt Arrernte-wide incorporations. The income from Tjuwanpa's CDEP in the financial year 1998–99 was around $3.8 million. In relation to UB, CDEP brings to Tjuwanpa both additional capital and operations support. It also brings the ability to manage income support on a family basis, important in funding outstation services. Managed saving is extensive at Tjuwanpa and is now being turned to fund maintenance and improvement projects that also create employment.

Within PRC, Tjuwanpa's is the largest of 12 CDEPs (PRC 1999: 15). The council's annual report for 1998–99 listed 335 participants for Tjuwanpa with the next largest being Yuendemu (135) and then Willowra (78). Overall Tjuwanpa's list accounts for about a third of the region's participants, and just over 27 per cent of regional CDEP budget allocations (PRC 1999: 27). In the Papunya Region, CDEPs have almost doubled in the last six years and PRC has a waiting list of communities (PRC 1999: 15). Regional conditions and its relative size place pressure on Tjuwanpa both to comply with ATSIC rules and also to develop profit-making concerns. The way forward is difficult, however.

Some problems in the outstation scheme

Problems are so numerous that I propose to focus on just two areas: resources and management. The first condition for an outstation CDEP is that people actually be on their outstations and then, preferably, with meaningful activities. This baseline requirement is hard to realise. With a municipal CHIP grant of less than $300 000 per annum, servicing the outstations is very difficult. The task includes maintaining access roads, generators, solar systems, bores, other forms of water catchment, houses, and other shelters. Inevitably the line between project initiatives and service maintenance is blurred, with CDEP staff spending most of their time on the latter. Palmer has described this dilemma in terms of 'a management style that is responsive and even . . . defensive, rather than strategic' (1998: 185), though this description hardly addresses the role and resource problems involved.

An important aspect of these resource issues is the maintenance of vehicles. The average life of a work vehicle is between three and four years, and it is common for such a vehicle to travel well over 100 000 kilometres in two years. During the past decade there has been a notable decrease in four-wheel-drive work vehicles attached to outstations and an increase in two-wheel-drive sedans, many of which have a very short life. An outstation group that lacks a vehicle will inevitably live for a period in Ntaria, although most such groups are normally away from Ntaria only for a few days at a time. Foraging and hunting are recreational pursuits now, and people are dependent on purchased food.

Vehicles are also crucial to Tjuwanpa. The pressures that bear on CDEP staff are due in part to the fact that they are constantly making decisions on the use of scarce vehicles. The pressing maintenance needs, especially of generators and solar systems, tend to be given priority thereby relegating supervision of outstation projects. Moreover, outstation heads, some of them management committee members, often request Tjuwanpa vehicles for personal use when their own vehicles are disabled. These requests are resisted, but not always successfully, heightening the scarcity of organisation vehicles.

Management problems also abound. At the local level, outstation heads who act as CDEP supervisors are also senior kin to those whom they supervise. There is no provision for training or support of these heads and one field officer cannot cover all the outstations on a very regular basis. Like its welfare counterparts, a CDEP offers to all participants a modest degree of autonomy. This makes it difficult for outstation heads to maintain authority either as CDEP supervisors or as senior kin who are required in any case to look after their relatives. This simply exacerbates a more general feature of wage support schemes: it is hard to sustain rewards on a graded scale for degrees of skill or work input. A few become stable wage or salary earners while the majority have little incentive to be other than minimum benefit recipients.

At the organisational level, Tjuwanpa's management committee has the substantial influence in hiring and firing the manager. However, beyond a growing sense of ATSIC-required accountability, members of this committee have had little engagement with the values and practice of asset management or commercial enterprise. As the management committee is comprised of outstation heads, the organisational and local dynamics tend to intersect. Outstation heads involved with the management committee are also involved in a resource politics to cater to kin through the acquisition of grants. The emphasis is on capital rather than on human capital accumulation. The manager must be keenly involved in acquiring grants. Yet grants are rendered mostly as forms of transitional benefit rather than as seed capital or assets. Land is the Arrernte's greatest potential capital asset. Its cultural significance and legal definition render it inalienable, however. These resource and management issues in conjunction with the limited possibilities of the region make it almost impossible for CDEP to work well. It is a substitute for economy rather than an economy itself, presenting a major challenge to Aborigines and non-Aborigines alike.

CDEP and the Western Arrernte: Some proposals

When two CDEPs were established on Western Arrernte land, the Tjuwanpa scheme was attractive to many for a number of reasons. Many Western Arrernte sought autonomy from an Ntaria increasingly controlled by one particular family. Although new housing came gradually to the outstations, it was distributed more widely than housing in Ntaria. Vehicles were acquired through the Aboriginals Benefit Reserve and its predecessors so that, at the outset, transport was accessible. Moreover, factors already mentioned meant a more limited capacity at Tjuwanpa to enforce the 'no work, no pay' rule that is operative in Ntaria. This provided false autonomy as workfare became welfare.

It is now evident that it is extremely difficult to resource the outstations and that resource and management problems make it unlikely that CDEP as presently organised can be an effective framework for outstation maintenance. At the same time, the lack of proper supervision on outstations has become destructive, especially for youth. Young people draw their CDEP pay from Tjuwanpa but spend most of their time in Ntaria and Alice Springs. These problems are exacerbated by the fact that Tjuwanpa is divorced from the settlement resources of Ntaria which sustains only a tiny CDEP in comparison with Tjuwanpa's project.

The populations of Ntaria and the outstation system are overlapping rather than separate. Most Ntaria residents have outstation relatives. People frequently move between an outstation on country and Ntaria, and Alice Springs. In fact it is difficult to imagine an outstation life that does not also involve Ntaria. The health clinic is there. Two supermarkets are there. The church is there and, although some outstations have their own regional schools, many outstation children attend the larger Ntaria school. Sporting facilities for youth, though meagre, are centred on Ntaria. A reintegration of these organisations within a single CDEP could produce a more effective use of Western Arrernte resources. Notwithstanding the political and cultural difficulties involved, it is of interest that recently Tjuwanpa's management committee has been thinking about a more regional approach to both CDEP and local government. Current negotiations on a joint approach to roads and local airstrips might be extended to housing, power, and other forms of maintenance.

These organisational issues also bear on CDEP and the local economy. It is unrealistic to assume that there can be equal activity on all outstations. Moreover, given the demands of supervision, most work that is not locality-based would be better centralised especially where that activity involves youth not concerned with the care of dependents. The outstation activities that are constant and successful to some degree are feral mustering, art and craft, and alcohol rehabilitation. Feral mustering might expand on both a domestic and export basis especially if there were a way to reduce prohibitive transport costs. Camel meat is an expanding export market for Australia and the domestic market for horse meat remains constant. The issue of regional infrastructure for these activities, including slaughtering and storage facilities, is worth a second look. These initiatives grow out of the pastoral industry but are fresh forms of activity. At the same time they employ well-established local skills, could be profitable, and are enjoyed by participants. Art and craft and rehabilitation are smaller concerns but each involves examples of local success and should be supported for this reason.

Tjuwanpa is currently negotiating contracts for 13 kilometres of walking trail in the Western MacDonnell Ranges and, following the successful Palm Valley land claim, Arrernte involvement in the Palm Valley tourist enterprise. The most viable local industry, however, is repair and maintenance of infrastructure both for communities and for the tourist trade generally. Further development of the building team and growth of the steel shop have potential for genuine enterprise. In conjunction with regional road contract work that would allow the Western Arrernte to engage with regional tourist infrastructural development, R&M could become a viable local industry. Such an aspiration would be more feasible if Tjuwanpa and Ntaria formed the core of a larger local government that integrated the service demands both of Ntaria and of the outstation system. Once again, these are activities that, on a smaller scale, have sustained some élan among workers as centralised projects. In conjunction with the administrative work required to run a settlement and outstation system these activities have the chance to realise real employment opportunity and possibly investment opportunity as well.

It may be that Ntaria and the outstation system can provide between them only a limited number of full-time equivalent positions for the resident population. If this is so, then it should be acknowledged and attention given to other forms of support required by a remote community: how to improve school attendance, manage flexible employment, care for the aged, deal with substance abuse, and find constructive outlets for youth. Understanding and accepting that in marginal economies the lead time to any form of regular employment is quite long would be a helpful starting point. In short, this support requires careful and innovative thought, real resources, and national recognition that for the Western Arrernte and like populations, staying put in an economically marginal region is an option of Aboriginal citizenship and not an irrational response or a moral failing.

Conclusion

I have not suggested horticulture for the Western Arrernte or the highly personalised 'home visit' tourism that has worked in some other Indigenous localities. My diffidence springs from the fact that in the last decade or so these activities have been tried as small businesses and petered out. I have focused on the more constant activities that Arrernte themselves engage with and enjoy. My proposal is that in enterprise, as well as on the larger issue of migration, the Western Arrernte make choices using their own local knowledge. It is now more important than ever to attend to and support those choices. For their own part, Western Arrernte must recognise that their own politics and practice do have implications for the younger generation. The intensity of family conflicts, and inability to build authority structures not dependent on encompassing orders, such as ATSIC, are major impediments in local development. Finally, I underline that education and work practice go together. Schooling and training become desirable in the company of opportunity, not in a social and economic vacuum.

Notes

1. Research pertaining to this paper was funded by an ARC Large Grant, A59700469. For their help in the course of that research I thank the Western Arrernte and especially the Tjuwanpa Management Committee. Elva Cook, Mavis Malbunka, Ralph Malbunka, Patrick Oliver and Conrad Ratara gave me useful insights. In particular I also thank past and present staff of Tjuwanpa. John Nicholas has been especially helpful along with Glen Auricht and Ivan Rieff. ATSIC staff in Alice Springs have been generous with their time and advice regarding documentary research. In particular I wish to thank Richard Preece, Wally Litvensky and Bill Muddle.

2. Different orthographies are used in different communities of the Arandic-speaking area. 'Arrernte' and 'Arranda' are two currently used variants. In his contribution John Nicholas uses the latter, which corresponds to the practical orthography in use at Ntaria (Hermannsburg). The spelling Arrernte is preferred here.

3. The PRC reports that only 1 per cent of Aboriginal children in the region over the age of 15 years are pursuing further education. The statistic is not disaggregated according to language group. It is likely that the Western Arrernte figure alone would be a little higher than this.

4. The total population figure is produced from Ntaria Health Clinic statistics. Because these are calculated on regular visits over time, the resulting figure is more reliable than a census figure. This is not the total number of Western Arrernte in central Australia, but the number involved in regular interactions in and around Ntaria.

References

Australian Bureau of Statistics (ABS) 1998. 'Fact sheet 16: Labour force status', *1996 Census of Population and Housing*, ABS, Canberra.

Palmer, K. 1998. 'Appendix 5: Resource agency funding options, resource management and cost recovery', in J.C. Altman, D. Gillespie and K. Palmer (eds), *National Review of Resource Agencies Servicing Indigenous Communities, 1998*, ATSIC, Canberra.

Papunya Regional Council 1999. *Annual Report, 1998–99*, ATSIC, Alice Springs.

Pearson, N. 2000. *Our Right to Take Responsibility*, Noel Pearson and Associates, Cairns, Qld.

Peterson, N. 1998. 'Welfare colonialism and citizenship: Politics, economics and agency', in N. Peterson and W. Sanders (eds), *Citizenship and Indigenous Australians*, Cambridge University Press, Cambridge.

Sanders, W. 1985. 'The politics of unemployment benefit for Aborigines: Some consequences of economic marginalisation', in D. Wade-Marshall and P. Loveday (eds), *Employment and Unemployment*, NARU, ANU, Darwin.

—— 1993. 'The rise and rise of the CDEP scheme: An Aboriginal "workfare" program in times of persistent unemployment', *CAEPR Discussion Paper No. 54*, CAEPR, ANU, Canberra.

Sommerlad, E. 1973. Community Development at Hermannsburg: A Record of Changes in the Social Structure, Unpublished report, Centre for Continuing Education, ANU, Canberra.

Taylor, J. and Bell, M. 1997. 'Mobility among Indigenous Australians', in P.W. Newton and M. Bell (eds), *Population Shift: Mobility and Change in Australia*, CSIRO, Canberra.

Young, E. 1988. 'Aboriginal economic support in remote arid land settlements', in T.B. Brealey, C.C. Neil and P.W. Newton (eds), *Resource Communities: Settlement and Workforce Issues*, CSIRO, Canberra.

18. CDEP in Victoria: A case study of Worn Gundidj[1]

Raymond Madden

In 1992, when Will Sanders looked at CDEP across the country (Sanders 1993), there were only two CDEP schemes in Victoria, both based in Gippsland in the east of the State. Since that time the scheme has expanded rapidly, and now there around 750 participants involved in about a dozen CDEP schemes across the State. The subject of this paper is a corporate CDEP scheme in Western Victoria which operates under the mantle of the Worn Gundidj Aboriginal Co-operative.

Worn Gundidj CDEP

Worn Gundidj is located in Warrnambool, in south-west Victoria. Warrnambool is a rural city with a population of 28 000 people, and a rich agricultural hinterland. Through its light industry, retail outlets, government bureaucracies and educational facilities it services a wide area of the south-west. Warrnambool has two Aboriginal co-operatives: Worn Gundidj (CDEP), and Gunditjmara Aboriginal Co-operative. The Warrnambool Aboriginal community has strong links to the Framlingham community located about 15 kilometres to the north-east; indeed the bulk of Warrnambool's Aboriginal population either came from Framlingham, or had ancestors who came off the Framlingham Aboriginal Station.

As a corporate CDEP, Worn Gundidj has a central office that services a number of satellite schemes (also referred to as outstations in CDEP-speak). The central office is the grantee and has the responsibility for administering the scheme's wages, on-costs and the specialised software program 'CDEPManager'. However, the Worn Gundidj central office is not just an administrative arm; it also has its own work programs and participants.

The structure displayed in Fig. 18.1 represents the totality of Worn Gundidj's operations. I conducted fieldwork only in the Warrnambool-based section of the scheme and so will focus on that part of the scheme's operations. I will refer to the central office and its operations as 'Worn Gundidj' and to the outlying operations as the 'satellites'. Fig. 18.1 shows that Worn Gundidj has a board of directors and chair at its decision-making apex. It is fortunate to have a regional CDEP coordinator based at its offices, who also sits as a board member. At this level the scheme is dominated by Indigenous voices. Yet at the next level—the executive and administrative level—the picture is reversed. Only two out of eight of the executive positions of program coordinator, finance manager, administrators (including receptionists), and supervisors are occupied by Indigenous people. Below the work supervisors come the participants. Worn Gundidj has around 110 participants on its schedule, and of that total between 40 and 50 are employed at any one time through Worn Gundidj's central office. The rest are employed through the satellites or in hosted positions elsewhere in the State.

Figure 18.1 Organisational structure of Worn Gundidj corporate CDEP, 2001

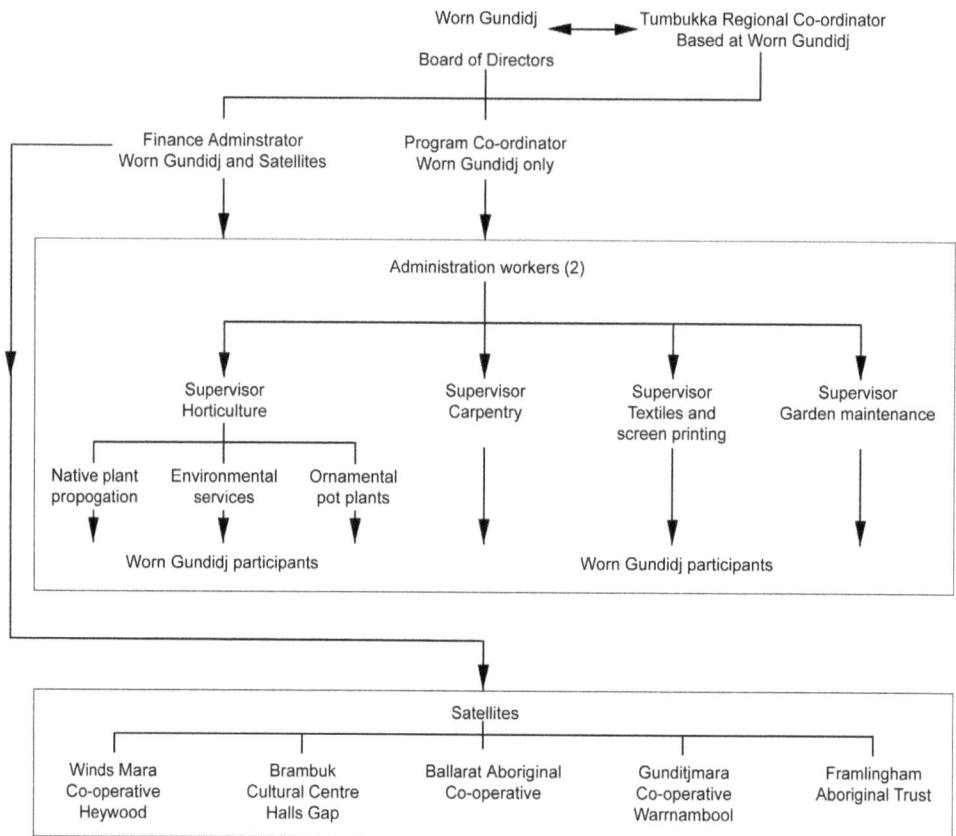

The Worn Gundidj work programs

The work programs undertaken by Worn Gundidj include three horticultural programs. One is devoted to the germination of native trees; the second concentrates on potted plants, both exotic and indigenous ornamental species. These are used to fill contracts with supermarkets and variety store outlets. The third program focuses on using the native trees and plants propagated on site to fill revegetation contracts—what Worn Gundidj calls Environmental Services. These work programs offer opportunities for participants to undertake a TAFE accredited horticulture course (Level II) or a horticulture apprenticeship. There are currently two participants undertaking horticulture apprenticeships at Worn Gundidj, and eight participants in accredited traineeships.

Worn Gundidj also has a carpentry program that undertakes private contracts, and maintenance around Worn Gundidj. This program offers participants either a place to undertake a carpentry apprenticeship, or basic training in building skills. Another work program is in textiles, and this stream of work can, like the horticulture, be combined with TAFE study in an accredited textile and screen-printing course. Here participants can learn the basics of dyeing, printing, assembling and designing for fabrics, and this work program allows artistic skills and culturally relevant design to flourish in a work environment. The final work program is a garden maintenance program which offers rubbish collection and gardening work in the local area.

The satellites

The satellites are located throughout the south-west of Victoria, and their relationship to the central office is important to the overall picture. The satellites are pre-existing Aboriginal co-operatives or trusts which have used CDEP wages to fund their administrative functions and maintenance work. Some also send workers out on work sites with Worn Gundidj workers. A brief word on Victoria co-operatives might be useful here. Across the State of Victoria there exists a regime of Aboriginal co-operatives dedicated to delivering Aboriginal-specific services through health workers, drug and alcohol workers, housing programs, cultural heritage officers, and so on. These co-operatives are funded by a mixture of ATSIC and State government dollars, the mix depending on the service provided.

In recent years the co-operative system has experienced funding reductions and a rationalisation of such things, for example, as the number of cultural heritage officers and the number of cultural heritage zones (in other words, fewer officers with bigger areas to look after). These funding reductions led to a loss of administrative positions in these co-operatives, not just in south-west Victoria, but across the State. These changes affected their ability to deliver the services they are charged with providing (see also Bartlett, Ch. 20, this volume). Some went very close to shutting their doors altogether, and some relied on volunteer administrative staff to keep operating. The integration of a cluster of south-west Victorian Aboriginal co-operatives into the Worn Gundidj satellite system, with the purpose of accessing CDEP wages to fund administrative positions, means that those co-operatives now rely on State, ATSIC and CDEP dollars to deliver a full suite of services.[2] I return to the theme of organisational integration below.

The satellites remain, on a day-to-day working basis, independent of Worn Gundidj with respect to their work program tasks. The satellites receive an on-cost component with their wages, and Worn Gundidj extracts an administrative component from the overall on-costs and administrative stream. This degree of local autonomy, coupled with regional co-operation, suits both the satellites and Worn Gundidj and accords with local political and cultural units of power and territoriality. But as all the satellites operate under the one grantee, they can provide staff for Worn Gundidj contracts without having the trouble of changing schemes, or notifying Centrelink. This arrangement has been in force recently with a revegetation contract in Portland and Heywood, an hour's drive to the west of

Warrnambool. In this case the contract was secured by Worn Gundidj from Warrnambool, but as it is in another mob's country, according to local reckoning of territory, they regularly use Portland or Heywood labour on these jobs. This is put forward as the culturally appropriate approach to dealing with contracts in the country of satellites. Thus labour pooling is one aspect of the relationship between the satellites and Worn Gundidj in addition to the administrative linkages.

Flexibility of staff movement between the satellites, when the need arises, and the localised autonomy over the day-to-day work as exercised by the satellites, provide an effective structure which can accommodate the economic reality of the need for short bursts of intensive labour on some jobs, and having workers based around their local CDEP satellite *co-operative* at other times.

ABSTUDY, training and CDEP

The management and directors at Worn Gundidj see the organisation not just as a place of employment, but also as a training and educational institution. The textiles work program at Worn Gundidj is an interesting example of this approach. The participants work their allotted CDEP hours per week (17.5 hours) but in addition a textiles and screen-printing course is delivered by the local TAFE college on site at Worn Gundidj. This qualifies as an accredited full-time course as it amounts to at least 14 hours per week, and therefore the participants are eligible for ABSTUDY. Although participants are not allowed to be on ABSTUDY when they come into the CDEP (they could not be classified as clients of Centrelink if they were in receipt of ABSTUDY), there is nothing to hinder them from going onto ABSTUDY once they have become employees of Worn Gundidj. In this manner Worn Gundidj can offer textiles participants both accredited training, and top-up money (in the form of ABSTUDY). Management at Worn Gundidj see this as a strong recruitment point, and it gives CDEP a real edge over Centrelink income support, especially for those adult participants who could get the same on income support, without having to work, as they would on CDEP. This training and top-up money cocktail has made the textiles program a vibrant hub of the organisation, as the classes and work are undertaken in the main office buildings. This work program, then, is in part dependent on ABSTUDY to make it a viable and attractive option for adult participants.

The other incentive that Worn Gundidj can offer is accredited certificates in horticulture for those participants under the horticulture work programs. Training for these participants is delivered by Wimmera and Grampians Group Training (a member of the Group Training Australia) who are based in Horsham. What it true of the textile stream is also true of the horticulture streams at Worn Gundidj—access to ABSTUDY dollars has made these programs very popular for both social and economic reasons. Thus, in these three work programs CDEP is closely linked to third party education and training providers, and is partly reliant on ABSTUDY dollars as a form of top-up.

Relations with Centrelink

Worn Gundidj, like all other CDEP schemes, has had to cope with a major administrative change. As of the 1 March 2000, all CDEPs now have to have data linkage with their local Centrelink office, and all CDEP participants have first to be clients of Centrelink (and have a customer reference number). In order to ensure parity between CDEP and mainstream work for the dole schemes, and to make CDEP participants eligible for a raft of concessions available to mainstream Centrelink clients, a $20.00 per fortnight supplement (CDEP Participant Supplement, or CPS) was made available to CDEP participants who became clients of Centrelink. This supplement was also payable retrospectively, to 1 March 1999, to those participants who had been on CDEP during that time. These payments came in two instalments known as 'retro one' (from March 1999 to September 1999), and 'retro two' (from September 1999 to March 2000).

This period of changeover threw a potentially serious administrative burden on Worn Gundidj (and on all CDEPs for that matter). Communication problems between Centrelink and Worn Gundidj led to a situation where Worn Gundidj only realised the extent of its responsibilities about three days before the final deadline for the CPS forms. Worn Gundidj then contacted Centrelink and began to negotiate a solution. It was pointless trying to get all the CPS claim forms and eligibility forms together in the time left—it was simply impossible to sign all their participants up with Centrelink in that time. The solution was that one of Worn Gundidj's administrative staff was seconded to Centrelink for two weeks to work on getting all the required paperwork completed. This person worked with the Centrelink Aboriginal Liaison officer and travelled to the satellites, gathering all the paperwork and bringing it back to the Warrnambool Centrelink office. This response to an administrative crisis was by all accounts very effective, and perhaps occasioned less waste of time and resources than if the changes had been managed over a longer period of time.

By having one of its employees inside Centrelink, Worn Gundidj was able to build a good relationship with two of Centrelink's officers who were charged with looking after the CDEP clients. Furthermore, the people involved in the rush to complete all the paperwork (both from Worn Gundidj and Centrelink) got, by default, an intensive course in what is required to manage data sharing between Centrelink and a CDEP scheme. Worn Gundidj now refers all its Centrelink enquiries to these two Centrelink officers, with whom they are able to communicate at a level of understanding that would not be possible if they were moved from one Centrelink officer to another. Another consequence is that Worn Gundidj is not reliant on the Centrelink Aboriginal Liaison officer, who is at times absent from the office on fieldwork to do with matters unrelated to CDEP. Having two office-based, well informed Centrelink staff to communicate with has meant that data sharing between Centrelink and Worn Gundidj is now a very smooth process, after what must have been a tumultuous initial period. Relations between Worn Gundidj and Centrelink are now described as very good, on/off notices and eligibility forms have 48-hour turn-arounds, and the system is now working as an ongoing process of data sharing rather than as crisis management.

Regional interdependence between Aboriginal organisations and CDEP funding

In south-west Victoria it is apparent that CDEP has made linkages with other Aboriginal organisations that are above and beyond simply providing employment. Diane Smith, in her 1995 study of the Redfern CDEP, shows that this scheme was more than just an employment program, that it had broader social and cultural elements of community development (1995: 12–13). In Western Victoria, we are seeing the beginnings of inter-community development under the auspices of CDEP wages. Indigenous organisations in Victoria are on the verge of a regional, multi-community approach to the management of development dollars. Interdependence is fostered through the use by the satellites of CDEP wages to run administrative positions in Aboriginal co-operatives that have a number of functions, some of which are unrelated to CDEP. It would not be too far-fetched to suggest that the operation of these co-operatives might be severely impaired, if not imperilled, by the loss of their CDEP-funded administrative positions.

Another interesting synergy is the one between ABSTUDY-funded TAFE courses and some of the work programs in Worn Gundidj. If the link between ABSTUDY and CDEP wages were ever to be broken by any form of prohibition on taking up ABSTUDY after being in receipt of CDEP wages, some of Worn Gundidj's core operations would be under threat (they would survive, but in a diminished form). And if a series of funding and function interdependencies develops between Aboriginal organisations across the south-west of Victoria, as it appears to be doing, then a threat to the operations of Worn Gundidj may also pose a threat to the operations of Aboriginal service delivery co-operatives, and a number of Aboriginal-specific training schemes. Aboriginal organisation sets are interlocked in a regional funding puzzle. If any piece of the puzzle were to be withdrawn, there could be serious ramifications for Aboriginal self determination.

Policy implications

The intermeshing, on a regional level, of CDEP schemes with other Aboriginal organisations creates policy implications. The challenge for policy makers is to understand the extent to which a decision regarding one stream of funding for Aboriginal development may affect another. For example, a change in the rules for ABSTUDY that precluded CDEP participants from being in receipt of it could have serious consequences for the operating size and viability of the Worn Gundidj enterprise. And because CDEP wages are used to fund administrative positions in other Aboriginal organisations in the region, any consequences of policy changes to CDEP may be felt across the region, above and beyond the constituency of CDEP participants alone. I am not suggesting that policy makers need to be able to make extra-CDEP decisions, or to go beyond the scope of what they see as their charter in formulating policy for CDEP. Rather, they should recognise that CDEP is more than an employment program, and that it has always had impacts beyond the income and labour force participation of individual participants. Furthermore, those who value CDEP need to be aware of its relationship to other Aboriginal endeavours, and be prepared to have input into the construction of policy for such things as training and education. The policy picture is complex indeed.

Notes

1. I would like to thank the participants and management of Worn Gundidj Aboriginal Co-operative for generously giving of their time and thoughts in support of this research project. In particular I would like to thank John Collier and Max Hall for their support and comments. A fuller version of this paper was published as Madden (2000).

2. CDEP funding stems from ATSIC. However, for the purposes of this paper I make a distinction between non-CDEP ATSIC funding and CDEP funding.

References

Madden, R. 2000. '"If it wasn't for CDEP": A case study of Worn Gundidj CDEP, Victoria', *CAEPR Discussion Paper No. 210*, CAEPR, ANU, Canberra.

Sanders, W. 1993. 'The rise and rise of the CDEP scheme: An Aboriginal "workfare" program in times of persistent unemployment', *CAEPR Discussion Paper No. 54*, CAEPR, ANU, Canberra.

Smith, D.E. 1995. 'Redfern works: The policy and community challenges of an urban CDEP scheme', *CAEPR Discussion Paper No. 99*, CAEPR, ANU, Canberra.

PART IV

COMMUNITY PERSPECTIVES

19. The community game: Aboriginal self definition at the local level

Frances Peters-Little

Introduction

This paper is based on a larger discussion paper (Peters-Little 2000) that I wrote for the Australian Institute of Aboriginal and Torres Strait Islander Studies (AIATSIS). The research I undertook focused on my mother's people, the Uralarai and Kamilaroi people from the north-west of New South Wales. I wanted to raise the question: 'What is an Aboriginal community, what are the boundaries, and how does one identify it?' I had always felt very strongly about the fundamental changes that have taken place in my community since my early childhood and the period I grew up there prior to the 1967 referendum and the introduction of 'government funded' community services.

Although I am an 'out-of-towner' and have lived most of my life in Sydney, I still identify with the north-west of New South Wales, in particular Walgett and Lightning Ridge, as my home and my community. As a Murri living in the inner-city suburbs of Sydney, I was familiar with hearing others talk about 'Redfern' or 'Glebe' or even 'Marrickville' as their Aboriginal community. I remember hearing phrases and even seeing posters sales-pitching 'Community as Unity' at me. This never quite sat right with me. I was particularly interested also in how much government policies and community organisations had impacted upon the shaping of 'who' and 'what' constitutes an Aboriginal community. It had seemed to me that it was the powers-that-be in Canberra that had been deciding who belonged to a community, that were instructing community organisations about who belonged in their communities and what their needs were. Is this problematic? To me, it was fairly evident that it was in my community, for four main reasons:

- most community organisations had boards with representatives from a restricted number of Aboriginal families, and many families were not represented on boards and committees;

- more often than not, the board members on one committee regularly sat on one or more other boards and committees in the town;

- there were fundamental problems and disputes between locals as to who their leaders were; and

- many people clearly felt that definite socio-economic groups had begun to develop in the town over the past 30 years, separating the 'haves' and the 'have-nots'.

I felt inspired by many to promote the idea for Aboriginal communities to redefine and identify themselves in terms of their own leadership, or eldership, for the purposes of a more effective and appropriate form of representation at the local level.

The 2000 discussion paper raises several questions including: 'What constitutes an Aboriginal community?' It examines how some Aboriginal people identify with communities, and explores how these are represented and conceptualised both internally and externally. I hope that this paper is read only as part of a continuing process of debate about community and identity, and to encourage further discussion about how one identifies and determines one's 'community'. The short-term goal of my research was to encourage Aboriginal people to critique what I believe have become romantic and imaginary notions of the Aboriginal 'community', encapsulated by slogans such as 'community as unity'. I wanted also to ask people to consider how recent historical events have impacted upon the development of our communities, and to question just how much of our contemporary notion of who and what the community is, has in fact been shaped by white government policies, and to ask how we should feel about government policies shaping our communities' identities.

My initial intention was to demonstrate and prompt discussion among community workers and researchers. I argue in the 2000 paper that Aboriginal people historically did not passively accommodate new, imposed, and artificial colonial boundaries, and I refer specifically to settlement history in the north-west of New South Wales. But it is clear, nevertheless, that the missions, reserves, and pastoral stations have since become Aboriginal communities that are fundamental to contemporary notions of Aboriginality. Also, while much of our factionalism, and long standing family and language group divisions existed long before self determination policies and community organisations, they nonetheless resurface in the everyday affairs of community organisations.

While my 2000 paper also requested white readers to challenge their desire to search for an 'authentic' Aboriginal cultural identity within the confines of a colonial framework, I also urged Aboriginal people to reject an uneasiness about what could be described as 'an airing of dirty linen', founded in fear of racial retribution from governments. I asked white readers to embrace Aboriginal people's legitimate claim to express their conflicts, internal disputations, and heterogeneity with the purpose of finding appropriate solutions for their concerns. Finally, I hoped to inspire Aboriginal people to develop their own definitions of Aboriginality at their own local level, and to redefine who and what constitutes an Aboriginal community, its identity, and its possible outcomes for a more accurate and appropriate system of self representation.

Elders

I first asked individual elders and leaders who they thought were Aboriginal elders. Today in many Aboriginal communities definitions of who and what elders or leaders are are extremely diverse. The towns of the north-west are no exception. A most typical concern can be summed up by my own elder June Barker from Lightning Ridge who said she thought she had never heard the word 'elder' used so much as she does now: 'These days you hear people call someone who is only 38 or 40 years old, and they call them elders' (Peters-Little 1998b). While there is much controversy over who and what an elder is, I was generally told that an elder was someone of my grandparents' generation and older. As

June Barker points out however, age alone is insufficient. They also have to be people who are perceived to be intelligent by the group.

Leaders

It was clear that many had strong, and various, points of view on who and what a leader was, and how one achieved this status. One comment, made by Aboriginal elder Harry Hall, clearly stated some of the impossible tasks required of Aboriginal leaders and community workers:

> So-called leaders in our communities are just there to answer the questions that the government doesn't want to answer. And those leaders can't win, they can't please blackfellas, they can't please the government. You're enemies with everyone, glory without power. If you had any brains you wouldn't get into the jobs, as window dressers. All the money is taken up by just running the organisations like cars, photocopiers etc. It's just about running the organisations, so they look like they're doing a lot of work but they are spending most of the money on just running the organisation and not the services. So it looks like we are busy doing things, but all we are busy doing is running the organisation. Like I say the glory without the power (Peters-Little 1998a).

Harry Hall, is not alone in his criticism of leadership. In their research for a leadership development program in Indigenous communities, Margaret Cranney and Dale Edwards from AIATSIS found Aboriginal people throughout Australia were frustrated with the ways in which Aboriginal people voluntarily or involuntarily emerged as leaders. The ways in which this happens include:

- someone who is already a 'cultural leader' is groomed or nominated by that community as a leader;

- someone is thrust into the role by peer pressure and expectations;

- someone is seen to be an expert on a subject or issue;

- people are elected to positions within community organisations or as representatives in their local governments;

- someone is perceived as a 'role model', who has gained the respect of the community and qualities of honesty and integrity in accordance to community wishes;

- someone is publicly in the forefront of media promotion;

- governments appoint a person formally or informally as an adviser; and finally

- individuals assert themselves and express opinions in the interest of self promotion (Cranney & Edwards 1998: 15).

There were two main thoughts on the issue of Aboriginal leadership: that Aboriginal people's notions of leadership clash with white concepts of leadership, and that conflict will always arise when Aboriginal people are expected to conform to the latter. Examples of this can be seen in communities like Walgett, where 'experts' in their fields cannot always act in accordance with the wishes of 'natural leaders' or elders, and vice versa. So they are faced with the impossible task of trying to take everyone's interests into account. Who becomes a leader is a highly vexing question, and being one is a laborious task.

Out-of-towners

The large numbers of Aboriginal people who have left Walgett permanently are referred to by some of the locals as 'out-of-towners'. Many of them still have relatives and elders living back home, but were encouraged by their families to leave the mission and the restrictions of small town life. Their reasons for leaving were either to pursue employment, further their education, or to raise their own young families. Although they may have been away from the area for several decades, when asked, 'Where is home?' they still identify their original town—for example Walgett or Lightning Ridge—as home. Many of them had intended to return equipped with their education and employment skills, but some (not usually their own relatives) feel that they need to familiarise themselves with the local situation before contending with local affairs. It is a limited mindset which rejects the skills of the out-of-towners, especially since an extraordinary number of Walgett's out-of-towners have made great achievements and have much to offer their 'home' community.

Self definition

It seems that the term 'community' became popular by the mid 1970s, after the Whitlam government established the Department of Aboriginal Affairs. It was used to help describe the way in which the government distributed funds for welfare programs and delivered services to Aboriginal people. It was seen as the focus which would automatically be culturally appropriate, democratic, and at the same time politically and socially acceptable to the majority of Australians (Smith 1989: 9). Since that time Aboriginal people across Australia have become so good at playing the 'community game' that many have begun to believe in it (Smith 1989: 3). Aboriginal community organisations have become the 'gate-keepers' of the communities they service, and they are somewhat problematic because the prominent and dominant families in the town tend to run them. They are likely to have an advantage over other Aboriginal families and consciously foster the use of the concept of 'community' for their own benefit and to the disadvantage of less powerful language groups and families (Gerritsen 1982: 21).

Since Aboriginal people have survived centuries of oppression and division, it is unrealistic to expect long-term inequities and cultural and political divisions among them to disappear just because they now have government funded organisations which determine their avenues of self determination. It is particularly unrealistic to expect all loyalties to kin and tribes to disappear if structures of 'community' boards are based on Western notions of 'representativeness' (Tatz 1977). The use of the term 'community' without Aboriginal consultation, self analysis and definition has in fact acted as a barrier to self determination, setting communities up for administrative failure, and thus denying Aboriginal people the opportunity to work through the development process, with specialised professional support, and in their own time (Smith 1989: 4).

The relationship between community workers and those who use the services raises questions of equity and privacy, both of which challenge those who idealise 'community as unity' and notions of 'sharing and caring' within Aboriginal communities. Aboriginal people are now not only economically disadvantaged when compared to whites, they are unequal even among themselves. Some families are more financially secure than others, and even within families some members are in a better financial situation than others. These concerns are not specific to and characteristic of the north-west of New South Wales alone. It could be argued that the provision of government funding to community services under the label of 'self determination' is creating further welfare dependency in Aboriginal communities, and widening the socio-economic gap between the people who fund the services, those who work in them, and those who depend upon the services. Many Aboriginal community workers feel that they are being torn between their positions as community workers and the people they service. By servicing their own community (and sometimes even family members) they are being placed in a position where they are actively participating in holding authority over their own families and friends, while relying upon the 'enemy' (government) to fund local self determination programs (these views were expressed by Michael Mansell, see Peters-Little 1987).

Finding a solution to the problem is a far-reaching and complex task. To automatically reject government funds and programs is indeed reckless. It is also naive and neglectful to overlook the tireless efforts of many Aboriginal community workers who are dedicated to Aboriginal self determination. Nevertheless, patterns must be broken if there is going to be a progression towards Aboriginal socio-economic and cultural 'independence', which can only work if its foundation is at a 'community' grass-roots level. I believe that the Aboriginal people of Walgett and the surrounding towns in the north-west can become critical thinkers and leaders towards this vision, for three reasons: Walgett has a long history of political activism; the Aboriginal people form a high proportion of the local population in the area; and there are many professionally skilled Walgett Aboriginal people who currently live and work outside of the town—the out-of-towners.

Conclusion

It is crucial that Aboriginal people themselves identify and define their community, and its distinctive features and history, and that they acknowledge the input they have had in the shaping of their community and identity. I would ask people be fearless in their attempts to raise questions about the impact that white governments and their policies have played in the development of popularised notions of 'community'. I would ask them to examine the cycles and 'rules' of the 'community game' and how it can become a win–win outcome for all Aboriginal people in a particular community.

We need to investigate why there are so many Aboriginal 'suburbs' or 'ghettos' in small rural towns and cities, and why has it become acceptable for poverty-stricken 'black suburbs' across Australia to be viewed romantically as a part of contemporary Aboriginal culture. More importantly I want to highlight the impossible tasks required of community organisations and their workers who are left as the proverbial 'meat in the sandwich'. In the 2000 paper, I hope to have offered a suggestion as to how the resourcefulness of local Aboriginal community organisations can be tapped. In this paper I have tried to address the various 'introduced and artificial boundaries' in our rural Aboriginal towns. I also want to urge these communities to clarify what and who their elders are, to nominate their leaders and their representatives as they see fit, and not as some outside body or policy would have them. And finally I have tried to acknowledge our 'out-of-towners', and to encourage them to take their skills back to their communities, with a view to tackling our internal issues productively and sensitively, bringing light to the myths of the 'community game', so that all players can be in a win–win situation.

References

Cranney, M. and Edwards, D. 1998. *Concept Study into an Aboriginal Indigenous Leadership Development Program*, AIATSIS, Canberra.

Gerritsen, R. 1982. *Blackfella and Whitefella: The Politics of Service Delivery to Remote Aboriginal Communities*, NARU, ANU, Darwin.

Peters-Little, F. 1987. A Collection of Oral History Interviews with Michael Mansell, James Cook University, Townsville, 1987 [edited version put to air as interview on *Radio Redfern*, January 1988].

—— 1998a. A Collection of Oral History Interviews with Harry Hall, Lightning Ridge, 1998.

—— 1998b. A Collection of Oral History Interviews with June Barker, Lightning Ridge, 1998.

—— 2000. 'The community game: Aboriginal self definition at the local level', *AIATSIS Discussion Paper No. 10*, AIATSIS, Canberra.

Smith, B. 1989. *The Concept of Community in Aboriginal Policy and Service Delivery*, North Australia Development Unit, DSS, Darwin.

Tatz, C. 1977. 'Aborigines: Political options and strategies', in R.M. Berndt (ed.), *Aborigines and Change: Australia in the '70s*, AIAS, Canberra.

20. CDEP and the sub-economy: Milking the CDEP cow dry

Phil Bartlett

Background

When I first set about researching material for this paper I searched through extensive reports, reviews, papers, comparisons, and sample budgets—these are CDEP history. For years now strong arguments have been put forward covering almost every angle of CDEP, every convincing argument. These are found in policy papers, analyses of grant conditions, and so on. Apart from these documents we know CDEP has been reviewed, reworked, revamped, changed, enhanced, audited, upgraded, downsized, made to fit, nationalised, regionalised, localised, centralised and decentralised.

What more, then, can be added to the mountain of information that already exists? There is no point in rehashing all the information that is available, explaining the changes, the constraints and the needs. There is no point in repackaging the information to display it with more diplomacy, greater feeling, or force. I do not want to re-tell a well-told story of neglect, retardation, exploitation, lack of funding, lack of training. At the time of writing, another review was taking place to consider vital funding for CDEPs throughout Australia to meet the essential costs of managing this program. No more information is needed, but rather, maybe, an awakening, an honest listening in a way that causes people to hear and to act.

Here are some facts which should be convincing enough to make people hear, to make them see the value of CDEP. First, it has continued as a program for over 20 years. No other initiative like it has survived so long. It provides activities, training and employment to about 33 000 Aboriginal and Islander people throughout Australia. It is far cheaper to run than other government programs that are similar to some degree, such as work for the dole, or Job Network. It has allowed the withdrawal of government services in rural and remote communities and the downsizing of government departments, saving vast amounts of money and allowing the redirection of funding. It provides a community development and infrastructure program and social support programs at isolated locations. These would be expensive for government to establish and support. In one case, the closure by a community of its CDEP led to the collapse of an entire regional network of community organisations and outstations. Without CDEP it was impossible to cover operational costs—vehicles, communications, maintenance, wages, infrastructure, power, and water supply.

Is CDEP worth funding? I would answer, 'yes'. Is there justification for additional operational costs? Again I would answer, 'yes'. Will government provide the money needed to support CDEP? Who knows. If CDEP is wiped out is there anything else to replace it in the diverse locations and circumstances in which it exists? The answer to that is, 'no'.

The main objective of CDEP—and other expectations

The 23-year path that CDEP has travelled down has been a long and hard one. Today the objective of the CDEP program, as defined in the Spicer Review and adopted by ATSIC is:

To provide work for unemployed [Aboriginal and Torres Strait Islander] persons in community managed activities which assist the individual in acquiring skills which benefit the community develop business enterprises and/or lead to unsubsidised employment (Spicer 1997).

Most CDEP organisations would accept this as the CDEP objective. However, other stakeholders have other objectives which place high expectations and demands on CDEP organisations:

- Centrelink uses CDEP as their unpaid agent to manage the unemployed in locations where others cannot;

- the Federal government sees CDEP as an opportunity to remove 33 000 people from the unemployment figures;

- DEWRSB views CDEP as an avenue to get employment outcomes at a far cheaper rate than from other contractors;

- ATSIC sees CDEP as a way of supporting other community based programs and funded positions that cannot be funded to needed levels;

- business projects see CDEP as a source of subsidised wages where no other avenue exists;

- Job Network agencies use CDEP as a place to park long-term unemployed Aboriginal and Islander people because their success with Intensive Assistance clients is limited;

- State governments (not all) view CDEP as a way to get out of the establishment of expensive community infrastructure and services program in isolated communities;

- local government gains cheap community services and a cheap labour pool.

The list could go on, but it is already sufficient to make clear that other stakeholders make great demands on CDEP and often enlist the support of ATSIC Grant Conditions to do so.

CDEP is a bit like the milking cow that is relied on to deliver nourishment. Initially in the early days of CDEP the cow was fat—it was well fed with only a small number of supply points.

Then as time went by the 'food supply' for the cow was depleted because of the drying up of government funding in other areas that enhanced or supported the CDEP program. However the demand for milk is now far greater. So the cow is now not only badly fed, but has many supply points.

Figure 20.1   The fat CDEP 'cow', as she was

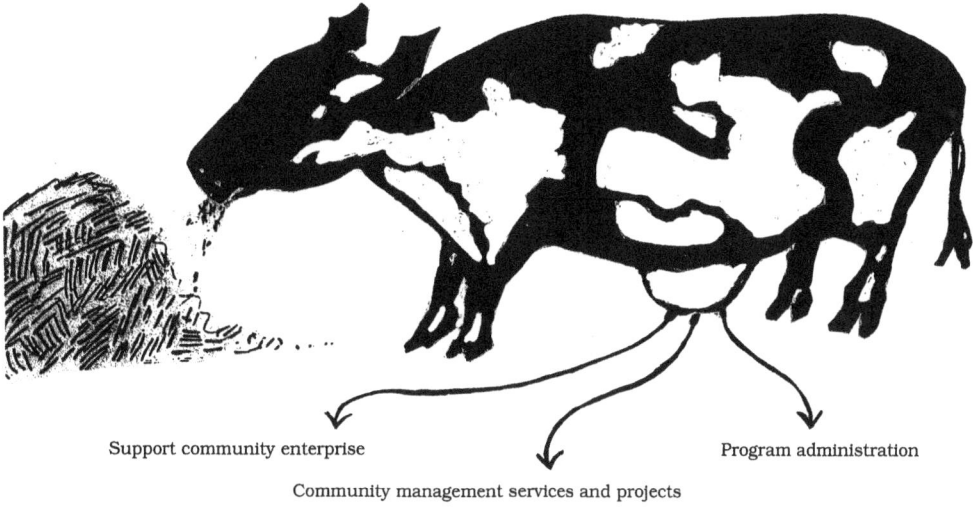

Support community enterprise

Community management services and projects

Program administration

Figure 20.2   The starved CDEP 'cow', as she is now

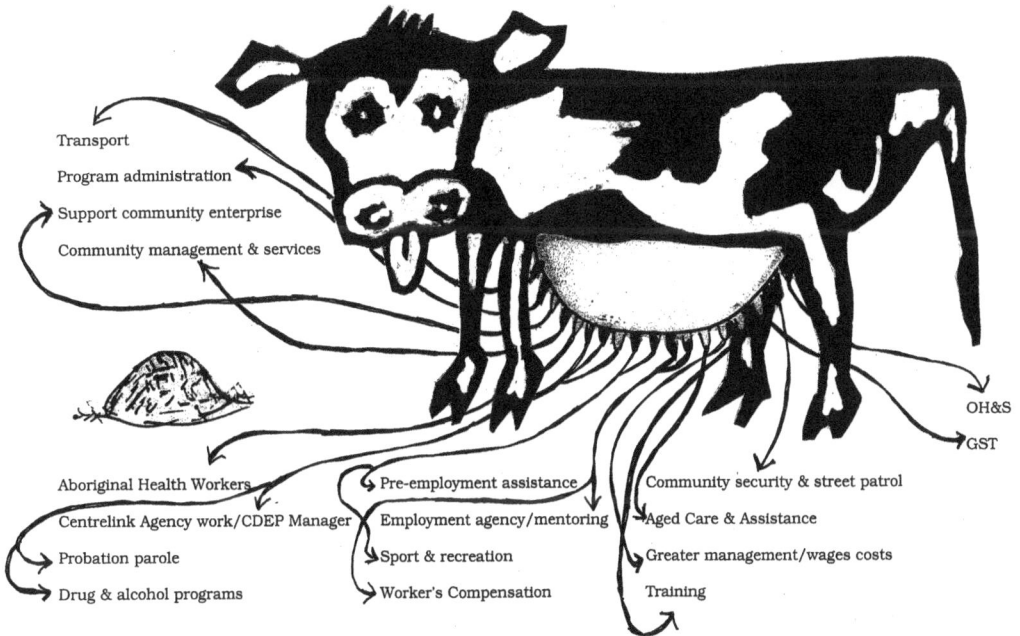

Transport

Program administration

Support community enterprise

Community management & services

OH&S

GST

Aboriginal Health Workers

Centrelink Agency work/CDEP Manager

Probation parole

Drug & alcohol programs

Pre-employment assistance

Employment agency/mentoring

Sport & recreation

Worker's Compensation

Community security & street patrol

Aged Care & Assistance

Greater management/wages costs

Training

CDEP: A sub-economy that excludes

I am not arguing that CDEP is worthless or a waste of time and that it should be scrapped. It has been the most stable and reliable program that has supported the Aboriginal economy. However, CDEP operates within a mindset that continues to exist in Australia, that determines where Aboriginal people and their organisations fit within the Australian economy and society.

This mindset views Aboriginal people and their organisations as customers of those engaged in business or service provision. This same mindset excludes Aboriginal people as business owners, proprietors, service providers. It sees them as welfare recipients rather than as dispensers of welfare programs and unemployed non-taxpayers.

Aboriginal people have been excluded from many things in Australian life so it would be surprising if it were different with regard to business and economic prosperity. My own experience has taught me this. I am 43 years of age and have always lived knowing that I am Aboriginal. I have been ever reminded of this fact by many events throughout my life that highlight the exclusion mindset.

- Early in life at school, playing cricket in the playground, I was not excluded from the game—that would be unfair or 'un-Australian'. However, although I was entitled to field the ball and even bowl, if I took a wicket the batsman would not be out. That was exclusion in the year 1964.

- When the latest Sting-Ray bike landed in our town the local supplier wanted to promote it to the kids. A group of boys gathered near his shop and all were given a test drive on the bike. I was not allowed to ride the bike because I might steal it. That was exclusion in the year 1968.

- When my family moved to live in the city my mother had to find rental accommodation through real estate agents. On the phone things always sounded promising but when we arrived with the deposit the houses were no longer available. That was exclusion in the years 1970 to 1972.

- When I left high school I eagerly sought work and went to many interviews. The employers were very positive over the phone and I would sometimes spend hours preparing and travelling for the interview, only to be told that the job was filled when I arrived. A subsequent phone call would reveal that the position was still available. That was exclusion in the years 1972 to 1973.

- When I turned of the age where you might like to drink a beer, I would often arrive at a pub only to be told: 'We don't serve Aboriginal people in this hotel. You have to drink in the black bar.' That was exclusion in the year 1975.

- When I joined the workforce I was well accepted as one of the workers and got on well with others. That was until I began to be promoted to positions of authority and all of a sudden others found it hard to accept an Aboriginal boss.

That would have been exclusion if I had bent to the pressure and rebellion. That was in the years 1980 to 1992.

- For the last seven years I have been working for Aboriginal corporations, managing CDEP and other development programs. My present organisation is involved in employment and training. Job Network agencies can earn up to $10 000 per client to do what we are doing for $2000 per client. This is exclusion, in the year 2001.

- Work for the dole projects get between $4000 to $6000 to do far less than we do for $2800. This is exclusion, in the year 2001.

- Centrelink will only do work in handling welfare clients if it gets paid to do so. Our CDEP organisation has these extra duties added to their Grant Conditions and gets no explanation or training, let alone any money. This is exclusion, in the year 2001.

- Our CDEP organisations are determined as employers for industrial relations purposes, and bear all the legal obligations and costs. Our CDEP participants work for $350 per fortnight, and when a national or State wage increase is approved to ensure Australian workers get a fair deal and are not living in poverty our CDEP participants do not get the increase. They have to work less hours to fit within the hourly rates of pay. This is exclusion, in the year 2001.

These examples are not presented as some sort of a political statement but rather to make clear the mindset that needs to be broken if Aboriginal people are to become real players and participants in the greater Australian economy. The events I have mentioned are just a small sample of typical events in the lives of Aboriginal people. The existence of an exclusion mentality has perpetuated a view that Aboriginal people and their organisations are the customers, or welfare recipients, and not credible participants in business. To involve Aboriginal people in economic and business side of Australian life we need to exclude the exclusion mentality. We need to fix the inequities that are present, and change the mindset.

The process of milking the CDEP cow dry has taken place over many years. It has not happened through drastic cuts nor by cancelling the program, but by demanding more and more of the program and the community managers of CDEP while at the same time not allowing CDEP to receive the same financial rewards as other agencies involved in management of welfare and community services.

What can we do about it?

I began by stating that all that needs to be said on CDEP has been said. In addition to detailed representations to ATSIC on a wide variety of issues, problems and policy matters by CDEP working groups, there were five national CDEP conferences in the year 2000, two State meetings in the 18 months up to the end of 2000, and three regional conferences. There is more than enough information to make some good decisions for the future good of all stakeholders involved in CDEP.

We now need action instead of talk, at national and regional levels, from ATSIC, DEWRSB, State Departments of Training, Centrelink, and DFACS. CDEP workers and those outside who are supporters of CDEP must give these and other relevant agencies a clear message. We must tell them that the major program in the development of Aboriginal people, that has existed for 23 years providing community development, employment, training, community services and mainstream employment, is starving to death, and that despite the unlimited numbers of papers, reports, reviews and conferences nobody is listening.

We must tell them that more and more expectations are being placed on the CDEP scheme, not through the fair payment for service provision but through non-negotiated Grant Conditions that bind us to the unworkable. There is a continuing inequity in Australia— a sub-economy that constitutes separate development, with far fewer resources than the mainstream economy. Inequality is entrenched, and institutionalised. Nelson Mandela could define this situation in just one word.

References

Spicer, I. 1997. *Independent Review of the Community Development Employment Projects (CDEP) Scheme* [The Spicer Review], Office of Public Affairs, ATSIC, Canberra.

21. Measuring expropriation: Enumeration of opportunity costs imposed on the remote community of Burringurrah, Western Australia

Dan Kean

Development of the economic base necessary for social empowerment requires four factors operating in unison: land, labour, capital, and knowledge. This paper sketches how European settlement in the Gascoyne pastoral region expropriated Aboriginal people from these means of production, how the dispossessed people returned to their lands and implemented development using their knowledge and a capital contribution from the State, and why this development is under threat from the imposition of bureaucratic decisions on the CDEP system. Finally it proposes that the opportunity costs of curtailing this development must be enumerated in order to support arguments in favour of continuing a workable CDEP program.

The Burringurrah Wajarri are the northernmost band of the Wajarri language speakers of the Yamatji nations. They enjoy custodianship of the lands surrounding Burringurrah, the largest rock in the world, named Mt Augustus by the Europeans and measured at over twice the size of Uluru. Springs under their care were the last source of water in the event of severe drought. Burringurrah provided refuge for stricken Yamatji throughout the region at such times. Rock engravings, cultural sites, and lore concerning Mt Augustus survive as reminders of the times before the European invasion.

Brutal land grabs in the Gascoyne from 1880 until 1910 expropriated their traditional lands. Outright killing and massacre and the rounding up and detention of other resisters and victims on the Bernier and Dorre Island VD–Leprosy concentration camps smashed all resistance. Survivors were then permitted to live on their ancestral lands under the European's terms—those of slavery.

Labour was expropriated by this slavery. If anyone doubts that a system of slavery existed they should consider the facts. Runaways, 'cheeky' recalcitrants, or those that refused to labour faced death, jail, or beating at the hands of the police, unofficially sanctioned posses, or overseers (who were often of mixed race, a feature common to many slave regimes). People were given meagre rations and families were punished through the withholding of rations if they bucked the system.

Prominent members of Western Australia's squattocracy owned stations on the Gascoyne and built their wealth on this system. In the 1950s this peaked at a pound sterling for a pound of wool. Most Gascoyne properties were shearing 15 000 to 30 000 head at the time. This expropriated wealth was available for investment in the minerals boom of the 1960s.

The 1967 referendum and the wage determinations of the 1960s resulted in the Yamatji families being thrown off the stations. They ended up as fringe dwellers in the regional towns of Meekatharra and Carnarvon. Knowledge, in the form of caring for each other in strong kinship groups and immutable (unbreakable) relationship to country, was the only thing left to them.

In 1987 there was a return to country by the families descended from the traditional custodians of the Burringurrah Wajarri. They took over the Mt James lease near the ancestral seat of Mt Augustus to escape the social problems of the fringe camps. Everyone lived in bough shelters and used their own funds and labour to survive. ATSIC finally invested heavily in the town, providing housing, power, water sewerage, an airstrip, and sealed roads after 1994. Now we have a fairly well set up town, and maintain our community using the CDEP program. Infrastructure and services that come within the sphere of State Government—health, education, additional housing, and law and order—remain inadequate.

ATSIC's investments might be seen as a form of mutual obligation or compensation by European Australia for the expropriation of land and labour and its manifestations—the very obvious and embarrassing social and economic deprivation suffered by Aboriginal people as a result. Now these services, reliant primary on CDEP, are under threat by those attacking ATSIC programs and demanding 'job outcomes', 'mutual obligation' and accountability. This economic-rationalist zeal for 'making them work' is strongly reminiscent of the ideologically driven activities of the missionaries, and even of labour organisers of the 1960s, who 'knew what was best' and did not listen, or pay attention to the consequences.

Policy makers removed from everyday life demand enumeration of job outcomes and mutual obligations. The CDEPManager computer system counts how many days the CDEP participants work. Even if hunting or social activity is included, as foreshadowed by the McClure Report (1997), how do you measure it and put it on a form? People going shooting on the spur of the moment or sitting on the veranda solving a family problem with Aunty are hardly going to write it down. We have a 'no work, no pay' policy, but take 'notional activity' into account when doing timesheets. It is pretty obvious who is putting in and who is not. We have a good mix of families in the office and among supervisors, so there are checks and balances on kinship obligations.

CDEP is being drawn into the mutual obligation matrix and is losing its thrust as a community program. This will make the program increasingly irrelevant to participants. They will lose ownership, and the forms and bureaucracy will make CDEP participation as onerous as being on Centrelink. Our workers will vote with their feet. Our funding base will shrink as our participant numbers decline. It is doubtful if the town's administration could continue without the core CDEP funding, and our organisation groans under additional bureaucratic imposts.

The bureaucrats—and academics—do not take into account how CDEPs are saving government organs in terms of opportunity costs. An example that springs to mind is the spread of CDEPs across northern Australia. Without CDEP, the coast would be empty and open to poachers, as well as harder for tourists to access, for example at Kakadu. The defence forces used these populations extensively during World War II. 'Populate or perish' justified post-war migration, but most arrivals settled in urban and regional areas. The continent would contain huge swathes of unoccupied land if it were not for the Aboriginal populations.

We are saving the government a lot of money on CDEP. The following is a partial list of our cost-saving activities.

- 250 members of fairly dysfunctional families are away from Meekatharra and Carnarvon with savings to the cost of social services, the education system, health, patrolling, justice, housing, fixing vandalism, and other such things that marginalised people impose on communities.

- The community by and large polices itself. Little police time is spent in Burringurrah.

- There are savings to the justice system, with less incarceration and the community's willingness to accept and supervise Community Service Orders, parolees and juveniles. Everyone by and large keeps out of trouble on the community.

- The Shire, with a population of only 400, receives substantial funds because of the 250 residents of Burringarrah, through the $80 000 that is received yearly for public roads.

- By using rangers and labour resident on the community, the recently expanded National Parks in the Gascoyne rangelands will make cost savings.

- Our intellectual property in the promotion of the Burringurrah story around Mt Augustus, and the increasing profile of Burringarrah Artists who are becoming a tourist attraction, promotes regional development in an area that has few prospects now that pastoralism has declined.

- We save Centrelink a lot of time and stress by acting as a go-between for welfare recipients, and taking 100 people off their books and onto the CDEP system. We recently audited ourselves and spent three hours a day liaising with Centrelink on issues outside the CDEP Management process.

- We rescue tourists and respond to other State Emergency Services call-outs, such as tracking lost walkers and car rollovers.

- The community provides a health clinic, swimming pool, and upgraded Telecom facilities to a poorly serviced region, to the benefit of surrounding pastoralists, kangaroo shooters and passing tourists, and service employees.

- CDEP enables the control of feral animals, the culling of kangaroo populations and other matters to do with looking after country such as fire regimes and control.

- CDEP resources the State government responsibility for water, power, sewerage, and environmental health.

- CDEP provides teacher's aides and ancillary staff to the school.

- CDEP provides the postal service.

- The only all-weather airstrip in the district is maintained by CDEP.

- The community store is supported by CDEP and is the only fuel outlet for 300 kilometres.

The scale of these activities is only possible with CDEP. My fear is we cannot enumerate this. CAEPR should extend its research into enumerating these opportunity costs to strengthen our arguments. ATSIC should redouble its efforts to see that community organisations are paid for the services they perform. The Public Affairs Unit should direct a massive publicity campaign highlighting the CDEP scheme to 'mainstream' Australia on our behalf.

The Department of Finance cannot be allowed to get away with the clawbacks that happen every year. The threat of a nationwide withdrawal from CDEP and return to welfare for a month is a tool that would show the present government's poverty of imagination and spirit, and it would only harm the politicians and bureaucrats. The National Working Group should be supported, and we should be prepared to go all the way if we cannot bring the appropriate government investment into our people and organisations through negotiation.

We have unrecognised skills, or intellectual capital, when it comes to dealing with our societies and our land. Give us our investment; let us use our social skills to bring our labour force up to scratch and give us the necessary rights to native title. Then and only then is there any realistic chance of development.

22. A part of the local economy: Junjuwa Community/Bunuba Inc., Western Australia

Rowena Mouda

In the Kimberley, we practice our law and culture right through the year. Our elders are very well respected and play a big part in decision making in the Fitzroy Valley.

Junjuwa Community receives funding from ATSIC for two programs. One is the Community Housing and Infrastructure program, and the other is CDEP. Junjuwa is further supported by the collection of contributions from the participants, or 'chuck-ins' as we call them. For example all CDEP participants have to chuck in from their CDEP wages for fuel and stores for their outstations, to help develop their communities. This is necessary because the money that we get from ATSIC is not enough to fund us right through the year. Therefore, because communities want to get their outstations developed, the community members chuck in for their fuel to get to and from their outstations.

In addition to looking after Junjuwa Community, Junjuwa looks after six outstations with the funding it receives from ATSIC. One of these is town-based, and there are five others out between 50 and 100 kilometres from Fitzroy Crossing, on dirt tracks that get closed during the wet season.

There are over 1000 CDEP positions in Fitzroy Crossing and outlying communities. This means that CDEP alone brings in just under $14 million each year to Fitzroy Valley. It is estimated that a total of $20 million in government funding is directed towards the Aboriginal communities in the area, so CDEP funding is a huge contribution to the economy of the area. Fitzroy Valley is very dependent on CDEP: if it were not for the 1000 CDEP positions, the official unemployment rate of Fitzroy Crossing would easily exceed 50 per cent.

As a community, Junjuwa has been in existence for 25 years. Its main purpose has been to provide housing and accommodation to Aboriginal people who have been relocated to the Fitzroy Crossing area. At Junjuwa, CDEP is used to deliver social services in the community. It provides services to youth and the old age pensioners, money management, construction training, office skills development, meals on wheels, and community administration. It also provides housing maintenance and construction to the community infrastructure. Some of our projects would be defined as self motivated or self supporting community service enterprises. Examples of such enterprises are the occasional care program—that is a CDEP-supported project that the women have asked for in our community—the housing and accommodation service, and meals on wheels.

CDEP gives the push needed to establish and maintain these programs, generating a high employment level that would be impossible otherwise. There is a social benefit from CDEP in communities like Junjuwa. Work projects in the community enhance the community, and there is also support for the administration of the community.

Participation in the CDEP is voluntary, but Junjuwa has set minimum hours that must be performed to obtain the full CDEP wage. CDEP encourages people to work together. Whereas social security payments are made to individuals, CDEP on-cost payments are made to groups. This encourages people to join together in family groups, to work together. Some family groups are in the process of establishing outstations, which takes some pressure off our town community housing, as well as giving people the opportunity to develop on their homelands. These smaller groups can join together under an umbrella group like Junjuwa, which creates the optimum size for achieving the best economies of scale. Pooling resources in this way allows for major capital projects to be undertaken.

It is not intended that CDEP be used to develop subsidised enterprises to compete with existing mainstream businesses. This goes against the CDEP spirit. However, where CDEP can be used to enhance an individual's skills, so that they may obtain unsubsidised employment, that is another matter. There is a potential for businesses to enter partnerships with Junjuwa, so that Junjuwa provides subsidy wages for the businesses, and the businesses provide skills, work experience and employment for the participants. For example we have a company called Leedal which has ownership of the local pub in Fitzroy Crossing, and the local supermarket. Junjuwa owns 40 per cent of Leedal. Indeed the long-term survival of the community hinges on developing partnerships with small businesses, industries, and government organisations, which will lead to a greater participation by Aboriginal people in the non-welfare sectors of the local economy. These partnerships can extend beyond wage subsidy to joint ventures in major projects.

Junjuwa has recently undertaken a major restructuring process, to establish a more stable community management structure. This will result in an emphasis on extended family groups as the foundation of the Bunuba language group. The community itself, as a place, is still known as Junjuwa, but from November 2000 our administrative and economic arm has been known as Bunuba Inc., that is by the name of the language group. Each family group will have permanent representation on the Bunuba Inc. Council. The long-term ambition for this community is, essentially, to establish a long-term economy, with sustainable social and commercial enterprises. Bunuba Inc. has the potential to achieve a high degree of economic independence. The community is aware of the many hurdles that it needs to overcome to achieve this, and initiatives have commenced to address some of these.

We see the health and success of Bunuba Inc. as being totally linked with the health and success of the economy of the wider Fitzroy Valley community. So we believe that it is in our interests to work together and support each other for our mutual benefit. With open communication, mutual encouragement and support we, as a united community, can achieve a more sustainable future for the Fitzroy Crossing area.

23. Self determination and CDEP: Tjurma Homelands Council, South Australia

Katalin Mindszenty

I would like to put Tjurma's situation in the context of self determination. Tjurma is a small, remote homelands community in the Musgrave Ranges, 500 kilometres south-east of Alice Springs. The community members want to keep a traditional homelands lifestyle. Most of our people are artists, and they also have other skills, which they put to full use. We have 45 people on our CDEP program. Prior to my arrival there had been about six or seven CDEP managers who came and went because of the uncertain situation and the local politics of the time. We have built up our CDEP from nothing, and hopefully the next move is to build up the homelands, which have been eroded.

To be viable, the homelands lifestyle requires a communications system, which means telephones at all the homelands. It requires access to transport, and it requires commitment by those who administer the funds, and also by people like myself, who are on the ground, working. It requires a commitment to teach the people any skills that we have as workers in the field so that they can take over on their own behalf. Putting this into practice, teaching the communications skills—and also to learning them—this is what self determination involves.

Self determination means, in part, 'giving the people a chance to give'. It is not just taking, but acknowledging and appreciating those gifts given in sharing their culture, knowledge and wisdom. That means we have to listen, it means we have to hone our communication skills, to sit down and take the time to understand what people who are from a different culture are saying.

People in Tjurma Homelands have to be empowered with resources, management skills, and money management skills. They face all the problems that prevail on the Anangu Pitjantjatjara Lands—substance abuse problems, and all sorts of other social issues, such as parenting, income levels, lack of opportunity for higher income levels and skills enhancement. These are all big problems, and perhaps bigger because of the remoteness of the community.

Tjurma Homelands is Honey Ant Dreaming. We operate from Amata. The Tjurma people are the people who have come from the Anangu Pitjantjatara Lands, and they are the traditional owners. There has been talk of merging with Amata, starting with our art centre. The Tjurma people do not want to merge with Amata, which is a larger community with a lot of problems. They want to keep their homelands lifestyle.

We have turned our art centre back into a community centre where everyone is welcome, not just artists. We are going to put back the kitchen for the aged, so people can work with other people coming and going, in the way that they are used to. Most of our people, and most of our councillors, are artists, for example Vera Bryan is a painter and Muna Kulyuru, is a batik artist. They are incredibly gifted in so many ways, and art is one of these. It is impressive that these talented artists are also active in community affairs.

24. Job creation and 'mutual obligation': Tapatjatjaka Community Government Council, Northern Territory

Harry Scott

My comments are directed at the policy makers. I want to challenge the notions of job creation and mutual obligation. Titjikala is 120 kilometres south of Alice Springs, in central Australia. It has a community of between 275 and 290 people, distributed between the main community of Titjikala and four or five outstations. We have 90 people on our CDEP program. We are at the limit, and we do not have, and probably do not intend to have, any jobs for them.

I will first list the various jobs that we do at Titjikala that are focused on service delivery for government organisations. We have CDEP people working in the administration, doing the work of local government, collecting rubbish for the council, and doing other local council work. We provide a vehicle to take patients in and out of town for appointments, to help out Territory Health. We manage the whole postal delivery service at Titjikala and the outstations. We provide assistance to the Education Department in the classrooms. We run our own night patrol, in the absence of a police presence. We organise the paperwork for births, deaths and marriages in the community. We deliver the aged-care program. We deliver the Jobs, Education and Training program for the creche. We provide the interface with Centrelink, and we do some work for Transport and Works.

The community budget is some $3.5 million. Of that, 68 per cent comes from ATSIC. CDEP funding is 42 per cent of that 68 per cent. In a remote community environment it is unrealistic to attempt to meet any of the 'outcomes' related to the concept of starting people on CDEP, moving them into top-up arrangements and then into full-time work. The only employment available is there because of government department funding. The closest connection with the 'real' economy in a lot of remote communities, including ours, is with the nearest major city, in this case Alice Springs. There are many diverse organisations, activities and enterprises possible under CDEP, but there needs to be a clear delineation for remote CDEP communities. They exist in part to ease the embarrassment of the unemployment rate but, more importantly, they exist because the local people are determined to build their community, and to protect their culture, their language, and their families.

We have people who work far in excess of the hours that are allowed under the rules, and they work because of the community. They work because of their families. The whole concept of mutual obligation is really a white-man's concept. As in the case in a lot of remote communities, for 93 per cent of the people at Titjikala, English is a second language. They have a significant and well-founded distrust of any white person coming onto the community because of what they have experienced. I can say only that I am sorry to have heard about it, and can only offer apologies for the degradation and insults, rapes, shootings and abuses that they have had to put up with. So when we get some fantastic gentlemen in suits coming in to tell us about a magnificent one-year program that is going to create employment, it is a long way from reality.

I would like to give an idea of some of the things that remote communities need. We are hamstrung by the rules that government places on ATSIC, in terms of the wage rates. We need some flexibility, to be able to acknowledge the extra work that various people in the community put in. I would strongly urge that the government acknowledge the benefit that they receive from the CDEP program, and consciously pay a CDEP remote rate greater than the unemployment rate.

The concept of 'one in, all in' should be supported in remote communities. CDEP is not about employment. CDEP is about community development. If anything is to come out of CDEP in terms of employment we have to start with community development. There is no mainstream employment, and the only real prospect for employment comes from enterprises. The biggest danger there is that the whitefella comes in and gets all excited and sets up an enterprise, then the whitefella leaves, and it all goes back down again.

CDEP on the remote communities is about self determination. It's about people establishing their own culture. We talk very freely about jobs, about work, about enterprise activities, and we carry a lot of cultural assumptions under those terms. We tend to forget that the Indigenous people had a very well organised economy—and an exceptionally well organised community. They had never experienced anything like the Protestant work ethic, they had no concept at all of nine-to-five work. They do what needs to be done, in the minimum time that it takes to do it. They are probably one of the most efficient groups of people that you could ever meet. They refuse to organise for something three weeks in advance; they organise it just before it is necessary.

We need to put the concept of community development back in front of the concept of employment for CDEP. Any employment that will come out of a remote community will only come because the Indigenous people have developed their community to a point where an enterprise would be able to subsist. What is more, any remote community that wants to seriously look at enterprise really has to address a three-year planning program, which requires a three-year funding program.

Finally, there should be an effort to stop stripping programs and dollars out of ATSIC. That little list of things given earlier is simply one of the service delivery areas that we do for government. There are a lot of other areas that CDEP is involved in, and we are hamstrung because when we go to ATSIC for funds we find that they just do not have the money. The training budget should be pulled out of DEWRSB and put back into ATSIC. Many of the programs which have been stripped from ATSIC need to go back in there.

25. Regional development and CDEP: Tjuwanpa Outstation Resource Centre, Northern Territory

John Nicholas

My topic is regional development. I want to put forward the proposition that within States and Territories where there are regions or sub-regions that are marginal economically, the CDEP has at least the potential to become important to State and Territory governments in terms of actually putting regional development policy on the ground.

The Northern Territory government has created a document called *Foundations for the Future*. And I am told by senior Northern Territory public servants that their jobs will basically be accounted according to how they succeed in laying those foundations. One of those foundations is regional development, and that is an important plank of that particular set of policies. A second one that they all say is extremely important is Aboriginal economic and social development. That this is important to the Northern Territory government is hardly surprising when you consider that, at the 1996 Census, 24 per cent of the Territory's population were Aboriginal and Torres Strait Islanders, and that proportion is more or less represented in the electorate. Perhaps this is an advantage that Aboriginal people in other part of Australia do not have.

For both of these policies, the Northern Territory government, and perhaps this applies to other governments as well, will find it very difficult to get their runs on the board without CDEP. Because in many of the areas that they are looking at in terms of regional development, it is CDEP that has the potential to be, and is, the engine of development.

We at Tjuwanpa have seen this as an opportunity to move towards practical results. Our committee has defined itself in terms of a region that covers the language and country associated with the Western Arranda people. This region of about 25 000 square kilometres has three local government organisations: one at Wallace Rockhole, one at Hermannsburg—or Ntaria—and one out at Areyonga. It has three CDEPs: one at Wallace Rockhole, one at Ntaria, and the last is Tjuwanpa, near Ntaria. We are the outstation resource centre rather than a local government organisation, although we have local government functions. In the region there are two gas fields and a pipeline, and there are busy gazetted roads, full of tourists going to King's Canyon, Glen Helen, and Palm Valley. There are the 40 outstations and about 300 kilometres of outstation roads. The region is fairly well defined geographically by ranges of mountains and a valley as well as being culturally bounded to the extent it is largely Western Arranda country.

We wanted to see if we could develop what happened in our organisation with regard to men who have an interest in yellow machinery—our roads and earth-moving gang. We have been talking to the Northern Territory government's Transport and Works Department not only with regard to what we need to do to look after our own roads, but also to get contracts for gazetted roads in the region. In order to do that we had to work with the government in terms of the two planks of government policy outlined above. We were told to talk about regional development: 'Talk regional, and we'll listen. Talk on your own and we won't.' The second plank, of course, was Aboriginal development policy. So we negotiated with the Northern Territory government, and have reached the point where the Minister has made an offer along the lines that if we come up with some sort of memorandum of understanding between the three CDEPs and the Areyonga community— an agreement between those four organisations which combines their skills and pools their machinery—and come back with a firm proposal, then they will give us what is called a Certificate of Expediency for as much roads maintenance work as we want on those hundreds of kilometres of gazetted roads. So in that way we were able to fit in with local regional development policy, to start thinking a bit regionally and co-operating in order to align ourselves with government policy, so that we could get the work.

We have just finished the first round of negotiations between those three CDEPs and Areyonga. It has gone well, and we all seem to be thinking together. We now need to go back, draw up the formal plan, and then put the proposal. We have also pretty well secured an offer from DEWRSB to provide us with a full-time dirt boss and trainer, whose job it will be to ensure that the quality of accredited training and dirt management is such that we can fulfil those bits of the contract that we choose to build on.

I can make a more general point from this local example. There is a potential for people to think a little bit sideways, about how CDEP can fit in with other things that governments do. If State and Territory governments have policies that CDEP can help to fulfil, then think hard about how to go for it. Because if you help them, they will help you. The Northern Territory government could not do this sort of thing without CDEP, and it would be nice if the Federal government realised that.

26. Catering for mobility and diversity: Bawinanga Aboriginal Corporation CDEP, Northern Territory

Rupert Manners

We have a large CDEP at Bawinanga, with about 350 people on outstations and 160 in Maningrida itself. As a result we probably see a lot of the problems which are found generally in CDEP schemes. The CDEP is a very multifaceted organisation: it is income support to some people, it is work to other people, to some of the other organisations in the community it is wages subsidy, and it is long-term employment for a lot of people. We should accept that this is the situation and we should not try to push CDEP in ways that it is not designed to go.

People are very mobile in the Maningrida area. They move to and from the outstations and Maningrida. Sometimes they work in the conventional way, and at other times they move out to their outstations and occupy themselves with hunting and gathering. We need a system which provides adequate rewards for the variety of activities people are engaged in. CDEP as it was originally run did not do that, so in Maningrida we are proposing to put in place a three-tiered system. People who are living on their outstations would get paid for 3.6 hours a day; those who are working in town, when they do the standard sort of morning, would get paid for 4.6 hours a day; and those who were sitting down would get paid for 2 hours a day, basically just to keep them going. Within that framework too, if people wanted to work full-time we would try to find them full-time work within one of our ongoing projects, or on one of the projects which the other agencies in Maningrida are running.

This framework suits the local people because it caters for mobility. At one time they might be at ceremony, and so they would get their 3.6 hours. Then they might come back and do some work for a while and they would get the 4.6 hours. Then they might take a break for some reason, and they would get the 2 hours. The outstation people like the concept because it means that people are encouraged to go out bush and look after their country. The town people like the concept because they get a better payment for working and get a reward for their effort. The only people who probably dislike it are those who are sitting down.

The framework gives people choice. We should not be telling people what to do, we should rather be giving them a choice as to what they want to do. If they have the choice between living out bush or working in town, then they can make their choice and get the rewards for that activity.

There is a risk for the CDEP organisation in running a program like this because if we ended up with 350 people on the outstations and 150 people all working like Trojans on 4.6 hours, we would not get funded enough by ATSIC to cover the bill. That is one reason why the $20.00 that is distributed to CDEP workers through Centrelink should actually be distributed by CDEP organisations, so that we can use it to provide top-ups. The CDEP in a place like Maningrida needs to be seen as a giant labour pool for everybody to draw on, and the businesses which are subsidised through CDEP wages should use those subsidies to create more enterprises, as we ourselves have done. That would provide a much fairer and equitable system for running CDEP within the context of a place like Maningrida.

27. Resourcing CDEP: The case of East Gippsland Aboriginal CDEP Co-operative, Victoria

Lionel Dukakis

I want to start off with a point, probably a political one, that was raised by my brother John Martin from Goulburn Valley CDEP. Victoria does not get the same recognition as the rest of Australia. For example it was said that the Chair of ATSIC would never come from Victoria because we were not black enough, or had no culture. So all credit to Geoff Clarke, he has done a great job. I am not saying that our needs are greater or less than those of our brothers and sisters in other parts of Australia. I just wanted to make that point that Victoria has the same problems—social, economic, housing, health and unemployment—as the rest of Australia.

I would like to concentrate here on the positive things that we are doing down in Bairnsdale. I am not so much focused on the negative things. Many of those are brought upon us—they are negative in that sense.

We are a CDEP with 97 participants from a wide range of age groups. We are 300 kilometres east of Melbourne, in a rural situation. In a range of about 200 kilometres there are three CDEP organisations working very well. About 50 of our participants work on CDEP within the organisation in administrative roles, and within the co-operative. I myself am on CDEP, because we do not have that money for administration from ATSIC. They only fund the CEO, and a couple of other things. It is not a bad thing to be on CDEP in itself, but if someone in my position has to go on CDEP then it is depriving someone less fortunate, who needs to acquire skills, of the chance to go on CDEP.

It has been reiterated time and time again that Aboriginal organisations have to use CDEP for administrative staff because the funding is being milked. Phil Bartlett's paper in this volume (Ch. 20) provides an excellent chronology of what is happening to CDEP generally.

We are a registered building company with three building crews, and we tender on the open market for contracts. We won a tender for the Aboriginal Housing Board of Victoria, which we are in the process of completing. The sad thing is that we are being scrutinised so much by the bureaucrats above us because we are blackfellas doing a job. That is very frustrating.

We also have a fencing crew who are working flat out. They have tendered and won quotes, and are actually knocking back work. We have 39 houses with East Gippsland Aboriginal Co-operative, and we do the maintenance work for the Co-operative. We have women's programs, including sewing, and practical skills around the home such as budgeting, cooking, and parenting.

As an ATSIC Councillor for the Binjirru region of Victoria I find it very frustrating that we could do more things and employ more people, if we had the resources. We have a waiting list of 70. One thing that we as Councillors have got to do is push our Commissioners to get those resources down our way. We are not an isolated instance, this is probably the case right across Australia. Some people put CDEP down, but there are people out there who can't wait to get on CDEP to get some skills.

In summary, the sooner the bureaucrats realise that the participants *are* the CDEP, and let them do things the way they think they should be done, the better things will be. Equity is a key issue. Equity is only a word to us Aboriginal and Torres Strait Islander people of today. What we get feels more like exclusion. We want the bureaucrats to make the change from a word, to reality for our people. I would like to think the concerns expressed in this volume will be looked at seriously, and actions taken for a better CDEP scheme. I would not like to think that my children, grandchildren, or great-grandchildren will have to sit down in the future talking about the same issues.

Although I have been critical of ATSIC, I am not pinpointing the staff. I know that in Victoria ATSIC is under-resourced, and the structure of the organisation has hurt their State office. I do not know if this is true throughout Australia, but certainly the morale of the staff in ATSIC in Victoria State office is so bad that we cannot get the full use of our support staff.

We have to think of the positive things that CDEPs are doing around Australia and go with them, but we should not forget the negative things. Hopefully in years to come the many positive things that we are doing, to better our people and to give our children a better future, will come to fruition.

28. Adequate funding as a question of equity: Lake Tyers Aboriginal Trust CDEP, Victoria

Siva Nalliah

The CDEP program is vital for the life of the Lake Tyers community. We have 73 participants in our community program. In 1998–99 the program was suspended for nine months, and we saw a marked increase in domestic violence, alcohol-related violence, and a general unrest in the community. This is also reflected in the police statistics. On the recommencement of the CDEP program we saw a marked decline in most of these social problems.

However, there are numerous inequities in the way that the CDEP program operates. Many of these arise from the heavy burden that is placed on CDEP programs by other essential services, namely Commonwealth and the local government services. We are in a remote community, so we are responsible for the municipal services, including garbage collection, road and path maintenance, sewerage pond maintenance, and water distribution. But we are not adequately funded, so we have to rely on CDEP participants to perform all these services. Most of the CDEP participants who deliver the services have gone through all the accredited training programs that are available. Unfortunately we cannot pay them award wages. If the CDEP participants who provide the services in our community went 35 kilometres to Lakes Entrance and provided the same labour, they would be paid about 300 per cent of what we pay them. And the irony is that Lake Tyers pays council rates and water rates, but we receive no service from the Shire. That is the reality.

The Commonwealth funds us to run a health clinic, and also after-hours patient transport services. Because we are in a remote area, there is no public transport. There are very few private vehicles available to transport patients. So we run a transport service 24 hours a day, seven days a week. Now what does the Commonwealth government give us? They give us money to buy two vehicles—and wages a for part-time driver. I cannot comprehend their logic. They give us capital money for two vehicles, but recurrent funding is only for a part-time driver. Our medical driver has got the First Aid Certificate, but I still pay him minimum wages. If he worked at Lakes Entrance, he would get a much higher income. Because we have inadequate funding, I ask CDEP participants to work the weekday night-shift, from five in the evening till seven o'clock in the morning, for $20. On Saturday and Sunday they get $50 per day, for a 24-hour shift. That is the reality. They do not even fund us for administration.

We run a day-care centre. There are three CDEP participants who are completing a two-year course. They will be getting their certificates shortly, but I cannot put them on permanency or full award. Because we have no funding. So they will complete their two-year course—and come back to CDEP wages. As an accountant, I am happy to keep them on CDEP wages because then I cannot be sued. Because, fortunately, CDEP wages do not have an award. So I can afford to pay them the minimum, even though they are qualified, and delivering the same service as qualified staff. That is another reality.

In addition to these commercial services we also provide social and welfare programs. We provide aged-care services and we provide meals on wheels to the elders. For the latter we are paid the grand sum of $1.10 for each meal delivered. It is possible to run the service only because we use CDEP staff to prepare the meals, we use the CDEP buildings, and we use the CDEP staff to transport them. We also provide the home care and home maintenance. All this is done by CDEP participants.

We have been successful in moving into income-generating activities. We have started a plant nursery. There are 15 participants in that, all of them undergoing accredited training. Training is delivered on-site, where the trainers sit and work with the participants. There is no classroom training, they work with the participants, and it has been very effective. Within the last three months we have sold about 40 000 seedlings, and we are really targeting to expand. We have also received some grants for revegetation projects. But the bottom line is whether this can be independently run and commercially viable. I have my doubts. We do not have the economies of scale to run a commercially independent operation.

We have started the production of pallets. We buy and saw the timber, and then we market those pallets. We have been reasonably successful, we have sold between $20 000 and $30 000-worth of pallets, but the enterprise cannot be commercially viable. We have to rely on, fall back on, CDEP subsidy that provides wages, electricity and everything. To be commercially viable, we would have to look at alternative arrangements like capital input, where we would be funded so that we could buy into already operating businesses, or network with other CDEP schemes and pool our resources to acquire businesses. We are too small to run a commercially viable business independently. There were a lot of incentives given for us to employ permanent staff out of the CDEP. I transferred four CDEP participants into full-time work, and at the end of the 26th week I took them back to CDEP. I had no money to pay them full-time wages. We do not generate that kind of money.

29. Supporting employment inside and outside the community: Woorabinda CDEP, Queensland

Elizabeth Young

Woorabinda is a community situated 200 kilometres south-west of Rockhampton, with a population of around about 1000 people. The largest group in the population is children up to 15 years old. The average age of death five or 10 years ago was 46 years of age, and it is probably lower now. The land at Woorabinda is in the form of a Deed of Grant in Trust lease. The community is situated near the Mimosa Creek and is surrounded by the Woorabinda property, an area of 40 000 acres.

Within this community there are a number of organisations and government agencies that operate, along with the local council, for the benefit of the whole community. Woorabinda CDEP is a public limited company that serves the community in a number of ways. We have 191 people employed in the Woorabinda Community Development Program, with the majority of those working within Woorabinda itself. This includes participants who are provided with the standard two days of employment and others who receive top-up wages on a regular basis. About 50 participants are employed outside of the community, mostly in Rockhampton or the surrounding areas such as Mt Morgan, Yeppoon, and Benaraby. At the moment Woorabinda CDEP is in the process of a name change to the Capricornia CDEP Ltd. This reflects the growth of our CDEP, which re-commenced in April 1997 with 101 participants.

Woorabinda CDEP operates in two ways. There is the normal CDEP operation where participants are supervised directly by supervisors and team leaders in their daily tasks. Then there are participants working with other organisations, companies, or government agencies outside the community, whose work is set by the host employers. This second option gives participants the opportunity to work in mainstream society. The normal CDEP operation in Woorabinda, which is a relatively closed and remote community, places less importance on improving work ethics. This is not only because of limited job opportunities but also takes account of the historical facts of the forced removal of Aboriginal people from traditional lands, and the destruction of Aboriginal societies throughout the State of Queensland.

In our community many of our people have a bleak outlook for the future. Lack of education, and alcohol and health problems are fairly well prevalent. There is still a welfare mentality in the community, and so there is a need to question whether CDEPs in remote communities should be regarded only as a stepping stone to mainstream society. If they are, this leaves a problem. In our case for example, if someone wanted to leave Woorabinda and make the move to Rockhampton there is no support system in place for them. As a result, people just become another statistic in areas such as the prison system, suicide, and unemployment. And for young girls the only way out is to have more babies to sustain a larger income. We have been working for the past three and a half years since the recommencement of the CDEP to bring about changes in attitudes, with some success. Unfortunately, again due to lack of jobs within the community, some of the success stories have been forced to leave Woorabinda.

Things have been made more difficult because of the poor financial situation of the past and present councils. Woorabinda CDEP has at present over 20 activities. These can be separated into two groups—basically the profitable and the non-profitable. The latter are administered directly by the Woorabinda CDEP Ltd, and the profitable activities come out under a subsidiary company called Yoogarnunni Yakah. This was set up to protect the not-for-profit status of Woorabinda CDEP Ltd.

We employ 12 workers in our administration activities. The positions include coordinator, assistant coordinators, accountant, administrative workers, newsletter editor and work supervisors. We are building an extension to our office, which finally will give everyone their own workplace. In the community care program there are a number of sub-activities. These include workers in a retail store, butcher's shop, women's shelter, aged care, primary and high schools, Woorabinda Council, and the Black Boy youth facility. In all more than $200 000 in CDEP wages is a direct saving to the Woorabinda Council. Other activities of benefit to the community are in the health areas, where we have workers in the health clinics, Health and Community Care buildings, and the hospital. A sewing group produces curtains for community members.

We have an active workforce in land care. Work performed includes the mowing of private yards, for which we charge a fee of about $20.00, through to the maintenance of public areas, airports and cemeteries, at no charge to the local council. Pastoral and fencing activities include the provision of a yard-fencing service which provides low-cost timber and chain-wire fences. Other crews carry out contract work, mainly for the Woorabinda pastoral company, but also for local property owners.

Our masonry plant produces masonry blocks which have been tested and meet Australian standards. These have been used in our office extensions and in a number of small jobs within the community. The wood products activity produces timber, tables, chairs, beds and other furniture items that are sent to Rockhampton for sale through our retail outlet, Murri Arts and Crafts. Aboriginal and Islander paintings and artefacts are also sold along with other lines through this shop.

Another activity of vital importance to our operation is that of the security workers who carry out a night patrol to minimise damage and loss to CDEP property. Our Undoonoo hardware store, which operates out of Woorabinda, is part of the 'Key Hardware' chain. It is well supported by community members as well as the nearby Duaringa shire, and government agencies. Locals are carrying out repairs and maintenance to the council-owned houses in which they live, because of the service we now provide.

We have people working for Woorabinda Pastoral Company, at Foley Vale, one of their properties near Duaringa. All types of fencing and cattle work are undertaken there by our workers. In Rockhampton we have a number of workers in a large range of different activities. These include the Christian Outreach Centre, Fitzroy Shire Council's Brothers Club Darumbul, and Darumbul youth services. We also have workers at local vehicle repairers, the Dreamtime Centre, and the university.

In conclusion I would note that large amounts are being spent to try and fix the problem of Indigenous unemployment, but nothing much seems to come of it. It must be understood there is a need to spend more at the grassroots level, with easier access to funding and less money being chewed up by bureaucracy and consultants.

30. Creating opportunities for training and employment: Tharawal Local Aboriginal Land Council CDEP, Western Sydney

Wendy Ann Lewis

Tharawal Land Council, along with five other organisations, took on the CDEP approximately nine years ago. Our aim was to create opportunities for training and employment for Aboriginal people. We have grown with that CDEP program, but we are going to be discussing whether or not we continue it. This is not because it has not been successful, but because a bureaucratic stranglehold has been put on something that was really for communities to develop and evolve—their CDEP program to suit their needs, and their aspirations. Those are different things, but they can be woven into one to create real benefits for Aboriginal people, no matter what community they live in and whatever that community's circumstances might be.

We have had our battles with ATSIC staff, we have had our battles with some elected people. We have our own elected representative on ATSIC Regional Council who goes to bat for us, but when the voting comes he has to leave the room. So he is of no direct benefit to us when funding is being allocated. We work on a policy where the Land Council's business is set by the members, and the CDEP carries out and works with them and their program to achieve the wishes of the Land Council. The other four organisations that I mentioned abdicated their responsibility to the programs seven or eight years ago. We are prepared to put outreach stations with them if they are prepared to acknowledge that the participants have a say in the direction of the type of work and the type of training that they do.

We are very big on training. We have a partnership with TAFE, which provides us with additional equipment and particularly with very good skills and a TAFE place for the supervisor, who is the teacher. We also have people attending university. We have people attending courses that have got nothing to do with our programs, because that is what they want to do. And all of our programs have been successful. One of the girls in the office recently got a job at University of Western Sydney because she has been doing her BA in social welfare. She is now working at that university and has achieved a real job. We will not be putting in for the $2000 exit payment with DEWRSB, because the form is a terrible little thing that would involve a lot of time and effort, and we do not have the time. And from what I have heard, another organisation that did put in claims only got 12 out of 39. We placed 35 people last year in real jobs, and we have a turnover in participants. People stay for nine months on average, and the longest we have had a participant in CDEP is four years.

Our management changes as well. I took leave from TAFE to work for the CDEP as the coordinator when someone left in a hurry. I then left TAFE to stay on there, and I see my role in the next year or so as moving on. We have developed people as well. Our bookkeeper is almost a trained accountant, and she was originally a CDEP participant. Our new bookkeeper in training will be running our hospitality area and our conferencing. She has got six bookings for conferences in 2001, which will cost $60 000 to put on. We will probably make $2000 on each conference, so that's about $12 000 profit for us in that year.

So we have now got the year's planner up, and it's really good because things start to move. But we are still going to have the debate about whether we continue. What we have to do is say to DEWRSB and ATSIC, and to Centrelink: 'You are not going to load us with any more work.' We as Aboriginal people are entitled to the same health, welfare, education and housing as every other Australian. We pay the same taxes, including GST—our programs are now paying that as well, and we used to be exempt. We are entitled to those services, and just because we use the CDEP to provide a service to our community, does not allow government agencies to abdicate their responsibility for providing them.

That is the philosophy we have taken on board. We tendered on the market with everyone else to do the meals on wheels delivery, and we were successful. Through that we got some more equipment for our CDEP, which is totally under-resourced with respect to its capital budget. We tendered to Homecare to mow the lawns, just of the Aboriginal clients at first. We did it so well that we were asked to tender for the mainstream. We got that, so we now do 120 lawns a month.

We have moved to the position now that we are in business, and if you want our services then we are like every other business person, we are going to tender. We are going to invoice you, and you are going to pay us. Because before we had expectations put on us: 'Oh can you go and do Mrs So-and-so's lawn …' Homecare are paid to mow her lawn, they get the funding for it, so now we tender. We have also been asked to now tender for Veterans' Affairs because Homecare, who pay for the lawns, have tendered to take on Veterans' Affairs. So they've rung us to say: 'Could you handle another 30 or 40 lawns?' Of course we can, but we will tender, and they will pay. We are not going to run out and suddenly start mowing lawns now for nothing. We cannot even get our own lawns done at our premises because we are so busy with these things!

We continue to want to have control of the CDEP and keep it in the hands of the people that the program belongs to. The exclusion of women—and men—on sole parent, old age pension and disability pensions from the dollar for dollar has debarred around 40 people from our program, and that is something that really needs to be addressed.

We run alcohol-free, and have a no work, no pay rule. However, we are compassionate. We do hear grievances. The participants make the rules, and therefore it always goes back to them. I just administer what the participants say. However I do get my say at a Land Council meeting. Because I am a member I can say something there, as a community member. So we wear different hats through the day.

This leads to the point I will conclude with, just one of the problems that we have faced. The thing that has made our CDEP a success is the thousands and thousands of hours that are put in voluntarily by the members of the Land Council, by our office bearers—we don't call them the executive—and by the committee people of the CDEP. We are accountable, we have no problem with dealing with accountability. Once again, Aboriginal people are doing voluntary work to set up a program and keep it going. There is no pay for this, and none of us expect it. But the expectation on us is that we can just keep doing those voluntary hours, and there comes a time when we are physically exhausted. We want to achieve things and we are running out of time. We have reached the point where we're going to say, 'enough's enough'.

31. Using the system to our advantage: Redfern Aboriginal Corporation CDEP, Sydney

Bruce Loomes

The topic I want to address is networking, playing the system, and being strong together. Redfern is an urban CDEP in the centre of Sydney. It is a small CDEP with about 80 participants and an annual turnover of about 200 per cent. Our people come from all over Sydney, and some of them commute for an hour and a half to get to work. The CAEPR report by Diane Smith (1995) showed that the people in Redfern suffer as great if not greater levels of poverty than the people around Alice Springs. We have a mix of community goals, of community development and economic development. We have been going just over three years in our present form; just over three years ago we were suspended with massive debts. We have come out of that, worked our way out of it.

We have got three businesses going, providing training and employment for our people. The first of these is a construction company that turned over $3 million in the last two years, through playing the system. We have accreditation to run our own training for apprentices and trainees. We are now starting joint ventures with Tharawal CDEP in Western Sydney (see Lewis, Ch. 30, this volume). We do town planning out in the general market.

We have a cruise boat on the harbour, which we bought out of project-generated income, by being smart. We have got a screen-printing and sewing department that produced $60 000-worth of goods for the 2000 Olympics. We have recently shipped off $6000-worth of goods, bought by the Italian Consulate, to the trade fair at Milan in Italy.

It is really a case of being smart. Government bodies talk about self determination, self management, about triennial funding, but these things are not being put into practice. Every area interprets government policy in a different way. A lot of the staff we are dealing with are straight out of university, are Gubbas (non-Indigenous people), have no experience of culture, and no experience of business. We had 12 project officers in the first 18 months after we started up again. One of those was there for nine months.

In my 15 years around CDEPs, whether in a rural, semi-urban, or urban environment, I've never come across a surplus. The push for demanding that surpluses be returned, and for certificates of compliance to be able to spend any surplus over $5000, makes it impossible to run business enterprises. How do you run a business if you have no cash flow, if you have to spend all of your budget by the end of the financial year, and if you cannot get triennial funding? We had a case where we had to renew over $5000-worth of equipment on the boat and we had a cruise running two days later. Spending at the end of the financial year often goes on things that are not a priority, and then you have no cash flow when you have a breakdown, or if a business opportunity comes up at the start of the financial year.

You need to be able to make instant responses to run a business. The whole talk of 'mutual obligation' is going in two directions at the same time. It seems as if some of the government organisations are trying to say: 'Well, for the sake of the public we want you to go towards enterprise and employment, but on the other hand we want you to be a welfare organisation, because we are not going to let you spend the money that the participants have earned.'

It is a case of using money cleverly. We try to do this as much as we can. We try to network as much as we can. There has been some discussion about losing participants through losing dollar for dollar. Some of our people decide to stay on, earning just under the cut-off point. So they keep their pension benefits and at the same time they are getting an income each week. It is a matter of playing the system.

Marketing support is another important issue. I have probably visited 100 CDEPs over the years, and a lot of them produce great stuff that would really meet the market. But like all of us, they have no money, often have no support. It is worth considering the idea of starting to network to put together forms of marketing on a regional basis for CDEPs. Good enterprises flop because of a lack of marketing. But if we are smart, and work together, we can start to deal with marketing.

It is like the situation with the $2000 payment for getting people into full-time employment. Unless people get together and support each other, it is not going to work. At the last count, we had 48 per cent of people on full-time wages, on award wages. We put numerous people out into the workforce, but we do not have the money to chase up on that payment. We have people dying every second week, we have people overdosing every week, we have 350 000 needles put onto the block in a year, on top of all the other social problems. The only way CDEP can work is if we all get together and be strong, and start to network and learn from each other how to play the system well.

References

Smith, D.E. 1995. 'Redfern works: The policy and community challenges of an urban CDEP scheme', *CAEPR Discussion Paper No. 99*, CAEPR, ANU, Canberra.

32. CDEP: A journey not a destination

Stephen Humphries

Perth Employment and Enterprise Development Aboriginal Corporation

There are two different organisations involved in providing employment and enterprise support within the Perth Metropolitan area, through the use of the CDEP. First there is the Perth Employment and Enterprise Development Aboriginal Corporation (PEEDAC), which was incorporated on 6 July 1997, and is run by an elected 20-member management committee. The PEEDAC management and members are all representatives from the five ATSIC Perth Regional Councils, which are classified as wards. The wards are Bibra in the inner-southern suburbs, Gnangara in the northern suburbs, Walunga in the north-western suburbs, Wungong in the southern suburbs and Yunderup, which encompasses the Peel–Mandurah areas.

The Perth ATSIC office decided that PEEDAC should have a company that ran the business side of the organisation, and in 1997 it started the company which is now called Peedac Pty. Ltd. PEEDAC's chief role is to provide policy guidance to the Peedac Board of Directors and continued development of CDEP. PEEDAC is also the sole shareholder in Peedac Pty. Ltd., but does not have any direct input into the day-to-day operation of the company's enterprises and projects.

Peedac Pty. Ltd.

The second organisation, therefore, is Peedac Pty. Ltd., which is an incorporated body under the corporations law and is directly funded by ATSIC to administer the CDEP to the Perth Metropolitan Region. Peedac Pty. Ltd. is governed by a Board of Directors and is solely responsible for the day-to-day management of its participants, projects and contracts. It actively pursues employment, training, and enterprise development opportunities. Peedac is a company limited by shares. The capital of the company is $1 million, divided into one million shares. It is solely owned by PEEDAC, the Aboriginal Corporation.

Peedac Pty. Ltd. currently administers a total of 510 CDEP positions, for an area containing approximately 19 000 Aboriginal people. Income that is generated from its enterprises goes directly back into the Perth Aboriginal community, through the incorporated body, to provide and enhance employment opportunities. The general aims of Peedac are to establish or purchase enterprises, provide job placement in private businesses or companies, provide training placements, provide part- and full-time employment, support community-based commercial joint ventures, and strive for economic independence.

The development of business enterprises to provide employment for CDEP participants is the prime focus for Peedac Pty. Ltd. Commercially viable Aboriginal business is seen as a foundation of economic independence for participants. To achieve that goal Peedac will continue to examine all business opportunities that are presented and where possible assist the person presenting the idea to access the relevant government assistance. Where appropriate, Peedac may enter into a joint venture partnership with mainstream or Aboriginal enterprises.

Presently, Peedac Pty. Ltd. operates a number of independent business units throughout the suburbs of Perth, from its central headquarters at Cannington. The enterprises currently provide approximately 60 full-time employment positions for the Perth Indigenous community, and between 50 and 60 part-time positions and numerous work experience positions. Each business site is structured to accommodate apprenticeships and traineeships which provide a solid training foundation for Indigenous persons moving through the program. Peedac actively pursues New Apprenticeships for participants by developing relationships with Registered Training Organisations and Group Training Companies.

Peedac Pty. Ltd. enterprises

Some of the enterprises include:

- Boola Wongin Nursery (native retail nursery) at Forrestdale;

- Bundi Art & Ceramics (production and design) at Bayswater;

- Karlarak Screenprinting & Graphics (production and design) at Bayswater;

- Midvale Upholstery (new and used) at Midvale;

- Armadale Monumental & Fabrications at Armadale;

- Shapecraft Automotives (mechanical workshop) at Rockingham;

- APEEL Clothing (manufacture and design) at Rockingham;

- Classic Resprays (automotive spray painting) at Maddington;

- Panel Beating Workshop at Malaga;

- Peedac Distributors (wholesale distribution) at Wangara; and

- four local and State government contracts (commercial mowing and maintenance), Metropolitan-wide.

The company continues to work actively with other government bodies to assist some members to buy their work projects as a franchise for later. This makes it possible for them to own their own business, which will increase their and their family's financial security. The company is able to share its management experience, administration and skills to help other Perth-based Aboriginal communities develop new commercial enterprises, so their long-term business enterprises are planned around their families and communities.

Company vision

Peedac Pty. Ltd. is the business partner for government and industry, for Indigenous people, to help meet their equal employment opportunity obligations. We provide practical work skills, employment opportunities and enterprise development for Perth's Indigenous community.

Aims and objectives

The aims and objectives of the company are the creation of new job opportunities for Aboriginal people within the Perth ATSIC Nyungah Region, the creation of Aboriginal enterprises, and increasing training opportunities linked to regional economic and employment opportunities.

Mission

Peedac Pty. Ltd. is committed to:

- promotion of Indigenous culture within the Perth Metropolitan region;

- providing, opportunities, choice, security and self esteem;

- ensuring a balance of enterprise and employment opportunities for both men and women; and

- encouraging initiative, innovation and team work, from within a safe, learning environment.

Values

Peedac participants and staff are committed to:

- understanding and respecting diversity in the workplace;

- empowerment, self respect, and the rights of individuals;

- honesty, integrity and accountability; and

- loyal, tolerance, harmony and compassion.

Participants are aware that the CDEP is not a destination but a journey to full-time, unsubsidised employment.

> Only with a spirit of goodwill and co-operation will more people in the new millennium reap the rewards from participation and being involved (Neil O'Donnell, Managing Director, Peedac Pty. Ltd.).

Postscript

Tim Rowse

In Chapter 9 Terry Whitby poses the question: 'Who represents CDEP?' He gives an all-inclusive answer: 'Everybody represents CDEP'. Yet, competing representations of, or descriptions of, CDEP emerge from this volume, and the resulting diversity makes it a very interesting document. In this Postscript I want to put the emphasis on 'competing'. The conference on which this book is based, like Parliament or the Press, was a political arena in which people tried out different ways of describing CDEP. Those exchanges of competing representations of CDEP made the conference a political process.

In the current political climate, or in any political climate, there are approved and unapproved ways of stating needs. One of the things that self determination policy is about is teaching Indigenous Australians 'correct' and 'incorrect' ways of stating their needs. Some will be rewarded with funding, others will be punished by a lack of funding, and the applicants will be sent back to rewrite their submission. So there is, in self determination policy, a politics of representation—an effort to teach the Indigenous person be a certain kind of political being who articulates Indigenous needs in a language that agrees with the available frameworks approved by the government of the day. The deployment of those frameworks, and the opposition to them from others, were very evident throughout the conference, and are reflected in these pages.

Here is an example. One of the dominant themes in the main government approach to thinking about CDEP at the moment, is to emphasise that there are some kinds of outcome that are more 'real' than others; and 'real' means 'more valued'. To quote Terry Whitby again: 'While the CDEP continues to demonstrate successful social, economic, and community development outcomes, the ATSIC Board does not see it as a substitute for real employment.' So there is something called real employment—but Terry does not define it. Peter Shergold (Ch. 8) emphasises that the best possible outcome for CDEP is to graduate people into what he calls 'private sector employment' which he appears to define very narrowly as employment to which government makes no possible contribution. This is his notion of 'real' employment.

In the language of some of my colleagues at CAEPR I have noticed the appearance of the jargon now employed by Noel Pearson. He talks about the 'real economy'—a term that is very poorly defined in his work, and that researchers would do well not to adopt uncritically. This is a debate that is going on within CAEPR—a friendly debate, I might add. For example, in Chapter 11 John Taylor and Boyd Hunter do not make a distinction between CDEP and other kinds of employment. Their overall analysis is based on the premise that participation in CDEP is no less 'real' than any other kind of employment, and that the way to raise Indigenous employment in Australia could therefore include putting a lot of resources into CDEP.

There is nothing that is necessarily second-best about CDEP, and yet this distinction between real and unreal jobs and outcomes puts CDEP and its proponents on the defensive, as if what they are doing is not good enough unless it leads to participants finding employment in the 'real' economy. The language of the 'real economy' is terribly tendentious, and it should be questioned, not accepted as an unchallengeable description of the 'facts'.

I now turn to a brief summary of some of the main themes that came from the contributions by the community representatives. People were very concerned about equity with another program—that is, 'work for the dole'. If that is getting a certain amount of government support, why should CDEP not receive similar support? Community sector contributors clearly want equity with some programs in the mainstream welfare field.

A second and even more important theme, that is elaborated in almost all of the community contributions, is that CDEP must be recognised for having multiple objectives. It is not just a matter of graduating people into the so-called 'real economy'. CDEP has many objectives, and they should be recognised and properly resourced. This makes it difficult to provide a succinct definition of what CDEP is all about, and it makes it easy for the media to misrepresent CDEP as if it were a one-dimensional program. The struggle for the recognition of the multiple objectives of CDEP is very important.

Another theme that comes through from the community representatives is a plea for a more respectful engagement with CDEP schemes from other government agencies and other programs. This respect takes many forms, but it includes dollars: when CDEP is doing a job it should be properly paid for.

The final theme that I want to highlight is that the CDEP managers and leaders are starting to network on a national basis, as a self conscious political lobby group. This is a very positive development, and the reader of Part IV of this volume cannot fail to be impressed by the consistency and the persuasiveness of the words of people who are obviously amongst the leading activists in that lobby.

At the moment CDEP is in both a strong and a weak position. It is in a very strong position in a practical sense, in that, as a number of contributors point out, if the government decided that the CDEP had to go, what would they put in its place? CDEP is doing so many necessary jobs, in so many different ways, in so many places, that it is quite entrenched in the Australian system of government. It may not be getting the recognition it deserves, but it is going to be very hard to get rid of it. So in this practical sense, CDEP is in a very strong bargaining position.

But CDEP is in a weak position in terms of the politics of representation. That is, the CDEP managers find it difficult to articulate an account of what they think CDEP is. What they are actually doing is not well described by the dominant message about CDEP that comes from the government—that CDEP is a failure if it does not graduate people into mainstream jobs. That is a very strong message coming out of government today, and it is very evident in Peter Shergold's contribution. His remarks and remarks by other people from government, including some from ATSIC, are part of the process of redefining CDEP so that it is all about employment.

CDEP is practically strong but theoretically—or ideologically—a bit weak, in the sense that it is very difficult to get out from underneath the government's representation of CDEP, and to articulate an independent community-based conception of what CDEP is all about. The potential for articulating a community-based view obviously exists, because there are so many community representatives saying the same things, over and over again.

CAEPR could play a good role by helping the CDEP leaders to consolidate, to make persuasive arguments for and to back up with facts the kind of things that they are saying in this volume. CAEPR can help to formulate political and cultural rationales that CDEP managers can present to government, backed by solid research.

The interaction, in my opinion, would also be very good for CAEPR. One of the strengths—but also one of the weaknesses—of CAEPR is its very close proximity to the central agencies of government. That is of great benefit to CAEPR in many ways, but it is also a fault that should be balanced by more exposure to the views and concerns of the people who are delivering services at the community level.

There is a worry that we must not be seen to be other than neutral academics, but it is very hard to identify the neutral ground in this debate. The language and categories of government or the language and categories of the CDEP managers are all that is available. We have to use somebody's language, so we must make some self conscious choices about what kind of language and frameworks of analysis we use in our future research.

Index

A

abbreviations, xiii–xv
Aboriginal and Torres Strait Islander
  Peoples Training Advisory Council
  (ATSIPTAC), 109–10
Aborigines
  elders, 188–9
  exclusion, 196–7
  leaders, 189–90
  organisations & CDEP funding, 182
  out-of-towners, 190
  self definition, 187–92
ABSTUDY, 180
acronyms, xiii–xv
Altman, Jon, 125–33, 243
ANU
  conference on Indigenous Welfare
    Economy & the CDEP scheme, iii
  RAI project, iii
  relationship to CAEPR, iii
Arthur, Bill, 135–41, 243
assimilation, definition, iv
ATSIC
  administrative culture, 44
  CDEP authority, 44
  expenditure on CDEP, 14
  financial services, case studies, 83–91
  IEP responsibility, 70
  monitoring of CDEP, 78
  Office of Evaluation and Audit (OEA)
    definitions of work, 39
    survey of coordinators, 40
  principles for welfare reform, 6
  relationship to CAEPR, iii
  review of CDEP scheme, 13
  role in combating racism issues, 8
  support for CDEP, 75–7
  support for mutual obligation, 8
  see also Spicer Review
Austin-Broos, Diane, 167–75, 243

Australian National Training Authority
  Research Advisory Council
  (ANTARAC), 109–10

B

banking *see* financial services
Bartlett, Phil, 193–98, 243
Bawinanga Aboriginal Corporation,
  211–2
Broos *see* Austin-Broos
Burringurrah, costs imposed, 199–202
Butler, Brian, 5–9, 243

C

Campbell, Shirley, 109–21, 243
Canada, financial services for
  Indigenous people, 87, 91
Canadian Royal Commission on
  Aboriginal Peoples (CRCAP), 16
Central Australia, financial services,
  83–4
Centre for Aboriginal Economic Policy
  Research (CAEPR), iii
  research monograph series, 247–8
  research project, 55
  tenth anniversary conference, iii
  views on social costs, 16–17
Centrelink
  access difficulties, 6, 68
  administration of CDEP, 49
  financial services, case studies, 83–91
  participants, 70–1
  registration of CDEP
  relations with CDEP, 181
  WFTD, 44
Committee on Economic, Social and
  Cultural Rights (CESCR), 14
  targeted assistance, 16

Commonwealth Grants Commission (CGC), exclusion of Indigenous peoples, 5

communities
Community Participation agreements, v
community perspectives, 187–229
control of programs & policy, 9
development in the welfare context, 31–6
leaders, 189–90
out-of-towners, 190
political dimensions of development, 39–46
research projects, 55–7
self definition, 187–229
see also individual communities

Community Development Employment Projects (CDEP) scheme
ABSTUDY, 180
administration, 49
application of *Workplace Relations Act*, 43
ATSIC's desired outcomes, 76
careers in Torres Strait, 135–41
community concept & development, 33–6, 187–229
comparison with TANF, 54, 62–3
comparison with WFTD, 42–4
costs & expenditure, 14–15, 39, 43, 7–9
  de facto financial services, 84–5
  see also economic issues
definitions of work, 39–40
demographic challenges, 95–107
description, 12, 15, 77
economic issues, 126–7, 193–8
employment, moves to employment, 70–2
industrial democracy, 40
industrial relations aspects, 45
inequities, 13
mutual obligation, 31–3
objectives, 194
observations, 26–7, 196

origins, 1–2, 11, 41
outcomes, 39
outstation movement, 168–72
overviews, 5–50
participant motivation, 40
performance monitoring, 78
policy perspectives & issues, 53–121
  broad policy context, 14–17
  policy history, 47–8
political dimensions, 39–41
progress over twenty years, 47–50
reform *see individual heading*
regional studies, 123–84
relations with Centrelink, 181
results of case studies of successful projects, 60–1
role as government provider, 15
satellites, 179–80
social costs, 16–17
support for cultural aspects, 15
targeted assistance, 16
training by doing, 109–21
urban CDEP, 225–6, 227–9
see also Bawinanga Aboriginal Corporation
see also Burringurrah
see also East Gippsland Aboriginal CDEP Co-operative
see also HREOC Review
see also Junjuwa Community
see also Kuranda
see also Lake Tyers Aboriginal Trust
see also Perth CDEP
see also Port Augusta
see also Redfern Aboriginal Corporation
see also Spicer Review
see also Tapatjatjaka Community Government Council
see also Tharawal Local Aboriginal Land Council
see also Tjurma Homelands Council
see also Woorabinda
see also Worn Gundidj

see also Yuendumu

conference, iii
  aim, 1
  participation, 1–2
Corporate Leaders for Indigenous
    Employment initiative, 69, 70, 72, 85

D

Dept of Employment, Workplace
    Relations & Small Business
    (DEWRSB)
  implementation of IEP, 17, 67
  responsibility, 70
Dept of Family and Community Services
    (DFACS)
  administrative culture, 44
  relationship with CAEPR, iii
  relationship with WFTD, 43, 44, 49
Dept of Social Security, aims of CDEP,
    42
Dukakis, Lionel, 213–14, 243

E

East Gippsland Aboriginal CDEP Co-
    operative, 213–4
economic issues
  CDEP and the sub-economy, 193–8
  costs imposed on Burringurrah, 199–
    202
  cost-saving activities, 203–4
  economic reform, basis for welfare
    reform, 27
  impacts of CDEP, 126–7
  see also funding
employment
  availability, 7
  cadetships, 70
  Corporate Leaders for Indigenous
    Employment initiative, 69, 70, 72,
    85
  creating opportunities for training &
    employment, 221–3
  decline in attractiveness of work, 20

demographic changes, 95–105
  effects of growing population, 14,
    96–7
  estimates of outcomes, 96–105
  expenditure, 14, 16–17
  inequality & unemployment, 19–21
  OECD rates, 19
  private sector employment, 67, 69
  stepping stone to unsubsidised
    employment, Port Augusta, 143–52
  Structured Training and Employment
    Projects (STEP), 69, 72
  unemployment rates, 7, 14–15
  wage assistance to employers, 69
  see also IEP
equality
  inequality & unemployment, 19–21
  principles of equality, 12–13
  see also human rights

F

financial services
  international comparisons, 86–7
  recommendations, 85
  regional & remote areas, 81–93
  Traditional Credit Union (TCU), 83–5
  Aboriginal organisations & CDEP
    funding, 182
funding, 213
  Aboriginal organisations & CDEP
    funding, 182, 193–8
  adequate funding & equity, 215–16,
    219
  see also economic issues

G

government
  empowerment & control, 9
  role in combating racism, 8
  role in mutual obligation, 77
Gray, Matthew, 143–51, 243

H

Human Rights and Equal Opportunity
Commission (HREOC), Review of
CDEP, 11, 12, 13–14, 15, 48–9
human rights
principles of equality, 12–13
rights-based approach, 17
Humphries, Stephen, 227–9, 243
Hunter, Boyd, 95–107, 243

I

Indigenous Employment Policy (IEP),
67–73
industrial relations, mutual obligation
concept, 44–6
industry
exclusion, 196–7
role in Indigenous employment, 78
inequality & unemployment, 19–21
International Convention on the
Elimination of All Forms of Racial
Discrimination (ICERD), 12
concept of reasonable differentiation,
15, 17
International Covenant on Economic,
Social and Cultural Rights (ICESCR),
8, 14
introduction, 1–2

J

Job Network, use by Indigenous
people, 67–8, 72
Jobsearch Allowance, 43
Jonas, William, 11–18, 243
Junjuwa Community, 203–4

K

Kardiya *see* Yuendumu
Kean, Dan, 199–202, 243
Kimberley region, 203–4
Kuranda, 54, 55–7, 59, 63

L

Lake Tyers Aboriginal Trust, 215–16
legislation
Social Security Act, 13
addressing inequities, 14
Lewis, Wendy Ann, 221–3, 243
Little *see* Peters-Little
Loomes, Bruce, 225–6, 243

M

Madden Raymond, 177–83, 243
Manners, Rupert, 211–12, 243
Martin, David, 31–6, 244
McClure report
McClure strategy, 128–33
see also welfare reform
Mindszenty, Katalin, 205, 244
Morphy, Frances, 244
Mouda, Rowena, 203–4, 244
Murdi Paaki Region, financial services,
84
Musharbash, Yasmine, 153–65, 244
mutual obligation concept, iii–iv, 7–8,
21–3, 42–4
ATSIC support, 8
Burringurrah, 200
CDEP, 31–3, 78
government obligation, 77
industrial relations comparisons, 44–6
job creation & mutual obligation,
207–8
lessons from community research & an
overseas initiative, 53–65
remote areas, 125–33
safety net, 6
social obligations, 34

N

Nalliah, Siva, 215–16, 244
National Aboriginal and Torres Strait
Islander Survey (NATSIS), 54, 59
New Enterprise Incentive Scheme
(NEIS), 67

New Start Allowance (NSA), 43, 48
Newman, Senator, welfare dependency, 27
Nicholas, John, 209–10, 244

O

overviews, 5–50

P

Papunya, 161
Pearson, Noel
  effects of rights without
    responsibilities, 11
  effects of welfare dependency, 5, 26, 27, 32
  Pearson strategy, 128–33
  publication, 31
Peedac Pty Ltd, 227–9
Perth CDEP, 227–9
Peters-Little, Frances, 187–192, 244
policy
  Asian experience, 24
  changing social security policy
    context, 19–29
  European experience, 23
  implication of intermeshing of CDEP
    with Aboriginal organisations, 182
  Indigenous Employment Policy (IEP), 17, 67–73
  parallels with USA & UK, 23–6
  policy history of CDEP, 47–8
  policy perspectives & issues, 53–121
  Social Policy Research Centre (SPRC), attitudes to change, 22
political dimensions of community
  development, 39–46
population
  demographic challenges, 95–107
  growth, 15
  Indigenous share of the outback
    population, 82
Port Augusta, stepping stone to
  unsubsidised employment, 143–51

postscript, 231–2

R

racism, 5
  CDEP, racism & social justice, 11–18
  policy & program delivery, 8
  role of government agencies, 8
Redfern Aboriginal Corporation, 225–6
references, 10, 18, 27–9, 36–7, 46, 50, 64–5, 79, 92–3, 105–7, 121, 133–4, 141, 152, 164–5, 175, 183, 192, 198, 226
reform, iv–v, 75–9
  efficacy, 7–8, 75
  HREOC Review, 11
  see also Spicer Review
regional & remote areas
  access to training, 111–13
  definition of remote Australia, 126
  financial services for Indigenous
    Australians, 81–93
  mutual obligation, 125–33
  regional development, 209–10
  regional studies, 123–83
  see also Bawinanga Aboriginal
    Corporation
  see also Burringurrah
  see also East Gippsland Aboriginal
    CDEP Co-operative
  see also Junjuwa
  see also Lake Tyers Aboriginal Trust
  see also Port Augusta
  see also Tapatjatjaka Community
    Government Council
  see also Tharawal Local Aboriginal
    Land Council
  see also Tjurma Homelands Council
  see also Tjuwanpa Outstation
    Resource Centre
  see also Western Arrernte
  see also Woorabinda CDEP
Reshaping Australian Institutions, (RAI), iii
Rowse, Tim, 39–46, 231–2, 244

S

Sanders, Will, 47–50, 244
Saunders, Peter, 19–29, 244
Schwab, Jerry, 109–21, 244
Scott, Harry, 207–8, 244
Shergold Peter, 67–73, 244
Smith, Diane, 53–65, 244
social costs, 16–7
social justice
    CDEP, racism & social justice, 11–18
    rights-based approach, 17
Social Policy Research Centre (SPRC)
    attitudes to activity test requirements,
        22–3
    attitudes to change, 22
social security
    declining attractiveness of work, 20
    necessity for change, 20–1
Spicer Review, 16, 41, 43–4, 49, 75–7,
    97
    industrial relations, 45
    suggested reform, 75–6
    training, 110
statistical information, Yuendumu,
    155–6

T

Tapatjatjaka Community Government
    Council, 207–8
taxation
    Earned Income Tax Credit (EITC), 24
    effect of unsubsidised employment on
        revenue, 17
    GST, 20
    Working Families Tax Credit (WFTC),
        25
Taylor, John, 95–107, 238
Temporary Assistance for Needy
    Families (TANF), 24, 54, 61–2, 90
Thacker, Elaine, 143–55, 238
Tharawal Local Aboriginal Land
    Council, 221–3
The Job Still Ahead, 7

Tjurma Homelands Council, 205
Tjuwanpa Outstation Resource Centre,
    209–10
Traditional Credit Union (TCU), 83–5
training
    access to information 118–19
    Bungala, 149
    CDEP & careers in the Torres Strait,
        135–41
    creating opportunities for training &
        employment, 221–3
    implications of socio-economic
        disadvantage 112–13
    relevance 113–15
    resources 116–18
    training by doing, 109–21

U

unemployment see employment
United Kingdom (UK), policy
    comparisons, 23–6
United States of America
    income inequality, 19–20
    financial services for earners of low
        incomes, 88–91
    lessons from welfare initiatives, 61–3
    poverty in work, 22, 24–5
urban CDEPs, 221–3, 225–6, 227–9

V

voluntary work, 58–9, 222–3

W

Walpiri see Yuendumu
welfare
    community support, 22
    costs to the Government, 7
    dependence, 5–6, 7, 31–6
        historical transition, 54–5
        lessons from community research &
            an overseas initiative, 53–65
        lessons from U.S. welfare initiatives,
            61–3

participation, 6
reform, iii–iv, 6, 19, 21–3, 26, 27
  ATSIC principles, 6
safety net, 6
service delivery & participation, 8
see also mutual obligation
Westbury, Neil, 81–93, 245
Western Arrernte, 167–75
Whitby, Terry, 75–9, 245
Woorabinda CDEP, 217–19
Work For The Dole (WFTD),
    comparison with CDEP scheme, 12,
    34–5, 43–4
work
  CDEP definitions, 39–40
  declining attractiveness, 20
  definitions, 39
  efforts to increase attractiveness, 24
  see also voluntary work
Worn Gundidj, 177–83

Y

Young, Elizabeth, 217–19, 245
Yuendumu, 54, 55–7, 59, 63, 153–65
    CDEP projects, 157

Notes on the contributors

Jon Altman is Director of the Centre for Aboriginal Economic Policy Research at The Australian National University.

Bill Arthur is a Research Fellow of the Centre for Aboriginal Economic Policy Research at The Australian National University.

Diane Austin-Broos is Professor of Anthropology at the University of Sydney.

Phil Bartlett is Corporate Manager of Wila Gutharra Community Aboriginal Corporation, Geraldton, Western Australia.

Brian Butler is the ATSIC Commissioner for the Adelaide Region, and holds portfolio responsibility for social justice.

Shirley Campbell was a Research Fellow of the Centre for Aboriginal Economic Policy Research at The Australian National University during 2000.

Lionel Dukakis is an ATSIC Regional Councillor on the Binjurru Regional Council in Victoria. Since January 2000 he has been an Operations Manager of the CDEP program at East Gippsland Aboriginal CDEP Co-operative Ltd. in Bairnsdale.

Matthew Gray is a Principal Research Fellow at the Australian Institute of Family Studies and was previously employed at the Centre for Aboriginal Economic Policy Research at The Australian National University.

Stephen Humphries the Training Manager for Perth Employment and Enterprise Development Aboriginal Corporation CDEP.

Boyd Hunter is a Ronald Henderson Research Fellow, and a Fellow of the Centre for Aboriginal Economic Policy Research at The Australian National University.

William Jonas is the Aboriginal and Torres Strait Islander Social Justice Commissioner and Acting Race Discrimination Commissioner of the Human Rights and Equal Opportunity Commission.

Daniel Kean is Manager of Burringurrah Corporation, Carnarvon, Western Australia.

Wendy Anne Lewis is the CDEP Coordinator for the CDEP program of Tharawal Land Council in Western Sydney.

Bruce Loomes is a part-time participant at Redfern CDEP, Sydney.

Raymond Madden was a Visiting Fellow at the Centre for Aboriginal Economic Policy Research at The Australian National University from February to June, 2000. He is now a PhD scholar (anthropology) in the School of Sociology, Politics and Anthropology at La Trobe University.

Rupert Manners was until recently the Accountant for Bawinanga Aboriginal Corporation, Maningrida, Northern Territory.

David Martin is a part-time Research Fellow of the Centre for Aboriginal Economic Policy Research at The Australian National University, and an independent consultant anthropologist.

Katalin Mindszenty is the Coordinator of Tjurma Homelands Council Inc. CDEP, based at Amata in the Anangu Pitjantjatjara Lands of South Australia.

Frances Morphy is a part-time Research Fellow and Academic Editor of the Centre for Aboriginal Economic Policy Research at The Australian National University.

Rowena Mouda is the Bookkeeper and Office Manager of Junjuwa Community/Bunuba Inc., Fitzroy Crossing, Western Australia.

Yasmine Musharbash is a PhD scholar in anthropology in the Department of Archaeology and Anthropology at The Australian National University.

Siva Nalliah is the Finance Manager of Lake Tyers Aboriginal Trust, Victoria.

John Nicholas is the General Manager at Tjuwanpa Outstation Resource Centre, located close to Ntaria, Northern Territory.

Frances Peters-Little is a Centre Associate of the Centre for Aboriginal Economic Policy Research at The Australian National University.

Tim Rowse is a Fellow of the Centre for Aboriginal Economic Policy Research at The Australian National University.

Will Sanders is a Fellow of the Centre for Aboriginal Economic Policy Research at The Australian National University.

Peter Saunders is Director of the Social Policy Research Centre at the University of New South Wales.

Jerry Schwab is a Fellow and Deputy Director of the Centre for Aboriginal Economic Policy Research at The Australian National University.

Harry Scott is the Council Clerk of Tapatjatjaka Community Government Council at Titjikala in central Australia.

Peter Shergold is the Secretary of the Department of Employment, Workplace Relations and Small Business and was a Chief Executive Officer of the Aboriginal and Torres Strait Islander Commission from 1993 to 1996.

Diane Smith is a Fellow of the Centre for Aboriginal Economic Policy Research at The Australian National University.

John Taylor is a Senior Research Fellow of the Centre for Aboriginal Economic Policy Research at The Australian National University.

Elaine Thacker was an Indigenous Visiting Fellow at the Centre for Aboriginal Economic Policy Research during 2000, on an inter-agency placement from the Aboriginal and Torres Strait Islander Commission.

Neil Westbury was previously a Visiting Fellow at the Centre for Aboriginal Economic Policy Research at The Australian National University. He is currently the General Manager of Reconciliation Australia Ltd.

Terry Whitby is the ATSIC Commissioner for the Western Australian Region, and holds portfolio responsibility for employment and CDEP.

Elisabeth Young is the Chairperson for Woorabinda CDEP at Woorabinda, Queensland.

CAEPR Research Monograph Series

1. *Aborigines in the Economy: A Select Annotated Bibliography of Policy-Relevant Research 1985–90*, L.M. Allen, J.C. Altman and E. Owen (with assistance from W.S. Arthur), 1991.

2. *Aboriginal Employment Equity by the Year 2000*, J.C. Altman (ed.), published for the Academy of Social Sciences in Australia, 1991.

3. *A National Survey of Indigenous Australians: Options and Implications*, J.C. Altman (ed.), 1992.

4. *Indigenous Australians in the Economy: Abstracts of Research, 1991–92*, L.M. Roach and K.A. Probst, 1993.

5. *The Relative Economic Status of Indigenous Australians*, 1986–91, J. Taylor, 1993.

6. *Regional Change in the Economic Status of Indigenous Australians, 1986–91*, J. Taylor, 1993.

7. *Mabo and Native Title: Origins and Institutional Implications*, W. Sanders (ed.), 1994.

8. *The Housing Need of Indigenous Australians, 1991*, R. Jones, 1994.

9. *Indigenous Australians in the Economy: Abstracts of Research, 1993–94*, L.M. Roach and H.J. Bek, 1995.

10. *The Native Title Era: Emerging Issues for Research, Policy and Practice*, J. Finlayson and D.E. Smith (eds), 1995.

11. *The 1994 National Aboriginal and Torres Strait Islander Survey: Findings and Future Prospects*, J.C. Altman and J. Taylor (eds), 1996.

12. *Fighting Over Country: Anthropological Perspectives*, D.E. Smith and J. Finlayson (eds), 1997.

13. *Connections in Native Title: Genealogies, Kinship and Groups*, J.D. Finlayson, B. Rigsby, and H.J. Bek (eds), 1999.

14. *Land Rights at Risk? Evaluations of the Reeves Report*, J.C. Altman, F. Morphy, and T. Rowse (eds), 1999.

15. *Unemployment Payments, the Activity Test, and Indigenous Australians: Understanding Breach Rates*, W. Sanders, 1999.

16. *Why Only One in Three? The Complex Reasons for Low Indigenous School Retention*, R.G. Schwab, 1999.

17. *Indigenous Families and the Welfare System: Two Community Case Studies*, D.E. Smith (ed.), 2000.

18. *Ngukurr at the Millennium: A Baseline Profile for Social Impact Planning in South-East Arnhem Land*, J. Taylor, J. Bern and K.A. Senior, 2000.

19. *Aboriginal Nutrition and the Nyirranggulung Health Strategy in Jawoyn Country*, J. Taylor and N. Westbury, 2000.

20. *The Indigenous Welfare Economy and the CDEP Scheme*, F. Morphy and W. Sanders (eds), 2001.

For information on earlier CAEPR Discussion Papers and Research Monographs please contact:

Publication Sales, Centre for Aboriginal Economic Policy Research, The Australian National University, Canberra, ACT, 0200
Telephone: 02–6125 8211
Facsimile: 02–6125 9730

Information on CAEPR abstracts or summaries of all CAEPR print publications and those published electronically can be found at the following WWW address:

http://online.anu.edu.au/caepr/

www.ingramcontent.com/pod-product-compliance
Lightning Source LLC
Chambersburg PA
CBHW041428290326
41932CB00055B/3410